RECIPES FROM THE
INDIAN
SPICE TRAIL

•

RECIPES FROM THE INDIAN SPICE TRAIL

written and illustrated by

LESLIE FORBES

BBC BOOKS

To Andrew Thomas for surviving my personal monsoons.
To Matt Thompson, producer of the BBC Radio Three series that
accompanies this book, for his constant supply of Scottish wit.
To Gillian Wright in Delhi, whose hard work, good contacts and wide
knowledge of her adopted country made my work so much easier.
And to all those in India whose generosity, intelligence and
extraordinary food I have been privileged to enjoy.

•

If you have any difficulty in finding any of the spices
for the recipes, please contact the address below for a
mail order catalogue:

Steamboat Oriental Foods PO Box 452
West Yorkshire BD4 7TF, UK
Tel/Fax: 01274 619826

Published by BBC Books, a division of BBC Enterprises Limited
Woodlands, 80 Wood Lane, London W12 OTT

First published 1994
© Leslie Forbes 1994
The moral right of the author has been asserted

ISBN 0 563 36986 8

Set in Simoncini Garamond by Selwood Systems, Midsomer Norton
Printed and bound in Great Britain by Butler & Tanner Limited, Frome, Somerset
Colour separation by Radstock Reproductions Limited, Midsomer Norton
Jacket printed by Lawrence Allen Limited, Weston-super-Mare

CONTENTS

•

ATTOCK

KABUL

LAHORE

PERSEPOLIS

DELHI

BARBARICON

AHMEDABAD

BARYGAZA/BROACH

MECCA

BOMBAY

ADEN

HYDERABAD

MALABAR

MADRAS

CRANGANORE

COAST

COCHIN

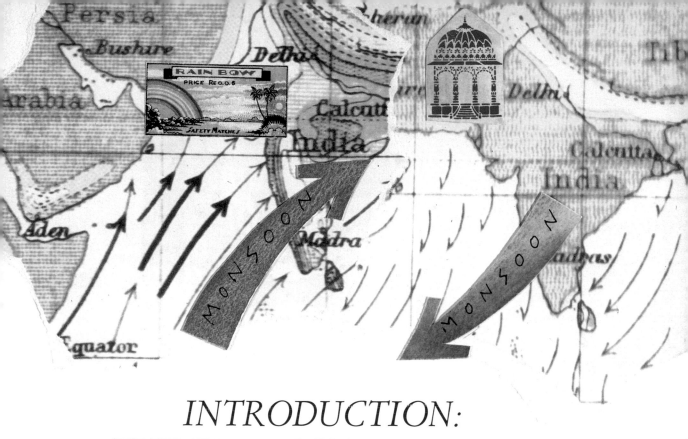

INTRODUCTION:
THE WINDS TO MALABAR

•

What is found in this epic may be elsewhere
What is not in this epic is nowhere else.

MAHABHARATA (XVIII, 50)

Emperors and kings, dukes and marquises, counts, knights and townsfolk, and all people who wish to know the various races of men and the peculiarities of the various regions of the world, take this book and have it read to you. Here you will find all the great wonders and curiosities of greater Armenia and Persia, of the Tartars and of India, and of many other territories.... We will set down things seen as seen, things heard as heard ... so that others who have not seen and do not know them may learn them from this book.

An enterprising travelling salesman and talented self-publicist, a Venetian, wrote that paragraph about 700 years ago. His name was Marco Polo, and he wove an epic of adventure of his travels and of his dealings with those men who, as he put it, 'made up their minds to conquer the whole world' – the Mongols. His tale of precious spices and gems and fabrics of beaten gold inspired Columbus (citizen of another great Italian spice-trading port, Genoa), who treasured a well-thumbed copy of Marco Polo's book and found the West by mistake, while looking for a spice route to the East.

This is the story of a quest to find the links in a chain of spices connecting India to its ancient trading partners in the Mediterranean. It began by accident, at the end of a typical peasant meal in Puglia, an isolated region of antique traditions in southern Italy. Instead of offering cake or pudding, my host brought in a tray of dried figs and green almonds and a little bowl of fennel seeds with a spoon in it.

'To freshen your breath and help your digestion,' he said. 'It is an old old custom in these parts, maybe a remnant of ties we had once with Greece and the Middle East.'

Something about the sweet anise flavour of the seeds inspired a vivid sensation of *déja vù*. I suddenly recalled an occasion eighteen months earlier on the Malabar Coast of India. A Muslim friend had passed me a dish of aniseed after dinner; 'to clear your palate.' His family had arrived in Malabar, so he said, as spice traders from Arabia in the eighth century. The presence of aniseed in Malabari Muslim dishes differentiates their food from that of other religions on the coast. 'In India', he said, 'they call it "foreign fennel" because it is a native of the Levant and was brought here by the ancient Arabs, Egyptians and Greeks.'

Flavours may persist where the people who shaped them have disappeared. 'The only way to distinguish a genuine Venetian risotto from any other region's,' a Venetian friend told me, 'is that in Venice it should contain, not saffron, as in Milan, but a pinch of curry powder' – all that remains of a trade which contributed to the fall of Rome and reduced Marco Polo's Venice from a great trading nation to a living museum.

When an Indian eats Western food today, he may, perhaps, be tasting his future. When Westerners eat Indian food, they are tasting their own past. For 1500 years or more, the West tasted of the East, of its hauntingly perfumed spice masalas and its curious blends of sweet and salt, sour and fetid. Look closely at the regions in Europe and America that have preserved their culinary traditions longest and you find spices leading, like signposts, to the Middle East and to India, where progress and fashion have not yet eliminated tradition. To paraphrase the *Mahabharata*, what is found in India may be elsewhere, what is not in India is nowhere else.

In a world shrunken by rapid transport, fax machines and international chain stores, we forget that people were once willing to risk their lives for a handful of spices, that something which simply made food taste better was so important it altered language and even geography. The greatest shopping centre ever conceived was Rome's Market of Trajan, built under the auspices of the Emperor Trajan sometime between AD 109 and 113. Rare and costly merchandise such as pepper and spices (*pipera*) could be found on its upper floors, and a ghost of this trade survived well after the market's destruction, in the name of a nearby road, the *Via Biberatica*.

One of the oldest of London's guilds, the Grocers, have as their symbol a golden camel bearing spices. They take their name from the old custom of measuring pepper and spices by the gross. First it was sorted for quality, a process known as 'garbling' (from the Arabic *gharbala* 'to sift, select'), and still called that in the city of Cochin on the Malabar Coast. In 1345 a request was made by merchants of Genoa, Florence, Lucca and Lombardy 'at present residing in the City of London' that London's official spice garbler henceforth come from outside the trade. Otherwise, they said, it was clearly in his interest to adulterate spices with less costly products. And, to ensure fair trading, the procedure should no longer be so secretive. In 1993 the assistant secretary of Cochin's Spice Board told me, 'No one likes you to watch the garbling in Cochin because how they do it is a secret.' In India there is always this percussive weight of documented fact; then, almost immediately, a lighter but insistent answering tap, an Indian drumbeat of the past still present.

History is full of emperors and their royal tastes. We know that the Mogul emperor, Akbar, liked cardamom; his prime minister kept a record of it. And according to the historian, Ajoy Kumar Singh, the Emperor Augustus was fond of black pepper. One year he received in Rome two Indian ambassadors bearing gifts: black pepper from Kerala, an enormous tortoise, some snakes and an Indian man with no arms. Augustus was pleased, Singh tells us, especially by the letter from a Hindu king offering Romans free entry to India's priceless spice trade, but how the man with no arms adjusted to his new life in Rome remains a mystery. The tastes of ordinary men and women seldom intrude on history, except where they have assisted in extraordinary events – or in emperor's kitchens. This is true especially of India, with its preference for troubadours and oral storytellers over scribes. No one sings a song of merchants or hawkers. So it may be because the North African merchant, Abraham Ben Yiju, was involved in the profitable Indian spice trade (like so many Middle Eastern Jews of the medieval period), a trade that interested emperors, that so many of his letters and trading documents were preserved in the library of Cairo's ancient synagogue.

In 1139 Ben Yiju was living in the city of Mangalore, on the Malabar Coast, worrying about a shipment of cardamom he had sent to Aden, a sophisticated metropolis that straddled the Indian Ocean's most important spice routes. He had made out a list of household goods he wanted to import from Aden and was very pleased to receive from a friend there an iron frying pan to replace one of stone whose case had broken. His friend, Khalaf, knew of Ben Yiju's sweet tooth, and of his dislike for Mangalore's local palm sugar. From Aden, Khalaf sent: two jars of raisins, a jar of almonds and two jars of crystallized cane-sugar, a product still known as *misri* throughout North India.

'Why is it called *misri*,' I asked Amitav Ghosh, the Indian author whose book, *In an Antique Land*, tells Ben Yiju's story, 'when the Arabic word *sukkar* is derived from a Sanskrit source?'

'*Misri*: in memory of men like Ben Yiju who first imported it,' he said, 'from Misr/Masr, the old name for Egypt.' There it is again, that soft, insistent drumbeat of another century.

Thanks to Ben Yiju's letters, we know one more thing. Probably to ensure the safety of a spice shipment, he sent his Malabari slave, Bomma, as emissary to the Middle East. Of the many Indians to have made this westward journey, the slave is one of the few who did not slip from the pages of history.

In Alexandria, delivering one of his most celebrated speeches, the famously charming Dio 'Golden-tongued' Chrysostom flattered the local population of 300,000 by calling their city 'a hinge connecting the whole earth and its widely separated nations'. Facing the Mediterranean, the city had a canal system linking it to the Nile, and thus, by a 400-mile arduous journey down that river, to Aden. It was the end of the first century AD and Alexandria was the greatest market in the world. 'In it,' said Dio Chrysostom, 'a visitor could see a settled population of men from lands as distant as India.' But Bomma's predecessors in the Middle East remain anonymous.

'It is more likely that they were Gujaratis rather than Malayalis (the people of Malabar),' said a Malayali friend. 'We always went out but always came back, just as we do still.'

Jews, Arabs, Phoenicians, Greeks, Gujaratis, Venetians, Egyptians – all the bravest sailors and merchants of the ancient world met in the ports of the Middle East en route to and from Malabar. For nearly 3000 years, until the British, Dutch and Portuguese took it over by force, the history of the spice trade in the Indian Ocean was an unarmed one. Its participants were largely men of peace who left their political differences at home and depended for successful trading on the mercy and good will of local sovereigns.

The book that changed the course of trade in the East and eating habits in the West was called *The Periplus of the Erythraean Sea*, written sometime in the first century AD. We don't know the author's name – he was probably an ordinary Greek or Roman merchant seaman – but he had a vision beyond his own individual enterprise. His book gave trustworthy accounts of how to trade in the Indian Ocean, so that other merchants might profit from his firsthand experience. He mentions the settlements around its shores – those prone to piracy and those to legitimate commerce. He lists the configuration of its coasts and its natural products. From Barygaza (modern Broach, on the coast of Gujarat), he writes, 'the produce to be shipped are beautiful girls for the harem, butter or ghee, ivory, fabrics and spices.' And he speaks of the winds of Hippalus, the monsoon winds, that blow for four months from southwest to northeast across the Indian Ocean and, three months later, reverse their direction.

Three months of the year, then, men from Athens, Alexandria and all over Italy lived in India, waiting patiently for the winds to take them home again. What did they bring back, I wonder? The fresh green herb pestos of the south – to be made in Genoa with olive oil instead of the cold-pressed coconut oil of Malabar? Or *piadina*, the flat bread of Romagna's plain, cooked on a terracotta griddle and eaten with garlicky greens, a mirror of the Punjab plains' chapatti, which is cooked over camel dung and eaten with garlic and ginger-flavoured mustard greens?

Before traders discovered the monsoon winds, ships would hug the coast of Arabia and Oman, going north around Gujarat's Gulf of Cambay to the port of Barygaza and down the west coast of India to Travancore, in modern Kerala.

'From Barygaza south,' warned Marco Polo, trying, as usual, to impress us with his courage while discouraging rivals, 'beware of pirates.' A hundred pirate ships a year, he claimed, bringing with them their wives and children, sailed out from Gujarat and Malabar to rob the spice ships.

'Let me tell you one of their nasty tricks . . . when they capture merchants they make them drink tamarind and seawater so they pass or vomit up all the contents of their stomachs.' The pirates had a logical explanation for this practice. They said that captured merchants often hid their gems by swallowing them.

Most merchants from Persia and the Yemen liked to disembark at Mangalore, where docks now cover the fine sand on which Abraham Ben Yiju beached his boats. The Sumatrans and Chinese preferred Calicut, farther south, a city 13 km (8 miles) in circumference when the Italian traveller Nicolo Contai visited it in 1430. It was, he said, 'a spice emporium for the whole of India and the East'.

A pillar marks the point at Malindi, opposite the clove island of Zanzibar, where an Arab pilot set off with Vasco da Gama to guide him on the last, 2000-mile leg of his voyage from Lisbon to Calicut. When da Gama arrived on the Malabar Coast in 1498, he presented a few gifts to its mighty Hindu ruler, the Samudrarajah, ('Sea-King'), whose ancestors had traded their pepper for gold, silks and Arab stallions from Cleopatra. Da Gama offered him six washbasins. The monarch decided to leave the spice trade where it was – in the hands of Muslim merchants.

The Portugese rapidly turned their hitherto purely commercial quest for spices into a holy war. Two years later, Pedro Alvarez Cabral arrived with a letter from the king of Portugal demanding that Malabar's ruler expel all Muslims. He was told that Calicut's pepper would continue to be available to any merchant, regardless of religion – even to the Portuguese, provided they paid the going rate. Cabral replied by sacking Calicut. Da Gama himself burned a Muslim pilgrim ship returning from Mecca, and the course of the spice trade, whose peaceful nature was seen by the Portuguese and other Europeans as one of weakness not of choice, changed forever.

'I want to travel down the Malabar Coast and into the Cardamom Hills,' I told an Oxford historian, 'just for the sound of it – it sounds like a road movie with Bing Crosby and Dorothy Lamour – and because I want to make some connections.'

'Did you know that you can trace the spice roads of India,' he said, 'what you might call *The Road to Malabar*, in the trail of gold coins left along them by Roman traders?'

I read that gold coins from the reigns of Augustus and Nero, many as fresh as on the day they were struck, had been found in hoards near the town of Kottayam on the Malabar Coast. 'If the wind called Hippalus be blowing,' Pliny had written, 'Malabar can be reached in forty days.' It took me just under forty hours.

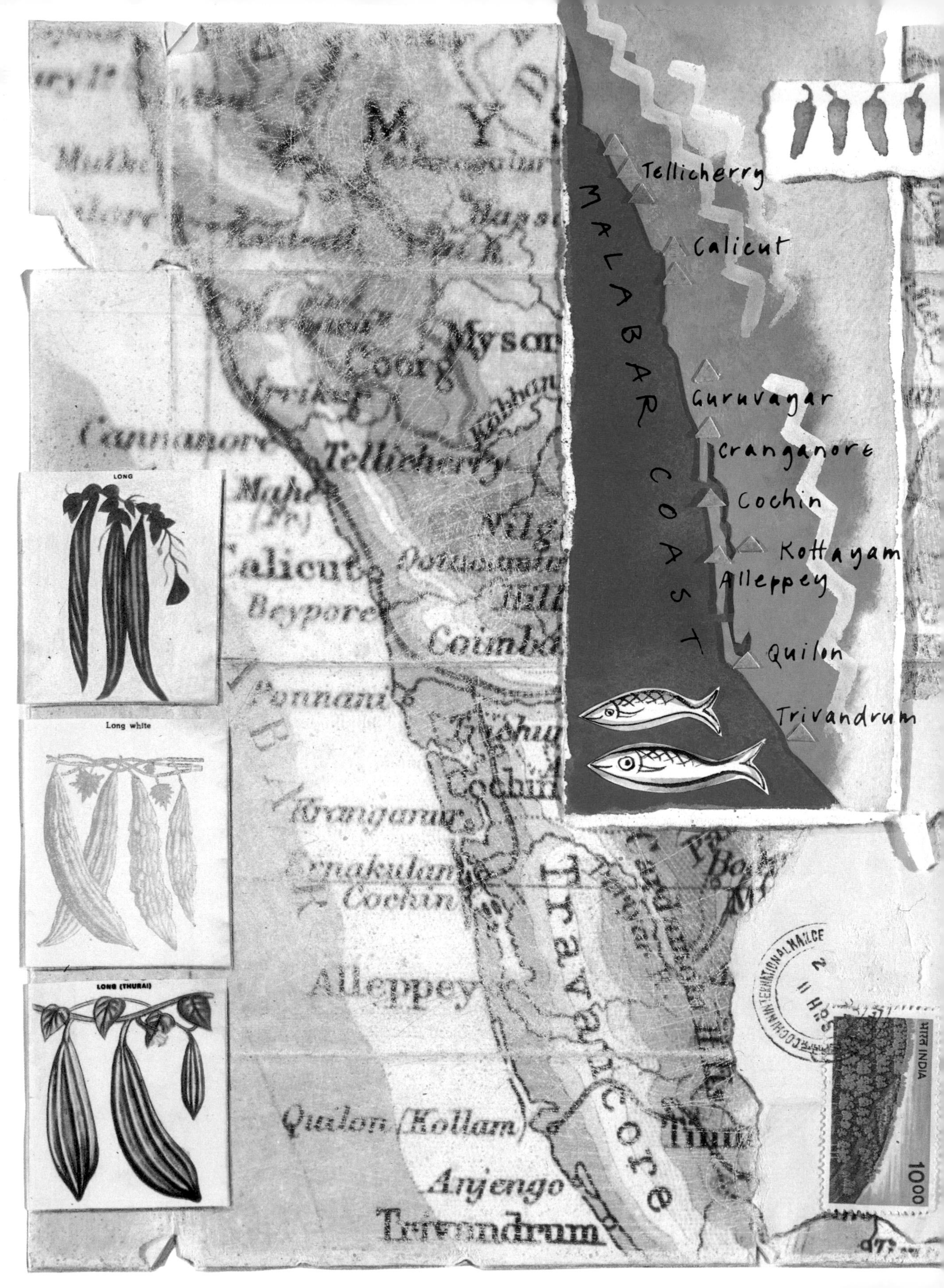
MALABAR COAST
Tellicherry
Calicut
Guruvayar
Cranganore
Cochin
Kottayam
Alleppey
Quilon
Trivandrum
LONG
Long white
LONG (THURAI)
Coorg
Cannanore
Tellicherry
Calicut
Beypore
Ponnani
Cochin
Kranganur
Cochin
Alleppey
Quilon (Kollam)
Anjengo
Trivandrum
Travancore
INDIA
10.00

CHAPTER ONE

INTO THE
CARDAMOM
HILLS

•

*In consequence of the great slope of Malabar up to the
Cardamom hills, the heaviest monsoon leaves little or no trace behind it,
so that lines of communication, once formed, are easily preserved.*

RICHARD FRANCIS BURTON, 1851.

'Once there was a time . . ,' Sugatha Kumari begins, like all the best storytellers, 'when the whole world was enamoured of the fragrance of Kerala.' Sugatha is a poet and ecologist in Trivandrum, the capital of Kerala. Like most Malayalis, she has the gift of epic poetry. Her local language, a sinuous bubbling that sounds like a stream running over pebbles, is appropriate for a region made up almost entirely of inland waterways and coastline and of fluid, elusive legends. 'Malabar,' wrote Sugatha's father, a famous freedom fighter and poet, 'where peppercorns glow in the forests like emeralds and coral.'

But the spice forests that brought Arabs and Europeans to Malabar on the monsoon winds of Hippalus were more valuable than emeralds. At the beginning of the nineteenth century, when Kerala's spice trade was controlled exclusively by British civil servants in Bombay, this coast was to have the reputation of making these individuals 'as rich as Croesus'.

A perceptive Indian politician said once that the coastal peoples of India, however widely dispersed, had more in common with each other than with their immediate neighbours inland, because they had learned tolerance from their constant contact with foreign merchants from across the sea. They never became 'small frogs in a deep well', as the Sanskrit saying goes.

In the sixteenth century, when the Dutch wanted to enhance the value of their own plantations in Ceylon, they managed to buy from a tolerant Malabari raja the right to destroy this coast's flourishing cinnamon forests. Tolerance is a very Keralan concept. The first place in the world freely to elect a communist government, it has India's lowest birthrate and its highest rate of literacy (about 90 per cent).

'Tolerance may be our downfall,' Sugatha Kumari said. 'We were, with Assam, the only state to have matrilinear succession. Since we let Delhi abolish it, Kerala is losing its identity.' Once, not long ago, this state was Eden. Every home was enclosed by jackfruit, mango, papaya and pepper, and within each compound, however small, was the 'sacred grove', a patch of jungle that had existed uncultivated from prehistory. 'These groves nurtured snakes and fruit and wild spices that maintained Nature's balance. But Westerners came and told us it was a backward idea, so we chopped down our groves and lost our soul. Spices used to be part of our culture. Now they are just one more commodity.'

The long sandy coast road from Trivandrum runs north through Quilon, one of the oldest ports on the Indian Ocean. Its most industrious traders were the Chinese, who established permanent posts here during the seventh century, and who later, under Kublai Khan, exchanged envoys with Quilon's rulers. Marco Polo travelled from the court of the Khan by dugout down the Malabar waterways looking for pepper and ginger. 'The heat here is so intense and the sun so powerful that it is scarcely tolerable,' he wrote. 'For I assure you that if you put an egg into one of the rivers you would not have to wait long before it boiled.' Marco Polo found ginger in Quilon – and noted the predominance of idolators, although he admitted that there were some Christians and Jews among them. The Christians were probably Nestorians from Baghdad. One of Kerala's watery legends relates that in AD 52, near Cranganore, St Thomas the Apostle landed, only to be martyred sixteen years later in Madras – stoned to death and then thrust through with a spear. But another, more probable story has it that the first Thomas was a Baghdadi merchant, who settled in Malabar in the fourth or eighth century to trade in spices, and took two wives, one dark and the other fair.

Certainly, there was a Christian church in Kerala when people in the West were still worshipping oddly shaped stones. In the eighth century, a group of Baghdadi Christians fleeing persecution, reached Quilon, led by the merchant Bar Yesu. They lived on land granted by the local raja, erected churches and built bazaars. 'Sometimes it is possible to find old settlements here,' wrote Leslie Brown in 1956 in an account of Malabar's Syrian Christian Church, 'by the persistence of Syrian names long after their buildings have vanished.'

Like Kerala's Muslims, the Christians began as coastal spice merchants, but over the centuries the capital from their trading enabled them to buy tenancies on land held by the Hindu and Muslim upper classes. Keralan women, even Muslims, did not leave their family homes after marriage, because of local inheritence laws. They took several husbands, who had visiting but not always residential rights, a practice scholars believe was adopted to prevent alienation of family property. 'The more lovers a woman has,' wrote Duarte Barbosa, a Portuguese traveller to Kerala in the sixteenth century, 'the greater her honour.' When the Indian government abolished matrilinear succession about thirty years ago, land was divided equally among sons, individual members of the landowning class were put, almost overnight, in charge of property they had neither the money nor the expertise to cultivate, and their Christian tenants easily bought up most of the big spice plantations.

Naomi Meadows is a Syrian Christian who spent her childhood on a farm seven miles outside Kottayam, a town at the end of a long inland waterway from the old spice port of Alleppey. East of Kottayam the road rises through pineapple, spice and coconut plantations to the Cardamom Hills. Cardamom, like tea and coffee, is a plant of the cool heights, but Naomi remembered many other spices in her grandmother's compound – and tractors with trunks.

'The elephants came every three months to shake the coconut palms. They knew exactly how many coconuts on each tree were ripe and they would collect and arrange them into pyramids with their trunks, putting one nut more to the left or right so it wouldn't fall.'

Keralans use coconut milk as the French do cream. 'The only thing we have more of here than coconuts is bishops.' said George Isaacs, a Syrian Christian friend of Naomi's who produces some of the state's best masalas and pickles. Before he made pickles, he was a Rhodes Scholar in philosophy at Oxford University. 'We export more bishops per square mile from Kottayam than anywhere else in the world, including Rome.'

George's mother, whose first cousin trained most of the cooks in southern Indian, started the family pickle business in about 1960, and his wife Susie controls it. 'I am just an ornament,' he said. In the old Dravidian traditions of Kerala, even the smallest goddess sitting passively under a tree is more powerful than a hundred-foot tall war god.

George's daughter drove us to the ancestral farm – once planted with rubber trees, now a myriad of greens: rice paddies the colour of a gecko's back, viridian-leafed coconut palms, the matt olive of creeping pepper vines, fuzzy lemon-green nutmeg husks – like tennis balls – concealing the ripening dark fruit. She was more interested in quantum physics than in farming.

'Why did you take out the rubber?' I asked.

'Because it drains the soil. My mother wanted to put something back.'

Her mother came from an extended family of small farmers who had long cultivated isolated forest land in central Travancore. Their farms were large enough to make them self-sufficient (unusually for India). The only thing they had to buy was salt. 'They grow all their own spices – in fact they use very few, mostly pepper,' George said. 'They press their own coconut oil; they have their own meat, fish, eggs, honey and rice, still with the pale pink husk clinging to it – it would be a tremendous loss of face to buy rice.'

'What do they do for medicine?'

'They concoct it from herbs and spices native to the region. And these are remarkably effective – they all live to be ninety and are as active as mountain goats. Before Susie moved to Kottayam she had never seen a fat person.'

Three centuries ago, the Dutch governor of Cochin, Heinrich van Rheede, who in the 1670s brought the rajas of Kerala under Dutch control, was also very impressed by the Keralan knowledge of medicine. He compiled a twelve-volume masterpiece of scientific literature, *Hortus Malabaricus*, containing information he had collected from local physicians about the flora of the country and the medicinal properties of its spices and herbs.

'I had the dubious distinction of introducing Susie's family to aspirin,' George said.

Kerala has always been full of storytellers and merchant poets. I took a passenger ferry across the harbour from modern Ernakulam to old Cochin, where the air was brown with ginger dust from the spice godowns (warehouses) nearby. At the end of a street of antique shops, a sixteenth century synagogue stood in a courtyard whose walls were lined with tombstones. The guide inside was Roman Catholic. Opposite the synagogue, in an old house with a Star of David grille over the window, lived seventy-nine-year-old Jacob Cohen. He struck a hard bargain.

'Pay me 400 rupees and I will tell you stories of the Jews in Kerala that no one else could tell,' he said, offering a glass of his wife's sickly sweet homemade wine, some cheese samosas called 'puffs' and a slice of her sponge cake. He said Solomon's fleet had come here for spices to the coastal village of Ophir, where he may also have obtained teak to build the Temple. He said he could tell me of copper plates presented to Kerala's Jews in the fourth century AD by King Bhaskara Ravi Varma, 'with a village he said would be theirs "so long as the world and moon exist". And I can tell you of the Portuguese who burned it – and with it, the records of our past.'

Jacob's family came from Baghdad two hundreds years ago to trade in spices and ivory in Madras. He still has the pale ochre skin of a Baghdadi merchant. For Sabbath, the next day, his wife was cooking a typically Baghdadi Jewish soup. In it floated *kubbah* – ravioli containing ground meat, chillies, mint (a herb rarely used in Kerala), saffron and a splash of vinegar to preserve them overnight in the heat. Her puffs, she told me, were also known as *pastel*, and her 12-egg sponge cake, scented with rose essence, as *cortina*, two words left over from the time of Portuguese rule in Kerala.

'Things the younger generation do not know,' she said. 'But we belong to an older time.'

I walked out past the antiques on my way to the pepper exchange around the corner, where six days a week, between 9.30 and 4.30 brokers auction up to 500 tons of 'black gold'. Many of the spice godowns here back onto the seas, so that briefly, through an open door, you will glimpse a shimmering wave and the silver flash of a leaping dolphin, or the skeletal silhouettes of the shorebound 'Chinese' fishing nets, arching and diving like prehistoric wading birds. In the courtyards, men and women dip dried ginger root into lime to preserve it, and blue, throat-catching lime

RIGHT: An inscription on the wall of the 16th century synagogue in Old Cochin.
ABOVE RIGHT: Bagdadi Jewish ravioli (kubbah).
FACING PAGE: Delivery of spices and local vegetables from the Cardamom Hills to warehouses or 'godowns' in Old Cochin.

בנה בנינו בית זבל לך מקוןלשב
עולמים שנת נדול יהיה כבורהבית
הזה האחרון מן הראשון ליצירההיום
כשלישיבשבת חמשה לכסלו בדהא

THE INSCRIPTION ON THIS
SLAB BELONGED TO
THE SYNAGOGUE IN KOCHANGADI
IT WAS BUILT IN 1344
THE OLDEST SYNAGOGUE IN COCHIN

COCHIN SYNAGOGUE
(1568)
1 Rs.

COCHIN SYNAGOGUE
(1568)
1 Rs.

786

powder rises up like smoke, flattening colour and life into mere fresco against the white-washed walls. This area is known as Jewtown, although no Jews work in the trade. 'Each year there are more antique shops and less Jews,' Jacob Cohen said sadly. 'Now we are only twenty-three. The young people, they have moved to Israel, our fatherland. But Kerala has been our mother for almost two thousand years. And what is a Jew without his mother?'

The first man from Vasco da Gama's fleet to set foot in Kerala was a Jew – João Nunez, a *degredado* recently converted to Christianity. On the shore near Calicut, two Muslim traders from Tunis were horrified to see a potential competitor.

'May the devil take you! What brought you here?' they asked.

'We have come in search of Christians and spices,' Nunez replied, in halting Arabic.

'But there never was a Jewish spice trade here,' said Mr Kishor, whose Gujarati Jain family have traded spices here for generations. 'They were always investors, the brokers between India and the Middle East.'

Even had I not already known that he was Gujarati, the cup of spiced tea Mr Kishor offered me would have revealed this. In Gujarat, every family has its own blend of *chai masala*. Keralans drink tea plain and prefer their coffee from their highlands. Mr Kishor smiled when I mentioned it.

'Here in Cochin they call it Gujarati tea,' he said. 'And if you cross over from the old Dutch palace in Mattancherry you will see a sign saying "New Road". For as long as I can remember this has been known as Gujarati Street, because you can find market stalls selling the food we like.' In this region of rice and fish and fresh herb masalas, the Gujarati spice traders stick to their wheatflour chapattis and dry-spiced dals. 'You will even find Rajasthani Jains here eating *dal batti*, the traditional food of their desert homeland.'

It seemed strange that the Jains, a religious group known for their austerity, should wind up surrounded by the voluptuous smells of cardamom and ginger, yet for years the spice trade in maritime Kerala has been dominated by Jains from the great northern deserts. Mr Kishor reminded me that Gujaratis were India's greatest navigators. Originally they may have come to Kerala's jungles looking for timber for their boats. He knew for certain that one maharaja of Travancore had invited them to deal in pepper here in an effort to break the Arabs' stranglehold. 'Perhaps you will find your answers in the north,' he said.

Before following the spice roads out of Kerala, I went to have lunch with George Isaacs. He told how, after leaving his Scottish missionary college in Madras years ago, he had taken his favourite Kerala spiced pickles with him to Oxford to flavour post-war British food. Now he sat in his family's old teak house, eating local river fish cooked in coconut milk and black mustard seeds. Above his head was an oar from his rowing days in Oxford in 1952–54. He still dreams in English.

'I would be an exile in my own land if this was any other country in the world,' he said. 'But the Hindu culture is so comprehensive it can absorb the British Raj and Balliol without the least effort. Now, you are a half-Scot; shall I give you a road song from my past to see you on your way?'

Then, with just the trace of a Scottish burr, he sang:

> *O, ye'll take the high road and I'll take the low road*
> *and I'll be in Scotland afore ye,*
> *But me and my true love will never meet again*
> *On the bonny bonny banks of Loch Lomond.*

In India, they say, you find what you are looking for, and what you find is a reflection of yourself.

Views of fishing boats and so-called 'Chinese' fishing nets on the beach at Old Cochin.

Flavours of Kerala
·
FISH, COCONUT AND FRESH GREEN MASALA

*T*he flavours of Kerala are more redolent of Thailand than of India: sweet from bananas and coconut, and sour from lime, starfruit, fresh green mango, yoghurt, buttermilk and *kokum (Garcinia indica)* or its more succulent but less widely available variety, *kodumpoli*, both known as fish tamarind because of their affinity with Malabar fish dishes. A sweet-fleshed deep red fruit whose salted, sun-dried sour skin (the part used in cooking) smells like sweaty saddle – sweet, musky, smoky – fish tamarind is fruitier, more aromatic and less astringent than citrus or regular tamarind (scarce on the southwest coast, anyway). Kokum ground with chillies dyes Keralan fish stews a bright scarlet, described in Sanskrit as resembling in colour and texture the mouth of a beautiful woman. If you find kokum in Asian markets, add several pieces of rind to stews, soups and sauces.

What sets Kerala dishes apart from other southern regions that use coconut is the addition of fresh chunks of the nut in cooking, and a last-minute drizzle of cold-pressed coconut oil (to preserve its fruitiness, just as Mediterraneans do with olive oil). As coconut oil is highly saturated and the cold-pressed version is unavailable outside India (the version we get is horribly reminiscent of cheap beach resorts), use sunflower oil in delicate vegetable dishes and light sesame oil (or, sacrilegiously, olive oil) in more robust ones.

For ground spice masalas, I find that packaged creamed coconut is as good as what passes for fresh coconut in the West, except when the fluffy texture of grated fresh coconut is needed. However, as creamed coconut has a fattier taste and canned coconut milk can lack freshness, they both benefit from being whizzed with a little yoghurt or lime juice for tang. When grinding a coconut masala, add a very little amount of hot water or milk to soften the nut oil and help it blend more easily.

VEGETABLES PARBOILED IN SPICED-SCENTED WATER

A treatment for vegetables such as potatoes, carrots, yam, plantains and gourds that require longer cooking before their final flavouring with spices: ground spices that are subjected to prolonged boiling in water lose their pungency, whereas their aromatic oils are released faster and more efficiently into fat. Per 450 g (1 lb) of vegetables, cut in chunks, boil 450 ml (15 fl oz) of water with 2 dried red chillies and ¼ teaspoon of turmeric. For red sweetish vegetables (where colour will not be ruined) such as carrots, yam and pumpkin, a 50–100 g (2–4 oz) ball of tamarind paste may be added, soaked first in boiling water for 30 minutes, then sieved and seeds discarded. When vegetables are tender, finish them by frying for a few minutes in a cooked masala or simply drizzle them with a tempering (see below).

TEMPERING

A final tempering of spices – the most popular being peppercorns, black mustard seeds and curry leaves – cooked in a little oil and poured onto a dish before serving (what Tuscans call the 'blessing'), is popular all over southern India. Spices retain their freshness this way and, like the glaze on an oil painting, bring out the colours of the dish. Each of the following temperings will season a dish for 4–6. Just pour over food before serving and however simply it has been cooked it will taste better.

'Garbling' (sifting) pepper in Old Cochin.

PEPPERCORNS, Black (kali mirchi)
BOT: *Piper nigrum*

•

The grains that beggared Rome: berries red and green when unripe on the vine, sable-black after farm wives in the Cardamom Hills have spread them to sun-dry in front of their bungalows. Precursor of chillies (introduced by the Portuguese) in India, black peppercorns are more scented and aromatic, a subtlety preserved by adding them whole at the beginning or coarsely ground towards the end of cooking. In Kerala as few as 6–8 peppercorns may be used in a dish. Long pepper (*Piper longum*), resembling a small catkin, was known to the Romans and popular in Europe in medieval times. It is more perfumed but difficult to find, even in India, and is generally used whole. Both forms are hotter if food containing them is re-heated after freezing. White peppercorns, far less aromatic, are allowed to ripen

on vines from green to red, unlike black peppercorns, then fermented and skinned. They are rarely, if ever, used in the South.

Kerala's pepper is graded by sieving (the bigger the berries, the better the pepper), a process which also includes cleaning. The best export quality is MG1 (Malabar Garbelled 1), and even better is TGEB (Telicherry Garbelled Extra Bold).

ROASTED BLACK PEPPERCORNS

Earliest and simplest tempering: to bring out the perfumed oil of good black pepper, put a few tablespoons of whole peppercorns over medium heat in a dry frying pan and roast until they start cracking. Remove from heat, very roughly crush and serve in a bowl to sprinkle on food, or warm them in a few spoonfuls of oil before stirring into a dish.

CURRY LEAVES (kari patta, mitha neem)
BOT: *Chalcas koenigii (Murraya koenigii)*

•

While black pepper is used all over India, curry leaves – at once nutty, lemony and musky – are, with coconut and black mustard seeds, the taste of the South. They are available fresh and dried from Indian stores (double the quantity if using dried). Although technically a herb, they are often treated as a spice, fried in oil and ground into a masala or simply fried and added whole at the last minute as a tempering with mustard seeds.

MUSTARD SEEDS, Black (rai, aslrai, taramira)
BOT: *Brassica nigra*

•

Mustard's hot bitterness results when it is ground with water, a taste popular in northeast India, but not in Kerala, where the seeds are generally treated in one of two ways: added to a medium-hot dry frying pan until they pop (have a lid handy to prevent popped seeds all over your kitchen floor), then cooked with a wet masala to begin a dish, or, more often (to preserve their flavour) popped in hot oil or ghee and used as a final tempering. Treated in this way they develop the nutty sweetness of poppy seeds.

LIGHT TEMPERING FOR GREEN OR DELICATE VEGETABLES
1 tablespoon light sesame oil or 15 g (½ oz) ghee

½ teaspoon black mustard seeds

handful of fresh or dried curry leaves

Pop mustard seeds in medium-hot oil, remove from heat and stir in leaves until they begin to brown and crisp. For an oniony, garlicky flavour without the bother of chopping, stir in ¼ teaspoon of asafoetida powder with the leaves and cook until it no longer smells raw.

ANISEED (vilayati saunf – 'foreign fennel')
BOT: *Pimpinella anisum*

•

Anise adds a delicate sweet citrussy flavour to dishes, like a cross between mild licorice and bitter orange, ideal with fish. Used by ancient Arabs, Egyptians, Greeks and Romans, it identifies the meat and fish dishes of Kerala's Muslims, who are descended from Arab coastal traders rather than from Moguls and Turko-Afghans, as Muslims are in the North. When lightly toasted in a dry pan (as it should be if it is to be a final addition to dishes), aniseed loses this citrus quality and becomes more nutty, as do many of the anise-flavoured spices such as fennel and coriander.

GRILLED MEAT OR FISH/PRAWN TEMPERING

3 tablespoons light sesame or olive oil
1 teaspoon black mustard seeds
½ teaspoon aniseed
1–2 onions, finely sliced
handful of fresh or dried curry leaves

Over medium-high heat, pop the mustard seeds in oil. Lower heat, add aniseed and onions and stir-fry onions until caramelly. Remove from heat and stir in leaves until crisp.

STARCHY VEGETABLE OR LENTIL TEMPERING

40 g (1½ oz) ghee or butter or 3 tablespoons light sesame or olive oil
1 teaspoon black mustard seeds
3 garlic cloves, shredded
2.5 cm (1 inch) piece fresh root ginger, finely shredded
3–4 dried red chillies, seeded and crumbled
handful of fresh or dried curry leaves or fresh coriander

Over medium-high heat, pop mustard seeds in ghee. Lower heat and stir-fry garlic, ginger and chillies until lightly browned. Remove from heat and stir in curry leaves until crisp or coriander until wilted.

STARFRUIT COCONUT MASALA

Because delicate vegetables can be overpowered by strong aromatics, Hindu cooks generally prefer lighter spices (black mustard, pepper and coriander seeds) with curry and coriander leaves, fresh ginger and green chillies, ground fresh every day in the same way as Italian pesto. Starfruit (*carambola*), fresh green mango, lime and lemon juice are used when in season (starfruit is the mildest, most scented flavour), and when a pearly whiteness or golden colour is important – they do not darken sauce in the same way as tamarind. Thus, from March to May, colours on Kerala's tables change from autumnal brown and red to green and cream. To give tang to a bland dish or to freshen one made with canned coconut milk, 50 g (2 oz) of raw green mango (very similar in flavour and result to green damson plums) can be stirred in towards the end of cooking, or 1 large starfruit (puréed), 100 g (4 oz) of thick curd or 2–3 tablespoons of lime juice.

This is a very good fresh chutney to serve on its own or with fresh fish, or to cook any number of vegetables any number of ways. If starfruit is unavailable, substitute juice and zest of lime.

75 g (3 oz) fresh or creamed coconut
4–6 green chillies, seeded and chopped
big handful of fresh coriander, chopped
1 starfruit, chopped, or juice and grated zest of 1 lime
2 garlic cloves
2.5 cm (1 inch) piece fresh root ginger
½ teaspoon ground turmeric

1 teaspoon cumin seeds, toasted
8 peppercorns, toasted
½ teaspoon salt

Grind everything together to a smooth paste with 2 tablespoons of hot water. Best used within a few hours of making, but it will keep for 2 days in an air-tight container. If you are not using it immediately, add the garlic cloves just before serving.

——————————— *Uses* ———————————

• *Vegetables with fresh Masala* Cook 450 g (1 lb) of plantains or quartered potatoes in just enough boiling water to cover them. When they are tender but not soft, add Masala and 225 g (8 oz) green beans to the water. Simmer until sauce thickens and beans are cooked.

COCONUT CREAMED GREEN AND WHITE VEGETABLE STEW

Serves 4–6 cm

Avial – the ultimate recipe for using a coconut masala. Green vegetables – beans, fresh peas, drumstick gourd are most usual – but try green peppers, asparagus and baby broad beans. Simmer them with starchy vegetables such as potatoes, yam or plantains in turmeric-scented water, then finish with a wet coconut masala and the sour tang of thick buttermilk or yoghurt. Usually served with rice or the fermented rice cakes called 'hoppers', this is delicious with the Crisp Rice and Coconut Chapattis (page 27).

450 g (1 lb) new potatoes, halved, or plantains, cut in 2.5 cm (1 inch) chunks
¼ teaspoon ground turmeric
225 g (8 oz) green beans, cut in 5 cm (2 inch) lengths
225 g (8 oz) starchy green vegetable e.g. young broad beans and peas
275 g (10 oz) tender green vegetables e.g.

courgettes, broccoli, mangetout, cut in 5 cm (2 inch) pieces
1 quantity of Starfruit Coconut Masala (page 24)
250 ml (8 fl oz) buttermilk or 150 ml (5 fl oz) Greek-style yoghurt whisked with 125 ml (4 fl oz) cold water
TEMPERING
2–3 tablespoons light sesame oil
¼ teaspoon asafoetida powder
handful of fresh or dried curry leaves or fresh coriander

If not prepared already, grind together Starfruit Masala ingredients from recipe on page 24 with just enough yoghurt or buttermilk to achieve a pouring consistency.

Cook potatoes or plantains with turmeric in enough boiling water to cover. When just tender (cooking time will vary depending on age and variety of vegetables, but 20 minutes is about average), stir in Masala, and when it is incorporated, add remaining vegetables in order of tenderness (broccoli, courgettes, green beans, broad beans and peas will take about 10–12 minutes, mangetout and very new peas about 3). Simmer until cooked. Stir in remaining yoghurt or buttermilk and remove from heat.

Before serving, heat oil to medium-high, remove from heat, stir in asafoetida and curry leaves and while sizzling, pour over vegetables.

KERALAN WARM GREEN SALAD (THORAN)

Serves 4 as a side dish

A simpler method for cooking vegetables such as green beans, cabbage, spinach and green papaya (or any green vegetable which requires brief cooking) in their own steam. Most cookery books advise against touching the inside of chillies and to wear rubber gloves while handling them to avoid their burning oils. In fact, it is difficult to judge the heat of a fresh chilli without touching it to your tongue, at least briefly. Strength can vary depending on country of origin – whether Africa, India or Mexico.

1 small onion or 4 shallots
2–3 green chillies, seeded
2 garlic cloves
50–75 g (2–3 oz) fresh or creamed coconut
½ teaspoon salt, or to taste
1 teaspoon cumin seeds, toasted
¼ teaspoon ground turmeric
1–2 tablespoons oil
½ teaspoon black mustard seeds
450 g (1 lb) green vegetables

Grind together onion or shallots, chillies, garlic, coconut, salt, cumin and turmeric. Over medium-high heat, pop mustard seeds in oil. Add spice paste and fry until fragrant, stir in vegetables for a couple of minutes, then sprinkle 2 tablespoons of hot water over, cover and simmer over low heat for 6–8 minutes. Eat as is, sprinkle with fresh coriander or dress with one of the temperings on page 24. Another good one is ¼ teaspoon of asafoetida powder sizzled in 1 tablespoon of oil with 2 crumbled dried red chillies and a handful of curry leaves.

GREEN-SPICED COCONUT CASHEWS

Serves 4 as a side dish
or 2–3 as a main course

Cashews are one of Kerala's main cash crops. Here they are cooked as a vegetable dish with a very fresh green 'spring' taste. This would also make a delicious main course vegetarian dish, served over rice or noodles.

1 teaspoon coriander seeds
1 teaspoon cumin seeds

¼ teaspoon black peppercorns, roughly crushed
¼ teaspoon ground turmeric
½ teaspoon salt, or to taste
3–4 green chillies, seeded and chopped
4 cm (1½ inch) piece fresh ginger, grated
3 garlic cloves, chopped
8 tablespoons canned coconut milk
175 g (6 oz) unsalted raw cashews, soaked 30 minutes in water
juice of 2 fresh limes or 1 starfruit, puréed
1 tablespoon light sesame oil or 15 g (½ oz) ghee or butter
1 teaspoon black mustard seeds
large handful of fresh coriander, finely chopped

Over medium heat in a dry frying pan, toast coriander until it smells aromatic, add cumin and cook until it changes colour. Cool and grind to a fine powder.

Process together remaining spices, salt, chillies, ginger and garlic to a coarse purée, slowly adding a little coconut milk. Stir in remaining milk.

Over medium-high heat, cook spiced coconut masala until its sweetly spicy smell permeates your kitchen, then stir in nuts. Reduce heat to low and simmer until most of the liquid has been absorbed (about 15 minutes).

Just before serving, pour lime juice or starfruit into cashews and while it bubbles, prepare tempering: put oil in a small frying pan over high heat and when hot, add mustard seeds, keeping a lid handy so you don't wind up with a kitchen full of seeds. When they stop popping, tip immediately into the nuts and stir in coriander.

─────── *Variation* ───────

• *Red masala cashews* For a hotter, more wintry flavour with a sour fruitiness, leave out the green chillies, limes and coconut and substitute:

100 g (4 oz) tamarind paste
4–6 dried red chillies, toasted
2–3 good tomatoes, peeled and seeded, or canned Italian plum tomatoes
handful of fresh or dried curry leaves

Pour 10 tablespoons of boiling water over tamarind and soak 30 minutes. Sieve and discard seeds. Follow recipe above but purée spices with red chillies and tamarind liquid. Add tomatoes where you would have used lime and stir curry leaves into tempering to crisp them.

TANGY COCONUT CHICKEN STEW

Serves 4–6 as a main course

When I asked George Kuruvilla, probably the greatest living fan of BBC Radio, how to make chicken curry, he said 'First remove the feathers by dipping the bird in hot water. After that, you cut off the legs and remove the liver – a very fine thing to add, not as good as foie gras, but delicious.' The following is a faster version of his farmer's recipe, a hot and sour stew often served at Easter in Syrian Christian homes. The spices are put in a muslin bag to preserve the sauce's snowy whiteness – just flecked with green chillies and curry leaves. Usually served with equally snowy hoppers but excellent with rice or Crisp Rice and Coconut Chapattis (right).

½ teaspoon black peppercorns
4 cloves
2.5 cm (1 inch) piece cinnamon stick, roughly crushed
1 teaspoon coriander seeds
1×450 ml (15 fl oz) can of coconut milk or equivalent fresh
2 large onions, chopped
2 garlic cloves
5 cm (2 inch) piece fresh root ginger, ½ roughly chopped, ½ shredded

3 green chillies, 1 seeded, 2 sliced finely crosswise
2 tablespoons sunflower oil
2–3 large potatoes, cut in 5 cm (2 inch) chunks
750 g (1½ lb) chicken (legs, thighs etc.) skinned and cut in 5 cm (2 inch) chunks
salt to taste
juice of 2 limes
fresh coriander or curry leaves, to garnish

Tie peppercorns, cloves, cinnamon and coriander seeds in a small piece of thin cloth. If coconut milk has a thick layer of coconut on top, spoon this out and reserve. Mix remaining thin coconut milk with 125 ml (4 fl oz) of water. If milk is already blended, pour off 250 (8 fl oz) and mix with water. Grind onions, garlic, chopped ginger and 1 chilli to a coarse purée.

Over medium-high heat, fry onion mixture in oil until soft but not brown. Pour in thin milk, add spice bag, bring to a low boil, then slip in the potatoes. After 5 minutes, add chicken pieces and salt to taste. Simmer, stirring sauce from time to time, until potatoes are tender and chicken cooked through (about 20 minutes).

Raise heat and stir in thick coconut milk and remaining chillies and ginger. After a couple of minutes, stir in lime juice and remove from heat. Although not traditional, I often add the shredded zest of 1 lime. Garnish with coriander.

CRISP RICE AND COCONUT CHAPATTIS

Makes 12 (serves 4–6 as a side dish)

Rice 'hoppers', the traditional partners for Keralan fish, chicken and mutton stews, are savoury sponges shaped like flying saucers and fermented with 'toddy', a liqueur made from the coconut palm before it flowers. The stalk is cut for sap twice daily, the evening brew being sweeter. These chapattis are the local Muslims' alternative to hoppers; crunchy with coconut, faintly scented with aniseed, and perfect to mop up fiery sauces. To make them with fresh coconut, as they would be in Kerala, finely grate a quarter of a coconut, and add water instead of coconut milk – you may need less than 5 tablespoons.

225 g (8 oz) basmati rice
40 g (1½ oz) desiccated coconut
½ teaspoon aniseed, toasted and coarsely ground
¼–½ teaspoon salt
5 tablespoons canned coconut milk

Cover rice with hot water and soak 5 hours. Drain, rinse and grind with coconut, aniseed and salt, slowly adding coconut milk until you have a stiff, sticky paste. Roll into 12 balls and keep covered.

In a small deep saucepan, heat about 2.5 cm (1 inch) oil until a piece of dough dropped into it sizzles immediately and turns golden in about 40 seconds. Flatten one dough ball to about 5 mm (¼ inch) thick, lightly brushing your hands with oil if necessary to stop it sticking (it will be very crumbly – more like biscuit dough than bread). Slip it into oil and as it rises to the surface, gently press it down with a slotted spoon. Fry until golden brown, then drain on kitchen paper and keep warm while you fry the rest.

STIR-FRIED BEEF WITH COCONUT AND GINGER

Serves 4 with other dishes

Muslims and Syrian Christians use a lot of oil, fish and meat, even game, which can support the heavier 'warm' aromatics (clove, cassia, cardamom). But even these, unlike northern dry-fried masalas, tend to be fried first in oil, then ground to a paste with coconut, browned onion and green chillies. In Syrian Christian homes, this beef is cooked slowly first in a little spiced water until tender, then stir-fried until almost dry with caramelized onions and curry leaves. It winds up tasting like Chinese sweet-and-sour crispy-fried beef. But as most beef in Kerala is from ancient bullocks who have trekked from Tamil Nadu over the Western Ghats to be butchered legally by Keralan Christians, this is a faster version for more tender cuts. The addition of vinegar at the final stage is popular with Muslims, Jews and Syrian Christians, whose heavier dishes it suits.

450 g (1 lb) rump steak or other good cut of beef, trimmed of fat
4 garlic cloves
2 tablespoons wine vinegar
5 cm (2 inch) piece fresh root ginger
2 green chillies, seeded
3 dried red chillies, toasted and crumbled
½ teaspoon ground turmeric
1 teaspoon coriander seeds, toasted and coarsely ground
3 tablespoons light sesame or vegetable oil
2 medium onions halved lengthwise, finely sliced
½ teaspoon black mustard seeds or ½ teaspoon Garam Masala
25–50 g (1–2 oz) fresh coconut, finely sliced
1 teaspoon salt, or to taste
handful of fresh or dried curry leaves
handful of fresh coriander

Slice beef across grain into thin strips. Grind together garlic with half the vinegar, ginger and chillies and all the spices. Toss with beef and leave to marinate for an hour or so – but if you haven't the time, it will still taste good.

Shred remaining ginger and chilli. Over medium heat, fry onion in oil until golden, add ginger and chilli and continue frying until onion is light brown. While this cooks, put mustard seeds (if using) over medium-high heat until they finish popping.

Raise heat and add beef, coconut slices, salt and curry leaves, stir-frying to lightly brown meat. Stir in remaining vinegar, bubble for a second, remove from heat and sprinkle with mustard seeds or garam masala and fresh coriander.

─────────── *Variation* ───────────

• Muslims on the coast have a version with mutton. Use lamb instead of beef, omit the green chillies and coriander seeds and grind double the red chillies and 2 teaspoons of aniseed.

─────────── *Serving suggestion* ───────────

• Because of its dryness, stir-fried beef is always served in Syrian Christian homes with a mild yoghurt 'curry' called *moru kachiyade*: pop 1 teaspoon of black mustard seeds in 2–3 tablespoons of light sesame or olive oil, add 2 finely sliced onions and fry until lightly browned. Grind 50–75 g/2–3 oz of fresh or creamed coconut to a fine paste with ¼ teaspoon of ground turmeric (some add 2.5 cm (1 inch) of root ginger, which is very refreshing) and fry this just until fragrant. Remove from heat and stir into 300 g (11 oz) of creamy Greek-style yoghurt.

SAFFRON LAMB DUMPLINGS WITH CHILLI AND GINGER PESTO

Serves 4–6 as a main course

A recipe with all its roots showing (mint is rare in Kerala and soft pasta non-existent) – these saffron-scented ravioli-type dumplings called *kubbah* are a speciality of old Jewish families in Fort Cochin. Mrs Cohen, who made them for me, said the vegetables for the soup base could be anything from okra to tomatoes, although she made what was essentially a beetroot borscht, giving the final dish a Hindu temple palette of magenta, yellow and mint green. You can make the dumplings with fish (in which case it is better to substitute coriander for the mint).

100 g (4 oz) plain flour
¼ teaspoon ground turmeric (optional)
salt
big pinch of saffron threads
1–2 tablespoon light sesame oil
1 onion, finely chopped
225 g (8 oz) minced lamb or beef
4 green chillies, seeded
large bunch of fresh mint, about 50 g (2 oz)
½ teaspoon coarsely ground black peppercorns
2 teaspoons wine vinegar
4 garlic cloves
4 cm (1½ inch) piece fresh root ginger, chopped
handful of fresh curry leaves or coriander
about 2 litres (3½ pints) good soup stock (made with beetroot for preference)

First make (pasta) dough: sift together flour, turmeric and a pinch of salt. Stir in 3–4 tablespoons of cold water, just enough to bind flour. Knead for 5 minutes to a smooth dough, dust with flour and rest in a plastic bag for 30 minutes.

Soak saffron in a spoonful of hot water. Fry onion in oil until very soft, then grind to a coarse paste with saffron, meat, 2 chillies, half the mint, ½ teaspoon salt, pepper and 1 teaspoon vinegar.

Divide dough into 24 balls and keep covered. One at a time, flatten and stretch each dough ball until it is very thin, put 1 teaspoon of meat in centre and squeeze dough together like a little purse, twisting and gently pulling to remove excess dough, being careful not to tear dumpling. Repeat until you have used up both meat and dough.

Make pesto by grinding together garlic, ginger, curry leaves (reserve some for soup) and remaining chillies and mint. Bring soup to boil with a few more curry or coriander leaves and 1 teaspoon of vinegar, drop in dumplings and simmer for 10 minutes after they rise to the surface. Stir in pesto just before serving.

Steamed Coconut Fish in Rice Parcels

Serves 4–6 as a main course

The Muslims of northern Malabar, known as *moplahs* (meaning 'bridegroom' or a person held in esteem, so-called because the Arab traders who settled here inter-married with local women) cook a variety of rare dishes with steamed rice. This one, *meen pathiri*, a soft, sweet-spiced rice dough enclosing fragrant coconutty fish resembles Chinese steamed pork buns. Local legend says that the large 2-handled wok known as a China pot, *cinachatti*, was inherited from T'ang dynasty Chinese traders. Perhaps this recipe was as well. It is based loosely on one in Ummi Abdullah's unusual book *Malabar Muslim Cookery*, which uses local fish steamed in green banana leaves. Greaseproof paper, if less beautiful, works just as well (see photograph on page 30).

RICE DOUGH
350 g (12 oz) basmati rice

120 g (4½ oz) creamed coconut, cut in chunks

¾ teaspoon aniseed, roughly crushed

1 small onion

seeds from 3 cardamom pods, roughly crushed

½ teaspoon salt

FISH STUFFING
1½ tablespoons grated creamed coconut

generous ¼ teaspoon aniseed

½ teaspoon ground cinnamon

12 peppercorns

2 cloves

1 big onion, finely chopped

3 green chillies, seeded and finely sliced

1½ tablespoons light sesame or vegetable oil

2 cm (¾ inch) fresh root ginger, grated

Steamed Coconut Fish.

30

1 garlic clove, crushed
¾ teaspoon coriander seeds, coarsely ground
¼ teaspoon ground turmeric
350 g (12 oz) firm white fish fillets (e.g. haddock, cod, etc.), skinned and cut in 5 cm (2 inch) chunks
handful of fresh coriander or curry leaves, chopped
rice flour, for dusting

Pour rice into a large pan of boiling water, boil hard for 3 minutes, then soak for 3 hours. Grind to a smooth sticky paste with remaining dough ingredients, adding up to 2 tablespoons of hot water if necessary.

Grind coconut with aniseed, cinnamon, pepper and cloves, adding 250 ml (8 fl oz) of hot water when it is smooth. Fry onions and chillies in oil until soft and golden, stir in ginger and garlic and when you can smell them, add coriander seeds and turmeric. Mix well and pour in coconut cream. When thick, remove from heat and toss fish and leaves with sauce.

Pre-heat oven to 230°C/450°F/Gas 8. Have ready a deep roasting tin with a rack sitting above it and a piece of kitchen foil big enough to cover. Butter 4–6 sheets of greaseproof paper measuring 30×35 cm (12×14 inches). Divide dough into 4–6 pieces – it will be sticky, more of a paste. Divide each piece in 2, dip dough and your fingers in flour and pat out half the pieces on greased paper to 5 mm (¼ inch) thick rounds. Spoon on ¼–⅙ fish mixture, top with remaining rounds of rice dough, which will be even more crumbly, and press edges together to seal. Wrap loosely and set on rack. Repeat with remaining dough and fish. Fill pan with hot water, seal tightly with foil and bake for 30 minutes.

On the Malabar Coast this is served with fresh coconut milk but Green Coconut and Coriander Chutney (page 92) is even better.

Uses

- Stuff boned, skinned chicken instead of fish.
- At the famous toddy house called Mulapanthal (Canopy of Jasmine) outside Cochin, where all college boys go to get drunk, prawns, crab and freshwater mussels are steamed first in their shells then smeared with some of this rich dough and stir-fried. Try steaming scrubbed mussels until their shells open, spread a little dough inside and put under a very hot grill until brown.

Fish or Shellfish Masala

The most caustic thing one can say of a Malabar feast is, 'The fish was served without due honour.' Like the people of Tuscany and Provence, Keralans give fish a final drizzle of freshly pressed oil after cooking, although here the oil is from a coconut, which is even more versatile than the olive. This masala from the Malabari Muslim community can be used to make clams braised in cinnamon-scented coconut milk with coriander leaves – the Cochin version of *moules marinière*. Simmer scrubbed clams in coconut milk with a stick of cinnamon. When they open, stir in a few spoonfuls of masala and serve.

1–1½ teaspoons cayenne pepper
½ teaspoon ground turmeric
1 teaspoon aniseed, toasted and ground
½ teaspoon salt
4 cloves, toasted and ground
8 black peppercorns, toasted and ground
1 teaspoon coriander seeds, toasted and coarsely ground
1 cm (½ inch) piece cinnamon stick, toasted and ground
50 g (2 oz) fresh or creamed coconut
1 small onion, chopped

Mix together all spices and grind with coconut and onion.

Variations

• Spread onto 750 g (1½ lb) raw prawns and cook under a hot grill until pink (3–4 minutes). As you peel them, dip into melted butter and lime juice.
• Spread onto fish steaks and grill.
• Soak 175 g (6 oz) of basmati rice in water for 2 hours and grind with masala. Spread on mussels that have been steamed open, and grill on the half shell until sizzling.

DRY-FRIED PRAWN OR FISH MASALA

Serves 4 with other dishes

Even frozen prawns become less boring when marinated in this sweet and sour masala. This would be made with Kerala's delicious prawns or dense white fish and soured with *kokum*, but ordinary tamarind is more widely available. Eat with something wet – try a glass of cold beer.

> *50 g (2 oz) tamarind paste or juice of 2 limes*
> *1 quantity of Fish or Shellfish Masala*
> *(without coconut and onion) (page 31)*
> *450 g (1 lb) raw prawns, peeled (about 750 g/1½ lb with shells) or thawed frozen raw prawns or boned swordfish cut in 1 cm (½ inch) chunks*
> *50 g (2 oz) fresh or creamed coconut*
> *2.5 cm (1 inch) piece fresh root ginger, chopped*
> *4 garlic cloves*
> *4 green chillies, seeded and chopped*
> *1 big onion*
> *2 tablespoons light sesame, peanut or sunflower oil*
> *handful of fresh or dried curry leaves (optional)*
> *1 tablespoon white wine vinegar*
> *1 teaspoon black mustard seeds, toasted*

If using tamarind, cover in boiling water and soak 30 minutes. Strain. Toss together masala spices, prawns or fish and tamarind or lime juice. Leave to marinate 10–30 minutes (up to 1 hour if using frozen prawns).

Grind together coconut, ginger, garlic and chillies. Halve onion lengthwise and finely slice crosswise. Over medium heat fry onion in oil until soft and golden. Add ground paste and cook until fragrant and lightly browned. Turn up heat, add prawns and curry leaves and stir until prawns turn pink. Add vinegar and mustard seeds, let sizzle for a second and serve.

Variations

• Stir in 2 chopped tomatoes and 135 ml (4½ fl oz) of hot water instead of vinegar and simmer until sauce thickens. Instead of curry leaves, sprinkle with fresh coriander.
• *Fish or prawn curry* To turn the dish into a coconut curry, instead of creamed coconut, add:

> *450 ml (15 fl oz) fresh or canned coconut milk*
> *2 potatoes or plantains, cut in chunks*
> *handful of grated fresh coconut (optional, but creamed coconut will not do)*

Separate thick and thin coconut milk (the thick milk will have solidified on top of tin). Grind masala (as above) but without creamed coconut. After it has been fried, add potatoes or plantains, stir-fry for a minute or two, then pour in thin coconut milk and cook potatoes until just tender. Add prawns, thick milk and curry leaves and simmer until prawns turn pink. Stir in vinegar and mustard seeds and top with fresh coconut.

BANANAS AND CASHEWS IN CARDAMOM BUTTER

Serves 2–4 as a dessert

A 5-minute pudding, delicious with the Orange Cardamom Indian Custard on page 188. While Mysore contributes about three-quarters of

India's crop of bananas, Kerala has the widest variety – over 250 types from bright green through every shade of yellow to clay pink. They appear in stews, dumplings and a rice breakfast dish steamed in bamboo. They are the first item to be served on the banana leaf for a feast – banana chips made from slicing and deep-frying large unripe fruit, then salted and dipped in molasses – and the last to complete a feast, cooked with raw sugar and fragrant rice. The ivory-coloured male stem bud, *pindi*, is steamed in vegetable dishes and the flower, *kumbu*, used in fried dumplings.

juice of 1 lime
2–3 large firm bananas, halved crosswise then lengthwise, or a mixture of fresh pineapple slices and bananas
25–40 g (1–1½ oz) ghee or unsalted butter
1 teaspoon muscovado or dark brown sugar
seeds from 3 green cardamom pods, ground
12 raw cashews, roughly crumbled
small handful of raisins

Squeeze lime juice over the bananas to stop them browning. Over medium heat, melt ghee with sugar and cardamom. Stir in cashews and raisins until they start to brown. Add bananas, tumbling in the browning butter until well coated and caramelized on edges. Spoon onto dishes and serve.

STRIPED BANANA AND NUT PUDDING
Serves 6

Kerala's answer to bread pudding comes in caramel brown and cream stripes of cardamom-scented batter. This is based on *naiyada* in Umni Abdulla's book on Malabar Muslim cooking.

4 large eggs
150 g (5 oz) dark brown sugar
90 g (3½ oz) plain white flour, sifted
pinch of salt
seeds from 4–6 green cardamom pods, crushed
275 ml (9 fl oz) milk
50 g (2 oz) broken cashew nuts
50 g (2 oz) raisins
40 g (1½ oz) ghee or butter, plus extra for tin
1 medium banana

Pre-heat oven to 220°C/425°F/Gas 7. Butter a 7 inch springform cake tin and put in oven to heat.

One by one, beat eggs into sugar until well blended. In a separate bowl, whisk together flour, salt, cardamom and milk, adding milk a little at a time to ensure a smooth batter.

Fry nuts and raisins in butter until nuts are toasted and raisins puffed and crisp. Pour roughly one-third (about 7 tablespoons) of flour batter into hot cake tin, swirling to cover base. Sprinkle with a few buttery nuts and raisins and put in oven until set (about 2 minutes). Pour on one-third of egg batter, sprinkle with nuts and raisins and put in oven to set (about 5–6 minutes). Repeat with flour batter and melted butter instead of nuts. Continue layering and cooking, and lavishly spread the last layer (egg) with nuts, raisins and sliced banana. This puffs up while cooking then sinks back when removed from oven.

Remove from pan, serve warm sliced in wedges with cold Greek-style yoghurt or cream.

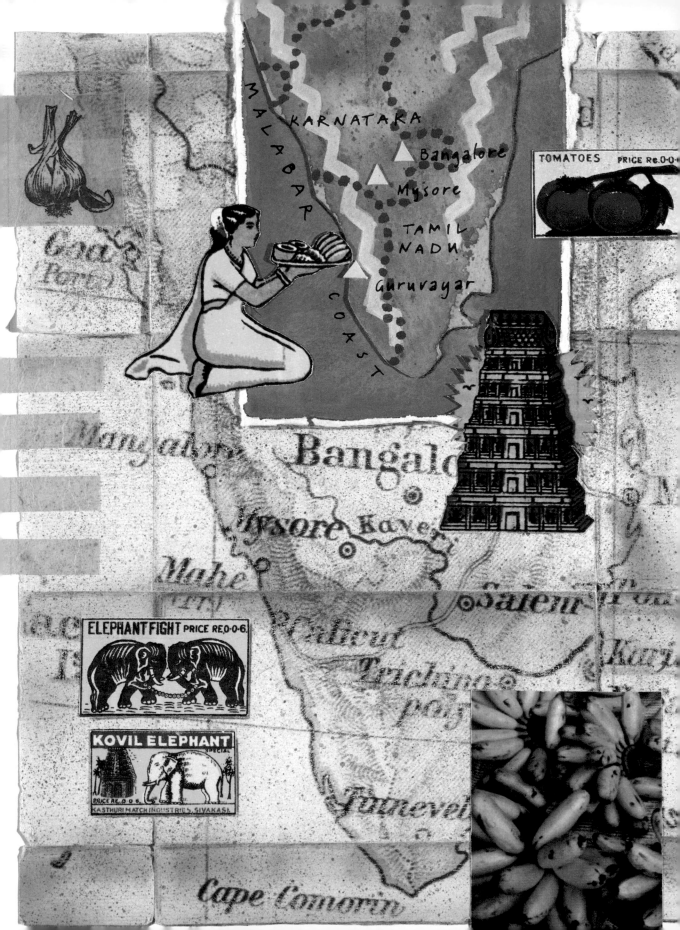

CHAPTER TWO

A
FEAST
IN THE
TEMPLE

•

Tuskers Run Amok Due to Overwork at Festival Time!

KERALA NEWSPAPER HEADLINE, MARCH 1993

Elephants are the celebrities of southern India. During the monsoon that precedes their busy festival season, they are fed meat as well as spices, an enormous biryani of goats' brains and chicken pounded up in rice with ginger, turmeric and pepper, considered to be good for their sensitive skins. When they carry the deity in the temple at festival time, of course, they revert to being strict vegetarians.

I went by taxi under a tarnished silver monsoon sky to a festival at Guruvayar, north of Cochin, once home of the most famous elephant in Kerala. While he lived, he was revered as a sort of cross between Elvis and God. When he died, people wept openly in the streets and all the newspapers had black edges. A movie was made of his life.

During Hindu festivals, highly decorated ceremonial umbrellas are borrowed from the Christians, I was told. In return for this favour, Hindus lend their elephants for use in Christian festivals. 'For what is a festival without elephants?' says a friend – and adds, bestowing elephant ratings like Michelin stars, 'It is only a three-elephant festival you are attending.'

As we surfed on rain-slicked tyres around rice paddies, the driver said that we were experiencing Kerala's 'season of sharp rain in the afternoons'. A sharp rain in India means that the telephone wires are down and cars float. Driving through such a rain in an old Ambassador with steamed-up windows and bad pirate tapes of Indian pop music has a surreal quality.

What can I say about this taxi ride? My advice is: when in India, always choose Christian or Muslim taxi drivers; they don't believe in reincarnation. Our driver was Hindu. He believed in *karma*. If it was our *karma* to be sent on to our next life by the lorry full of dangerous chemicals driving towards us at 200 km per hour on our side of the road, then mere brakes would not alter anything.

My guide to Guruvayar was Pepita Seth, an English photographer resident in India. They call her *Anamadama* 'the elephant memsahib', because she's mad about elephants. She once owned a share in an elephant with her friend Mr Menon, an insurance agent. He insures elephants as well as houses. As one of the few non-Hindus to have been allowed into the austere and traditional Kerala temples, Pepita has photographed rare snake rituals and spirit possessions, exorcisms and blood sacrifices.

'There is a government enforcement against blood sacrifices now,' she said. 'They still go on, but more people use turmeric instead. Mixed with lime, it turns blood-red.' This is one of the five colours in the intricate, ephemeral floor paintings called *kolums* used to invoke the deity, along with white from powdered rice, dense black from burnt paddy husks, green from ground leaf and yellow from pure turmeric.

Turmeric, with saffron, has been the most important spice in Hindu religious rites since pre-Vedic times. Its golden colour is known as *shubh*, meaning auspicious or beautiful, perhaps

linked originally to its antiseptic properties:
it is shaken over temples during festivals and
added to the vast tureens of rice and lentils
prepared daily in certain temples to serve
pilgrims. Some temple kitchens are so famous
that many houses in the immediate vicinity
do not have their own kitchens because they
were always occupied by high-caste Brahmins
who took all their meals in the temple.

Temple festivals are a favourite time for
weddings, and by noon the feast hall outside
Guruvayar temple had already fed 700
wedding guests. Food was served on banana
leaves – twenty-five rupees for a leaf, with
unlimited refills. We tried two of the traditional temple sweets called *payasum* – one
was a delicious liquid rice pudding redolent
of cardamom and raw sugar, the other one a
sickly sticky lentil porridge redolent of cardamom-scented wallpaper paste. An acquired
taste.

Guruvayar's classic Keralan over-
hanging roof gave it the Oriental demeanour
of a Buddhist temple transplanted from
Beijing. As a non-Hindu, I could not enter
with Pepita but from a balcony above, I

*BELOW: The Carmen Miranda head-dress of a cow
at Harvest festival in Karnataka.*
*FACING PAGE: Elephants are the film stars of south
India; here, a mahout rides his elephant past the
temple at Guruvayar in Kerala.*

watched snaking queues of people waiting to offer food to the deity. Hinduism is a kitchen
religion where gods as well as people have to be fed. Some deities are so coated with melted
ghee and turmeric by pilgrims that the figures lose their features inside golden stalagmites of
fat. And even gods like spices. The deity at Ayappa is said to favour pepper, while greedy,
elephant-headed Ganesh prefers sweets flavoured with cardamom. In one Ganesh temple,
cooks prepare cardamom cakes and run to offer some to him while they are still hot. Any that
he doesn't gobble up are offered to visiting pilgrims.

How can a Westerner grasp the intricacies of a country in which there are 36,000 gods
(more or less)? Where Brahma, Creator of the Universe, will be dissolved and the sun and stars
and all life extinguished after a predetermined span of one hundred celestial years (that's
311,040,000,000,000 mortal years)? Where harvest festivals feature cows with bunches of
bananas and peppercorns tied between their horns, Carmen Miranda fashion?

Hinduism, the Syrian Christian George Isaacs told me, is a system encompassing everything from human sexuality to the correct spicing of food to concern for the environment: 'the most complex effort mankind has ever made to reach an understanding of the whole of creation'. He saw Hinduism's cuisine as one of its greatest achievements. 'Without taking life, it satisfies all man's health requirements, his need for flavour and beauty, his desire for luxury.'

I met a genius in the North, a Brahmin called Dr Push Pesh Panth from a village in what he referred to as 'the hills' (the Himalayas), famous for its geniuses. He opened doors for me into the Hindu mind – and the Hindu kitchen. 'Before you start cooking with spices,' he said, 'you must understand *why* we use them.' It wasn't necessary to follow local recipes slavishly, because often the spices were added for their vitamin content as much as flavour.

Dr Panth was a university professor in international relations who had taken a sabbatical to write about Indian food, and his words had the resonance of lyric verse learned at school. 'In the Vedic texts' *materia medica* it says, "A hungry man will indulge in all the sins." You are sinner or saint according to whether you have eaten well.'

In the ancient Indian Ayurvedic (science of life) system of medicine, he told me, spices are used not only for flavouring; they can alleviate or prevent medical problems, enhance a certain mood or trigger a physical reaction. 'If you go to an Ayurvedic doctor with a headache, he will not give you an aspirin, he will ask why you have that headache at all. It may be that your diet does not suit your metabolism, your climate – or the season. Some spices, like nutmeg, mace, cinnamon and black cardamom are strong stimulants only suitable for regions whose winters are more extreme; in the south, lighter spices like mustard seed, turmeric and cumin are preferable. A whole chapter of the Hindu holy text, the *Bhagwat Geeta*, is dedicated to classifying food and spices and their correlation to personality types and modes of action.'

The doctrine propounded by Dr Panth might have seemed pure mysticism but for the current research into how diet can relieve stress or create hyperactivity in children. Nutmeg and mace for instance, are known to contain toxic myristicin, a stimulant and hallucinogen. The fact that traditional Indian texts describe its effect in religious rather than scientific terms does not make their prescriptions less effective.

Food, religion and theatre are not separated here, as they are in the west. An example is the southern dance-drama *Kathakali* and its more complex form, *Sanghakkali*, (whose performers re-tell the Hindus' great religious epics), which emerged in Kerala in the seventh century. The feast before their dances gave rise to a tradition of pre-dinner speeches in tribute to the coming dishes. One local historian called this a case of the stomach, instead of the heart, seeking lyrical expression. After the feast, while the replete performers danced about brandishing ladles, a poet especially expert in nonsense gourmet verse would enter. Unlike the dancers, he was non-vegetarian, as were his verses:

> *Trim off the tail of the skate,*
> *Fry it well on a spit,*
> *If she eats this with a coconut bit,*

I swear to you, mate,
The teen-ager will become a nubile wench.

Verse as menu: Indian culinary traditions being largely oral, many spice masalas and recommended menus were taught as sayings like this one to make them more memorable.

The temple compound becomes a theatre in the round during festivals, whereas the traditional Indian open-air kitchen is a permanent stage. If the participants are orthodox Brahmins, a division between performers and audience is strictly observed. Ash is sprinkled around the cooking area in a sacred square, symbolizing the structure of the cosmos, and no one must enter save the cook, lest they cast their polluting shadow over the rice pot.

'It's a magic act, cooking rice,' said Bill Aitken, a Scottish writer who had spent 11 years in a Hindu ashram, before being seduced away from austerity by an Indian princess.

'What if I were an English memsahib and dipped my ladle for a taste in an orthodox Brahmin's rice pot?'

'Your action would be followed by the house falling down and every dish in it being broken most dramatically. Even the cook must not taste the food. When he is frying a spice masala, say, he must rely on sight and experience alone.'

This strictly oral and visual approach applies only up to a point. Most information is acquired by sticking your hand in the chapatti dough. 'I cannot give you a recipe,' one cook told me. 'You must come and put your own nose over the pot. The cinnamon will tell you when it releases its aromatic oils.'

The ancient Indo-Aryans committed their prized records to memory rather than to papyrus or clay because they believed that every material, apart from the human mind, perishes with time.

There are many spice roads in Kerala. I chose to take the old medieval route northeast out of the succulent greens across the ancient, arid Deccan plateau – to the diamond mines of Golconda, through Mysore and the ghost city of Hampi, the Pompeii of India. Capital of the southern Hindu empire of Vijayanagar until it fell in the sixteenth century, Hampi monopolized the spice and cotton trade and rivalled the Moguls of the North. It is now a ruin the size of Rome.

Every road on the Deccan leads to a Hindu temple, each one densely carved in exuberant surface patterns depicting gods and goddesses. Some are austere in dove-grey stone. Some are painted flesh pink, chrome yellow, chocolate, peppermint. Some deities' heads are so encrusted with scarlet pigment they appear molten. The old bigot, Lord Macauley, did not approve. 'Through the whole Hindu pantheon you will look in vain for anything resembling those beautiful and majestic forms which stood in the shrines of ancient Greece,' he wrote in 1843. 'All is hideous and grotesque and ignoble.' The closer he examined Hindu religion and architecture, the more he found a muddled masala.

In southern India I found Italy: coffee as strong and frothy as a Milanese cappuccino; theatrical traditions to match the *commedia dell'arte*'s joyous vulgarity; the colours of Neapolitan ceramics; the sweet and sour flavours of medieval Sicily. It was a masala, but in the original Persian sense of the word, meaning all the things needed to prepare something such as a book. It was the architecture of storytellers.

Order lies in the details. A close look reveals themes in Mysore's crowded covered market that the first glance missed. In one corridor a kaleidoscope of Day-Glo colour resolves into neat cones of ground spices and pigments. In a second, small, muscular brown men hook huge branches of bananas over each shoulder like yellow Japanese armour, their legs bent under the weight. In a corridor apparently devoted to the colour green, women grade betel and banana leaves (the dinner plates of the South) by size, and a vendor carefully places one red chilli on every small pile of shelled peas. The Mysore masala shop looks like a giant's paintbox, with each variety of rice, beans, lentils and spice displayed in its own silver pan for inspection.

The selling and preparation of food is a folk art here. It is the poor of India, not the rich, who most appreciate the alchemy of spices – the ability of a handful of lentils and a few dried pods and seeds to transform bland boiled rice into a subtle feast.

LEFT: Edible folk art – pa'an leaves in concentric circles and volcanoes of ground spice and pigment are arranged in Mysore market as precisely as the masks below are painted for Kerala's Kathakali dance theatre.

41

The Muslim Tipu Sultan, 'Tiger' of Mysore, who united Malabar's Islamic spice merchants against the Hindu landowners and the British, would have enjoyed Mysore market. He was interested in agriculture as well as war, and while terrorizing the British pepper traders in Tellicherry, he made a few positive contributions to the local cuisine. In one letter he wrote, 'Clove and nutmeg seeds and plants must be brought back from Mauritius.' These were the aromatic spices beloved of Arabs and Persians, and not native to the subcontinent. He also introduced pineapples from Africa and avocados from Mexico and cultivated the *piper betel* creeper to fill the silver pa'an and spice box next to his throne.

Tipu died against the wall of his fortress of Srirangapatnam, 'Port of the Lord of the World', fighting a combined force of British and Hyderabadis. Never again throughout the years of the Raj would Britain lose its grip on India's spice trade. Nine years later, in 1808, an English Lord stopped off on his way to Bangalore and enjoyed a plate of strawberries from what had once been Tipu's garden, noting its abundance of fruit and vegetables.

The garden has now vanished – converted into a thousand peasant allotments around Mysore. But every year the last surviving member of Tipu's family makes the long journey from Calcutta to pay his respects at the domed tombs of his glorious ancestors. 'And it is very difficult for him,' said the guide who followed me around, 'because in Calcutta he is only a rickshaw driver.'

elephant. Mysore Palace.

Flavours of the Hindu South

•

TURMERIC, FENUGREEK AND SPICY TAMARIND

As one moves north or east out of fish-eating Kerala, away from the coast, the sweetness and perfumed quality of coconut oil is replaced by nutty sesame oil, and food colours change from the Malabar Coast's creamy whites and greens to the ochre and reds of lentils, beans and dried red chillies. There are still curry leaves and mustard seeds (the great southern spices), but in addition fenugreek and toasted pulses provide nutrition as well as sweet and earthy flavours to the vegetarian diet.

FENUGREEK SEEDS (*methi*)
BOT: *Trigonella foenum-graecum*
•

Actually a protein-rich, highly nutritious legume, orangey-yellow *foenum-graecum*, 'Greek hay', is used primarily as a spice. The taste it imparts to dishes is mild and bitter-sweet, with a golden colour like caramelized celery.

Together with asafoetida and fresh ginger, fenugreek is one of the spices believed by Indians to inhibit the windy effects of starchy vegetables and pulses, hence its inclusion in vegetarian dishes. Ayurvedic doctors recommend a few seeds soaked in water as a digestive. It must always be dry-roasted before use to get rid of bitterness and care must be taken to prevent it burning, when it turns from yellow to red and becomes bitter. Its leaves have a strong, pleasantly bitter flavour – delicious mixed into fried rice or noodles or stewed with sesame oil and a splash of vinegar.

FENUGREEK TEMPERING

To stir into earthy or starchy dishes like potatoes, lentils or cabbage.

40 g (1½ oz) ghee or butter or
3 tablespoons light sesame oil
1 teaspoon fenugreek seeds

Heat ghee until sizzling, stir in fenugreek seeds until they turn chestnut brown, then stir immediately into dish.

PULSES

In the South, 'spice' is re-defined: the lentil becomes the pulse not only in a culinary sense but in the sense of a heartbeat. It is both ballast – in breads, soups, stews, pancakes, sweets of cardamom and coconut – and spice: dry-roasted until its mealy texture is transformed into a warm and nutty pepperiness.

Sweeter than similar-looking *toovar dal*, the Indian species of yellow split peas (hulled split chickpeas), *channa dal*, is small and black when whole – called *kala* or *desi channa*. I have seen the same black variety sold in the markets of Puglia in southeast Italy. Like the Italians, Indians grind chickpeas into flour (*besan*) and use it instead of wheatflour to make sweets, fried pastries and batters. It is also ground with raw sugar and cardamom to make a filling reminiscent of marzipan. As a spice, it is generally dry-roasted until it changes colour, then mixed with mustard seeds and curry leaves fried in oil, a process that adds protein as well as nutty flavour. If it is to be used as a spice for slow-cooked dishes such as dals and soups, its initial roasting can be as little as 30 seconds, stirring often until coloured; if used as a final tempering, 10–12 minutes dry-roasting is better to make it digestible. Do this with enough peas to fill up a jam jar and save on last-minute preparation.

Yellow split lentils, *toovar/toor dal*, have a dark, earthy flavour popular all over India,

although the pink version cooks twice as quickly – useful when roasting it as a spice – and has a sweeter, spicier flavour. Both types cook to a smooth golden purée. Some Asian markets sell *toor dal* rubbed with oil as a preservative – wash off before use.

White/black grams or beans, *urad/urith dal*, are available 'washed' (split white) or whole black, both used in southern India as a spice to flavour vegetable and pulse preparations. Urad dal gives off a rather odd, musky, earthy smell while toasting and, like channa and toor dal, if used to spice slow-cooked dishes it needs only a few minutes dry-roasting in a frying pan but should be roasted for about 10–12 minutes as a final tempering.

DRY BEAN CHUTNEY

Makes about 2 jam jars

The salt and pepper of vegetarian South India: use it the same way and remember that it adds nutrition as well as flavour.

75 g (3 oz) each urad dal, toor dal, split or whole mung beans
1 tablespoon black peppercorns
1 teaspoon fenugreek seeds
50 g (2 oz) sesame seeds
2–4 green chillies, finely chopped
2 teaspoons sea salt

Roast beans together for 12–15 minutes over medium-low heat (or spread out on a tray in an oven heated to 190°C/375°F/Gas 5) until they change colour and smell toasty. Roast pepper and fenugreek until fenugreek darkens but watch it doesn't burn. Toast sesame seeds in a dry pan and add to fenugreek. Stir-fry green chillies until they are well browned and dried out but not burnt. Grind everything together to a coarse powder and store in air-tight jars. Taste – you may want to add more salt.

CRUNCHY LENTIL CHUTNEY

Makes 1 jam jar, enough for 8–12 servings as chutney or 6 servings as a sauce for pasta or vegetables

A moister chutney than the previous one – add a little more sesame oil to it and you will have a nutritious nutty pesto for pasta or rice. Pack it as a crumbly shell around hard-boiled eggs (quails' eggs are best) for a picnic; press it onto the surface of sliced sour green apples; stir it into grated mango and eat with grilled chicken – or spread over thin Indian bread, roll the bread tightly, pin with toothpicks, slice into little wheels and fry in hot oil until crisp.

175 g (6 oz) tamarind paste
50 g (2 oz) split red lentils
50 g (2 oz) desiccated coconut
50 g (2 oz) sesame seeds
1–1½ teaspoons coarse sea salt
1 tablespoon sesame or peanut oil
6 plump garlic cloves, chopped
½ teaspoon asafoetida powder
5–8 dried red chillies, seeded and crumbled

Pour just enough boiling water onto tamarind to cover, mashing fruit down well. Leave to soak 30 minutes, then sieve.

In a small dry frying pan, roast lentils for about 6 minutes until aromatic and lightly coloured. Add coconut, sesame seeds and salt and continue roasting until golden.

Heat oil and cook garlic over medium-low heat until it is pale golden. Stir in asafoetida and chillies, cook until chillies change colour, then grind coarsely together with lentil mix and tamarind. Keeps for several weeks in an air-tight jar.

TAMARIND: *imli*
BOT: *Tamarindus indica*

•

One of the main ingredients in Worcestershire sauce (which may explain why Indian cooks who worked for the Raj liked the sauce), tamarind is available as a dried paste containing the seeds and fibres of the pod. The paste needs a 30-minute preliminary soak in boiling water before use. Tamarind can also be bought as a smooth pre-soaked syrup: per ounce of dried paste mentioned in this book you can substitute 1 tablespoon of this syrup.

Although most cookery books (including this one) offer lime or lemon juice as alternatives, tamarind gives an altogether spicier, fruitier and less acidic note. It also thickens cream or yoghurt sauces without curdling them, although because of its rich, dark colour, it is not suitable in dishes where whiteness is important.

Served with fresh mint and watered down with plenty of ice, it makes a tart and cooling summer drink. In Gujarat and Bombay tamarind is frequently simmered until syrupy with raw brown sugar and chillies to make a typically sweet and sour dipping sauce, delicious with grilled fish or meat.

TAMARIND-STEAMED VEGETABLES

Kootu is a speciality of Tamil Nadu, a technique for cooking fleshy or starchy vegetables such as yam, cabbage or broccoli-like thick-stemmed spinach (for which you could substitute either broccoli or Swiss chard, with stems cut crosswise). The vegetables are sliced in bite-sized pieces and cooked until barely tender in water with turmeric and a plum-sized lump of tamarind paste. They are then drained (save the liquid for cooking pulses) and mixed with an equal quantity of cooked dal and a ground wet masala the size of a golf ball consisting of:

¼ teaspoon asafoetida powder
½ teaspoon salt
2 teaspoons Dry Sambaar Powder (page 47)
50 g (2 oz) fresh or creamed coconut
2–3 green chillies

A little water is sprinkled over the vegetable and dal mixture, and the dish is covered and steamed for about 2 minutes, then dressed with a tempering of mustard seeds, urad dal, dried red chillies and curry leaves fried in oil (see any of the temperings on pages 23 and 24).

TURMERIC: *haldi*
BOT: *Curcuma longa*

•

A rhizome of the ginger family, turmeric is a native of southeast Asia, one of the earliest spices to be transported overland through Arabia to Europe. In India, slices of the fresh root are often included in water for cooking rice and vegetables (see Vegetables Parboiled in Spice-Scented Water, page 20), a practice which preserves the spice's freshness. When dried and powdered (the form most commonly found outside India), it should be stored away from light and heat, as it loses its fragrance rapidly. Although frequently used as a colouring substitute for expensive saffron, the flavour is much more delicate and it lacks saffron's pungent overpowering aroma. For this reason turmeric is seldom included in strong-tasting meat or cream dishes which mask its subtle nutty woodiness. And unlike saffron, whose flavour is dissipated by prolonged cooking, turmeric must be cooked well or it can have the 'raw' flavour of floury gravy that is not browned first. It is *the* vegetarian spice, ever-present in pulses and vegetable stews.

GOLDEN TURMERIC BUTTER AND CLARIFIED BUTTER

If you come across fresh turmeric root (it looks like a red-gold version of ginger), peel it, slice it thinly and heat it gently with a teacup of ghee for about 15 minutes until it imparts both rich colour and subtle flavour. Even better is to do this while making your own clarified butter: heat butter until frothy, add turmeric and cook until milk solids separate and drop to the bottom. This is basic clarified butter. Indians take it a step further and allow the solids to brown for an even nuttier flavour. Whichever version you make, strain out the solids, pour the liquid into a small jar and reserve for stirring into creamy mashed potatoes, lentil soups, puréed celeriac, or as a final golden glaze for roast chicken.

SAARS OR RASAMS

The word *saar* (*rasam* in Tamil) simply means 'essence': a liquid essence of anything from lentils to rice. Seasoned with tamarind, mustard seeds, red chillies and garlic or asafoetida, it is the Southern vegetarians' answer to the Northern carnivores' meat stock, the basic instrument on which a tune is played (see recipes following) rather than the tune itself. I often use this method for cooking the tiny slate-blue French de Puy lentils, as well as their cousins from Castelluccio in Umbria, then reserve the cooking water for soup and serve the pulse itself with roast pork.

On the Karnataka coast I was served a *saar* in a teacup with tiny macaroni cooked in it – for all the world like an Indian-spiced version of the Tuscan soup made with chickpeas which is called *pasta e ceci*.

BASIC SAAR/RASAM

200 g (8 oz) toor dal or other lentils, rinsed well

2.5 cm (1 inch) piece root ginger

½ teaspoon salt, or to taste

Boil 2 litres (3½ pints) of water, add dal and ginger and simmer 15–20 minutes, or until dal begins to break up and soften. Season with salt. This can then be treated in two ways:

—————— *Uses* ——————

• Serve as soup (you may simmer it with a can of coconut milk first) with seasoning below. If *saar* is prepared ahead or frozen, add seasoning just before serving.

• Alternatively, strain dal and purée as a vegetable with seasoning below. Save liquid and use as a stock or soup base.

BASIC SAAR/RASAM SEASONING

15 g (½ oz) ghee or butter or 1 tablespoon sesame oil

½ teaspoon black mustard seeds

2–3 dried red chillies

½ teaspoon black peppercorns

½ teaspoon cumin seeds

¼ teaspoon asafoetida powder

handful of fresh or dried curry leaves

1 quantity Basic Saar/Rasam (see above), to serve

Over medium heat fry mustard seeds in ghee until they pop. Stir in remaining spices until they are fragrant and change colour, then add a ladleful of the Basic Saar/Rasam (above), swirl about until sizzling and whisk back into remaining mixture.

- You may also add 6 shredded garlic cloves and 1 finely sliced onion, fried until brown and caramelized.
- Tamil rasam has an additional ½ teaspoon of toasted, ground coriander seeds and 50 g (2 oz) of soaked and strained tamarind paste (or the juice of 1 lime) and a handful of chopped fresh coriander leaves.
- An excellent addition to rasam is 2 tablespoons of roasted cashews, roughly ground.
- The coastal people have their own sweeter, nutty version, adding 2 tablespoons of ground coconut.

- Add 6 peppercorns, crushed, 2 teaspoons of coriander seeds and 2.5 cm (1½ inch) piece of root ginger, shredded, with the chillies.
- For a creamier dish, substitute 200 ml (7 fl oz) of canned or fresh coconut milk for the stock.
- Upkari makes an excellent filling for the Honeycomb Popped Millet Crêpes (see page 122) or for ordinary thin French crêpes, in which case, grind the toasted spices with 50 g (2 oz) of fresh or creamed coconut before cooking the vegetables.
- The same urad dal spice masala is delicious if you stir 3–4 beaten eggs into it and scramble them as usual.

DRY SPICED VEGETABLES

Serves 4 as a side dish

Upkari are dry vegetable dishes commonly seasoned with an *urad dal* spice masala such as this. For 225 g (8 oz) of shredded cabbage or grated mooli radish or 450 g (1 lb) of diced potatoes or courgettes you will need:

15 g (½ oz) ghee or 1 tablespoon sesame oil
½ teaspoon mustard seeds
1 teaspoon urad dal
2–3 dried red chillies, crumbled
handful of fresh or dried curry leaves
½ teaspoon salt
pinch of muscovado or dark brown sugar
150 ml (5 fl oz) stock or hot water

Over medium-high heat fry mustard seeds in ghee until they pop. Add dal, chillies and curry leaves and stir-fry 30 seconds, then immediately stir in vegetables, salt, sugar and stock. Cover and cook over medium heat for 10 minutes. If there is any liquid left when you remove the cover, turn up heat and bubble it off. With potatoes, I like to let them brown as well. In Kerala, this would be sprinkled with fresh coconut before serving.

DRY SAMBAAR POWDER

Makes 1–1½ jam jars

Without the coconut this is nutty and spicy. With the coconut, it becomes rounder and moister and doesn't keep as long. Stir in 2–3 tablespoons of the sambaar powder towards the end of cooking lentils, or use it to thicken soups and vegetable stews. A mixture of urad dal and chickpeas is more usual in a sambaar mix, but I prefer red lentils for their spiciness and speed of cooking.

4 tablespoons split red lentils or urad dal
4 teaspoons coriander seeds
½ teaspoon fenugreek seeds
4–8 dried red chillies, seeded and crumbled
1 teaspoon cumin seeds
1 teaspoon black mustard seeds
2 teaspoons sesame seeds
1 teaspoon ground turmeric
8 tablespoons desiccated coconut, toasted (optional)

Over medium-high heat, stir-fry lentils in a dry frying pan until they start to change colour from orange to ochre. Add coriander, fenugreek, chillies and cumin seeds and continue frying until fenugreek is mahogany coloured. Empty into a bowl and add mustard seeds to pan. When they start to pop, pour in sesame seeds, put on a lid and wait for popping to stop. Remove from heat, add turmeric and stir with the warm mixture for a minute or two to remove its raw taste. Grind everything together with coconut and store in an air-tight jar up to 6 months.

--------- *Uses* ---------

- Indians would be horrified, but I heat 2–3 tablespoons of sambaar powder with a can of baked beans to zap them up. Stir in a squeeze of lime juice and scatter with fresh coriander leaves for instant lunch.
- Heat 3 tablespoons of light sesame oil or 40 g (1½ oz) of butter, stir in 2–3 tablespoons of sambaar powder and sizzle for 20–30 seconds. Pour into cooked lentils and toss well with fried curry leaves.
- Do the same but stir into mashed potatoes.

DRY CURRY LEAF MASALA

Treat powdery southern spice 'chutneys' as you would Parmesan cheese. They serve the same purpose – for adding bite, protein and ballast to bland rice, pulse and pasta dishes. This one is mildly spicy and gives a surprising bacony flavour to anything it is sprinkled on.

2 tablespoons sesame seeds
3 big handfuls of fresh or dried curry leaves
4 dried red chillies, seeded
½ teaspoon salt, or to taste
½ teaspoon muscovado or dark brown sugar

Toast sesame seeds, leaves and chillies separately in a dry frying pan until they change colour and smell aromatic. Grind all ingredients together to a coarse powder (not to a paste). Stored in an air-tight jar, the mix stays fresh for 3–4 weeks.

NUTTY YOGHURT CURRY IN A PUMPKIN

Serves 4 (see photo, right) as a light main course

A beautiful pale yellow curry, with green beans and orange pumpkin, and fresh leaves which turn crisp and papery in the hot oil. If you have any left over, serve it the next day over noodles tossed in sesame oil. This can also be made with buttermilk instead of yoghurt, as it is by the monks at the famous temple in Udipi, which spawned the *idli-dosai* chefs and gave its name to a whole school of South Indian cuisine.

1 whole pumpkin (about 1.5 kg (3½ lb)
3 tablespoons broken cashew nuts
3 tablespoons sunflower or melon seeds, toasted
50 g (2 oz) fresh coconut or 25 g (1 oz) desiccated
½ teaspoon ground turmeric
½–¾ teaspoon salt
about 450 ml (15 fl oz) Greek-style yoghurt
225 g (8 oz) green beans, cut in 5 cm (2 inch) lengths
SPICE TEMPERING
2 tablespoons light sesame or peanut oil
1 teaspoon mustard seeds
3–4 dried red chillies, seeded and crumbled
handful of fresh or dried curry leaves or fresh coriander

Pre-heat oven to 190°C/375°F/Gas 5. Cut a lid in stem end of pumpkin with a sharp knife and remove seeds and stringy pulp. Make a series of deep criss-cross slashes in the flesh (but don't cut through skin) to allow flavours to permeate.

Grind together nuts and seeds, coconut, turmeric and salt to a paste with a little yoghurt, then whisk in remaining yoghurt (how much you use will depend on how big pumpkin cavity is – if you

Kaddu: Hindi • Lal Bhopla: Marathi • Kumbelkai (Sarekai): Kannada • Tambde Duddi: Konkani • Mathan: Malayalam • Parangikkai: Tamil • Tiyya •

don't have enough liquid, add a little warm milk). Heat not quite to boiling and pour into pumpkin with beans. Put 'lid' back on and put pumpkin in a roasting tin just big enough to fit. Cook for 1–1½ hours or until interior flesh is tender.

To make tempering, cook mustard seeds in medium-hot oil until they pop, then add chillies and brown them slightly. Remove from heat, stir in leaves, allow them to crisp for a few seconds,

then stir into yoghurt mixture. To serve, scoop out some of the flesh with the sauce and a few beans.

ABOVE: Every part of the pumpkin is used in south India – the seeds are roasted with spices and crunched as snacks, the skin makes tangy pickles and the flesh, cooked here with coconut, turmeric and cashews, makes a creamy vegetarian curry.

GINGERY SPINACH IN COCONUT YOGHURT

Serves 4 as a side dish

Two seasonings: first the fresh spice paste, then the nutty tempering of mustard seeds. It makes a very good stuffing for the Honeycomb Popped Millet Crêpes (on page 122) – a sort of Indian-spiced version of spinach pancakes *alla fiorentina*.

2 green chillies, seeded and roughly chopped
75 g (3 oz) creamed coconut
2.5 cm (1 inch) piece fresh root ginger, chopped
450 g (1 lb) spinach
135 ml (4½ fl oz) Greek-style yoghurt
salt to taste

SPICE TEMPERING
1 tablespoon light sesame oil
1 teaspoon black mustard seeds
handful of fresh or dried curry leaves or fresh coriander

Grind chillies, coconut and ginger to a coarse paste. Wash the spinach well but do not drain. Put in a saucepan over medium heat, cover and cook until wilted. Squeeze spinach liquid into yoghurt, chop leaves finely and mix all together with yoghurt, chilli paste and salt.

Just before serving, cook mustard seeds in medium-hot oil until they are all popped, remove pan from heat and sizzle the curry leaves in the hot oil. Pour over spinach, stir and serve.

SPINACH AND COCONUT DAL

Serves 4–6 as a side dish

If you read the Indian train timetables, I was told by the Scottish author, Bill Aitken, resident in Delhi, who writes a column on great rail journeys that is carried by many Indian newspapers, you will find the letters BSW: B for bookstall, S for Refreshment stall, W for Waiting room. 'I call it the Brain, the Belly and the Bum.' he said, 'and the belly is always catered for in India. If you don't have a B or a W there will always be an S.'

As vividly coloured as a Fauve painting, this is a slightly more refined version of a dish with deep-fried puri breads sold in south Indian railway stations. Because it reminds me of Puglia's bean purée with wilted greens, I like to serve it as a dip, letting everyone scoop it up with toasted chunks of chewy Pugliese olive oil bread.

225 g (8 oz) yellow split peas
½ teaspoon ground turmeric
½ teaspoon cumin seeds
3 green chillies, slit lengthwise
2 tablespoons light sesame or olive oil
1 teaspoon black mustard seeds
1 small onion, finely sliced
3 garlic cloves, finely chopped
1 teaspoon salt, or to taste
200 ml (7 fl oz) fresh or canned coconut milk
225 g (8 oz) spinach, shredded

Bring peas, turmeric, cumin and chillies to boil with 900 ml (1½ pints of water). Cover, reduce

heat to very low and simmer 30–40 minutes, until peas are tender. Cook mustard seeds in medium-hot oil until they pop, then add onion and fry to a light brown. Stir in garlic towards end just to soften. Pour into peas with salt and coconut milk, stir well, then top with spinach and cook just until it wilts.

RED CHILLI TAMARIND NOODLE FRITTATA

Serves 4 as light luncheon with other dishes

South Indians have a soft rice vermicelli dish using these hot, wintry spices with the sweet smell of fenugreek and the musky beaniness of urad dal. In my version, the Italian frittata method of frying noodles into a 'cake' is used. It forms an almost candied exterior crust. Excellent with Spicy Tomato Chutney (page 52).

Cashew nuts in their shells.

175 g (6 oz) tamarind paste
1 tablespoon white urad dal
½ teaspoon fenugreek seeds
½ teaspoon coriander seeds
3 tablespoons light sesame or peanut oil
3 dried red chillies, seeded and crumbled
½–¾ teaspoon coarse salt
1 teaspoon muscovado or dark brown sugar
100 g (4 oz) Chinese rice noodles
½ teaspoon black mustard seeds
40 g (1½ oz) raw cashew nuts, roughly broken
3 garlic cloves, shredded
6–10 fresh or dried curry leaves

Cover tamarind in 350 ml (12 fl oz) of boiling water, mashing it down well with a fork, and leave to soak for at least 30 minutes. Press as much paste as possible through a sieve, then discard residue of pips and stalks.

In a 20 cm (8 inch) non-stick frying pan, cook dal for 5–6 minutes over medium heat until lightly browned. Add fenugreek and coriander seeds and cook until they change colour. Grind finely. Heat 2 tablespoons of oil and stir-fry fenugreek, dal, chillies and coriander seeds until fragrant. Add tamarind, salt and sugar and mix well, then add noodles, stirring and lifting them until they soften and absorb liquid. Cook without stirring until a light brown crust forms on bottom, then slide noodles out of pan onto a plate, and slide back into pan brown side up.

While frittata browns on bottom, cook mustard seeds in remaining oil over medium-high heat until they pop, keeping a lid handy to avoid being splattered. Lower heat, add cashews and cook until they turn golden, then stir in garlic and curry leaves off heat. Slip frittata onto a serving plate and pour seed and nut tempering over top. Cut in wedges to serve.

COCONUT NOODLE FRITTATA

Serves 4 as a light lunch dish with other courses

A cool summery version of the previous recipe. Cherry or Italian plum tomatoes give some of the sharpness and acidity of Indian tomatoes.

1 teaspoon black mustard seeds
1 tablespoon white urad dal
¼ teaspoon turmeric
2.5 cm (1 inch) piece root ginger, shredded
½–¾ teaspoon salt
juice and grated zest of 2 limes
2 green chillies, finely sliced crosswise
450 ml (15 fl oz) coconut milk or equivalent fresh
100 g (4 oz) rice vermicelli
1 tablespoon sunflower oil
1 teaspoon black mustard seeds
¼ teaspoon asafoetida powder (optional)
handful of fresh coriander, coarsely chopped
6 cherry tomatoes, halved, or 2 plum tomatoes, seeded and cut in strips lengthwise

In a 20 cm (8 inch) non-stick frying pan over medium-high heat, cook 1 teaspoon mustard seeds until they finish popping. Add dal and cook for about 6 minutes, until golden. Add turmeric, ginger, salt, lime, chillies and coconut. Stir well, then add vermicelli, lifting and stirring it to coat it with the aromatic sauce.

When vermicelli is soft, leave undisturbed for about 10 minutes or until it browns on bottom. Slip it out of pan onto a plate then slip it back into pan, uncooked side down, to brown. While it cooks, make spice tempering: in a small frying pan cook remaining mustard seeds in medium-hot oil until they pop. Remove from heat and stir in asafoetida and coriander. When the raw smell vanishes, stir in tomatoes and pour over frittata. Cut in wedges to serve.

Variation

● *Orzo (rice-shaped noodles) pulau with Indian spices* A good rice alternative to serve with grilled or fried fish steaks coated with Fish or Shellfish Masala (page 31): make the spice mixture above, stirring in 450 g (1 lb) of cooked orzo instead of vermicelli. Top with crushed cashew nuts in addition to the mustard seed and tomato tempering. Serves 6 as a side dish.

SAVOURY GINGER PATTIES WITH SPICY TOMATO CHUTNEY

Serves 6 as a light main course

One of the South's great treats are the crisp lentil patties, or doughnuts, called *wada* – and one of the best ways to eat them is off a banana leaf with a mug of frothy Mysore coffee at Maddur Tiffany's on the road from Mysore. They come with two bowls for dipping – one of the peppery tamarind-scented versions of Basic Saar/Rasam Seasoning (page 46) and the other of creamy white Coconut Chutney (page 56) flecked with black mustard seeds. I have substituted red lentils for the usual urad dal in this version because I like their spicy flavour and salmony colour.

225 g (8 oz) split red lentils
1 teaspoon salt
2 green chillies, chopped
2.5 cm (1 inch) piece root ginger, roughly chopped
½ teaspoon asafoetida powder
2 tablespoons fresh or creamed coconut (optional)
peanut oil for deep frying or light sesame oil for greasing

SPICY TOMATO CHUTNEY
2 tablespoons light sesame or olive oil
1–1½ teaspoons cayenne pepper
¼ teaspoon asafoetida powder

*6 medium plum or other well-flavoured
tomatoes, coarsely chopped*

*2 tablespoons muscovado or
dark brown sugar*

salt to taste

handful of fresh coriander, chopped

Cover lentils with water and soak 4 hours. Drain and grind to a paste with salt, chillies, ginger, asafoetida and coconut (if using). Form into 12 circular patties like mini-hamburgers. Either deep-fry over medium-high heat a few at a time in 4 cm (1½ inches) of oil until patties are well browned on each side – the crispest version – or lay in a single layer on a well-greased baking sheet and bake, turning once, in an oven pre-heated to 200°C/400°F/Gas 6 for 20 minutes until brown.

While patties cook, make chutney: heat oil, stir in cayenne and cook briefly over medium heat until it is less raw smelling, add asafoetida and remaining ingredients except coriander. Let it bubble and thicken slightly, crushing the tomatoes a bit with a fork. Remove from heat, stir in coriander and serve each person with 2 little patties and a dollop of chutney.

Note When no fresh tomatoes are available, use 2 cans of Italian plum tomatoes and add ½ teaspoon of turmeric with the cayenne, then simmer tomatoes until thick, adding a little wine vinegar or lime juice at the end to give some acidity.

——————— *Variations* ———————

• To make the popular doughnut-shaped *wada*, poke a hole in the centre of dough before frying it, wetting your hands first if it is sticky.

• A cooling alternative to the previous dishes is to roll the lentil dough into cherry-sized balls, deep-fry them and drain on kitchen paper. Then pop 1 teaspoon of black mustard seeds in 1 tablespoon of sesame oil. Stir in ¼ teaspoon of asafoetida, 2 finely sliced green chillies and a handful of curry leaves. Whisk immediately into 900 ml

(1½ pints) of yoghurt, add the crisp lentil balls and a big handful of chopped fresh coriander and eat with a spoon.

LAYERED LENTIL AND AUBERGINE CAKES

Serves 6

Although the elements in this are pure Indian, the presentation – stripes of red lentil cake and glossy purple aubergine – was inspired by a polenta dish of Anton Mosimann's. Makes 1 stack each – enough for a starter or light lunch.

*2 large aubergines, each sliced crosswise
in 6 rounds*

salt

3–4 tablespoons light vegetable oil

*1 quantity uncooked Savoury Ginger
Patties (page 52)*

*1 quantity Spicy Tomato Chutney (page 52),
coarsely puréed (reserve coriander)*

*Greek-style or other strained yoghurt,
to serve*

Salt aubergines and leave to drain in a colander for 1 hour (you can leave out this step but it does stop them absorbing so much oil). Pat dry.

Pre-heat oven to 190°C/375°F/Gas 5. Brush a non-stick frying pan lightly with oil, heat to medium-high, and brown aubergines on both sides. Oil pan again when you turn aubergines.

Repeat with lentil patties – the aim is just to brown and crisp them as they finish cooking in the oven. Make 6 layered stacks of lentil patties and aubergines, starting each with lentil and finishing with aubergine on top and sticking the layers together with a little tomato sauce. Place them in a greased ovenproof dish, surround with any remaining tomato sauce and bake for 20–25 minutes. Decorate with sprigs of coriander and a spoonful of yoghurt on the side.

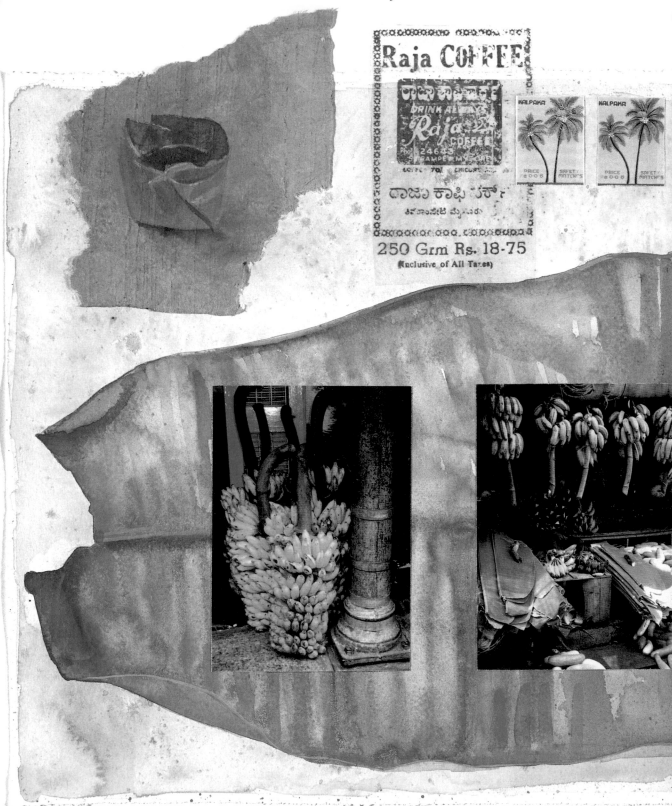

BELOW: *Uttapams (right), sourdough griddle cakes, served on the melamine tray of south India – a banana leaf.*

SOURDOUGH GRIDDLE CAKES WITH SEED CRUST

Makes 4 large pancakes

The south's superb, crispy griddle cakes called *uttapam* are made with sourdough fermented overnight. This is the lazy cook's version – almost like a giant Indian blini – the sourness coming from ginger and yoghurt instead of fermentation. Slice the cakes in wedges to make them go further. I use sun-dried or red and yellow cherry tomatoes for the tempering because good tart tomatoes are rare. *Uttapams* are usually served with a chutney such as Green Coconut and Coriander Chutney (page 92) and a bowl of Dry Sambaar Powder (page 47).

90 g (3½ oz) chickpea (besan/gram) flour

90 g (3½ oz) ground rice

2 tablespoons semolina

¾ teaspoon 'Easybake' (or other fast-acting) yeast

300 ml (10 fl oz) yoghurt

½ teaspoon salt

2 onions, finely chopped

¼ teaspoon asafoetida powder

4 cm (1½ inch) piece root ginger, shredded

2 green chillies, finely sliced crosswise

TEMPERING

4 tablespoons light sesame oil

1 teaspoon black mustard seeds

2 tablespoons dry-roasted peanuts, roughly crushed

1 tablespoon sesame seeds

handful of fresh or dried curry leaves or handful of fresh coriander, chopped

24 cherry tomatoes, halved, or 12 sun-dried tomatoes, cut in strips, or 2–3 good tomatoes, seeded, cut in fine strips lengthwise

Sift together flour, rice, semolina and yeast. Whisk yoghurt with 150 ml (5 fl oz) of water, heat until lukewarm and beat into flour. When batter is smooth, cover with clingfilm and leave in a warm place for an hour.

Stir salt, onions, asafoetida, ginger and chillies into batter and let rise again in a warm place for 30 minutes. Set oven at place-warming temperature. Heat ½ teaspoon of the oil over medium-hot heat in a 20 cm (8 inch) non-stick frying pan. When sizzling, pour in a quarter of the batter and cook until it sets on top. Slide onto a plate, add another ½ teaspoon of oil to pan and slide pancake back in, uncooked-side down. After 2 minutes, transfer pancake to oven and repeat process with remaining 3 pancakes.

To serve, fry mustard seeds in 3 tablespoons of medium-hot oil until they finish popping. Stir in sesame seeds, peanuts and curry leaves and brown lightly, adding tomatoes at end just to soften them slightly. Put a pancake on each plate, pour nuts and oil over top. If not using curry leaves, top with coriander.

——————— *Variations* ———————

• Do the same thing but fry shredded savoy cabbage or sweet red peppers with the seeds and nuts, and spoon them onto the uncooked top of the pancake just as it starts to set. Finish browning it under a grill.

• For a more substantial dish, fry 2 large diced potatoes in 2–3 tablespoons of sesame oil with 2 tablespoons of Dry Sambaar Powder (page 47) until crisp and browned. Spread a big spoonful on uncooked top of pancake when it starts to set around edges. Allow top to set lightly, then finish browning under a grill. Repeat with remaining pancakes and serve with fresh coriander and wedges of lime instead of the mustard seed tempering.

• A summer topping: cooked baby peas rolled in butter with spring onions, chillies and mint.

COCONUT CHUTNEY

The sweet and mild creamy chutney that comes with every snack in the South – from lentil doughnuts (see Savoury Ginger Patties, page 52) to *uttapam* (see Sourdough Griddle Cakes, page 55).

1 teaspoon skinned urad dal or split red lentils
2 dried red chillies, seeded and crumbled
100 g (4 oz) fresh or creamed coconut
salt to taste
135 ml (4½ fl oz) creamy yoghurt
1 tablespoon light sesame oil
1 teaspoon black mustard seeds

Dry-roast dal in a small frying pan over medium heat until lightly browned, add chillies and stir-fry until darkened. Grind to a fine paste with coconut and salt, then stir into yoghurt. Before serving, fry mustard seeds in medium-hot oil, and when they finish popping, stir them into yoghurt.

FRESH GINGER PACHADI

Serves 4 as a cooling sauce with other dishes

Pachadis are a cross between a chutney and a vegetable side dish. The grated vegetables (such as okra, pumpkin and aubergines) are stir-fried until tender with a pre-fried and ground wet masala. However, if using grated cucumber or ginger, this step is left out. The most commonly used wet masala is: 1 fried chopped onion, ¼ teaspoon of turmeric, 1 teaspoon of toasted cumin seeds, 2–3 toasted and ground red chillies, 2–3 fried garlic cloves, 2 green chillies, and salt. The vegetable mixture is then combined with an equal volume of creamy yoghurt, and topped with roasted cumin seeds and coriander leaves. Alternatively a tempering of mustard seeds, asafoetida and curry leaves is added, with a little brown sugar to taste.

This *pachadi* makes a very simple, refreshing accompaniment to everything from Sourdough Griddle Cakes with Seed Crust (page 55) to grilled chicken.

5 cm (2 inch) piece root ginger, finely grated
2 tablespoons canned coconut milk
(use cream from top of can)
275 ml (9 fl oz) creamy yoghurt
½ teaspoon salt, or to taste
½ teaspoon muscovado or dark brown sugar
1 tablespoon light sesame or peanut oil

1 teaspoon black mustard seeds
¼ teaspoon asafoetida powder (optional)
handful of fresh or dried curry leaves or
fresh coriander

Whisk together ginger, coconut, yoghurt, salt and sugar until well blended. Just before serving, heat oil in a small frying pan, add mustard seeds and cook over medium-high heat until they pop, stir in asafoetida and allow it to sizzle for a few seconds. Remove pan from heat, throw in the leaves, stir a couple of times and pour into the yoghurt.

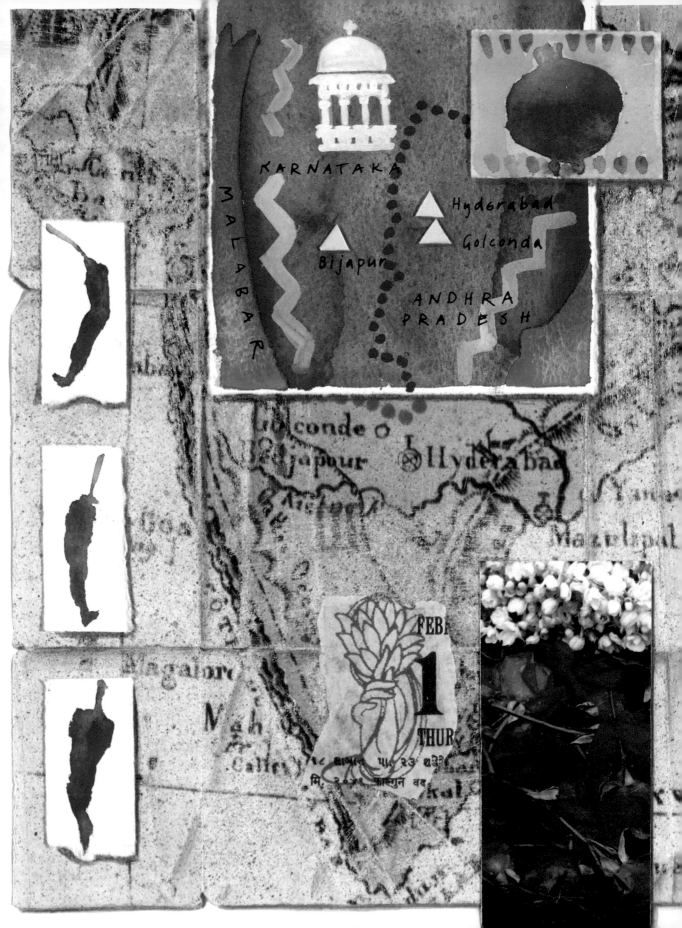

KARNATAKA

MALABAR

Hyderabad

Golconda

Bijapur

ANDHRA
PRADESH

CHAPTER THREE

THE LAST
MOGULS

•

*Every item of food was sprinkled with a profusion
of spices. There were numerous varieties of
delicious puddings, sweets, cakes, unleavened bread,
all beyond praise, description or exaggeration.*

MOGUL ENVOY AT A DECCANI BANQUET, 1604

Moazam Mir Hussein pointed across the tarmac car park to a set of broken steps in front of the rambling building that houses Hyderabad's Ministry of Irrigation. 'The last time I stood here, those steps were carpeted in red, this building was my grandfather's country palace, the parking lot was a French garden, and where those shacks have sprung up was the polo field. Nine hundred and twenty-seven people lived here with him, including his police force, his own army (the commander was chief huntsman at tiger shoots), and a battalion of cooks. The year was one long feast.'

A week before every formal banquet, sporting members of the family would be sent off to shoot game birds. 'My wife gave you quails on toast for lunch,' said Mir Hussein. 'Grandfather's banquets started with snipe on toast.' After the Western dishes would come the Moghlai; Mir Hussein's father-in-law, a famous Urdu scholar, recorded more than 2000 Mogul kebabs, although by the early twentieth century these had dwindled to two or three hundred. Finally there were the lozenge shaped sweetmeats of pure almond. 'The British only picked at these, but to us they were great delicacies, cooked by a very famous and highly paid man from Lucknow.'

Every year, the great elephant procession that marked the martyrdom of The Prophet Muhammad's grandson used to come to his grandfather's city palace for the family to view. 'Within that palace were seven more palaces,' Mir Hussein says. 'Bit by bit they were sold off after India's independence until finally even the walls disappeared.' He did not discover the loss until he returned in the 1970s after working abroad for thirty years.

'Has Hyderabad changed otherwise?' I asked.

'Times have changed. Where are the elephants now?'

Hyderabad's images of confinement – from the walls of legendary Golconda outside the modern city, to a silver pa'an box, each betel leaf pierced by a silver clove.

Mir Hussein's grandfather was a chief minister to the seventh and last Nizam of Hyderabad, which before independence was the greatest princely state in India. The Nizam, a ruler known among his detractors as 'the Miser', was reputed to have been the richest man in the world.

'So rich, he had a chain of lorries full of untouched gold ingots round his palace,' says his biographer, V.K. Bawa.

'A simple man,' said Mir Hussein's wife, the Begum, 'who never opened the trayloads of Paris toiletries bought for him in the Place Vendôme by my husband's grandfather.' They were found later stacked in cupboards and covered in dust. The Nizam preferred Sunlight Soap.

'So mean,' said a woman who knew him, 'he refused guests second helpings at state dinners and saved cigarette butts.'

This parsimonious ruler was the antithesis of his father: the sixth Nizam filled his court with poets of classical Persian and courtiers in antique dress endlessly salaaming – and lots of wives. The food he liked was flavoured with spices that sound like the harvest of an Arabian oasis – whole dried roses and cassia buds, sandalwood and vetiver, *kewra* (the sword-shaped leaves of the pandanus tree) and green cardamom.

Although the Persian opulence and elaborate manners of Hyderabad's court have been acclaimed as the last flowering of Mogul India, they pre-date that empire by centuries. Their origins can be found six miles outside Hyderabad, on a green hillside stepped with dove-grey walls and studded with the domed tombs of former sultans. These ruins are the physical remains of a legendary fortress – Golconda, once famed all over the medieval world for its diamond mines. Its cultural remains are more substantial.

Golconda's Muslim court was allied by trade with Shi'ite Persia and Arabia, not with Sunni Delhi. One of the greatest centres of Arab learning outside the Middle East, it adopted the courtly food, art, medicine and architecture of its allies, then filtered this culture through Deccan Hindu traditions. The result was a harmonious blend of imported formal elements and exuberant local ones, a stylized Persian miniature isolated and framed by the surrounding Hindu South. In one book of Urdu poetry, written in 1682, three and a half pages are devoted to a marriage feast in the nearby kingdom of Bijapur. It could have been narrated by Scheherazade. Tablecloths were as white and pure 'as the cheeks of angels', kebabs were emerald green with vetiver, the *kichri* golden with saffron. The flames in gem-encrusted lanterns flickered over rock crystal cups. 'Sweets were more beautiful than a lover's lips, and as the bride appeared, even the stars turned aside, she was so beautiful. If I start to describe the sweets,' wrote the poet, 'my ink will flow like syrup.'

In the late sixteenth century, water supplies to Golconda became inadequate and the city of Hyderabad was laid out as its suburb. After Golconda's defeat by the Mogul emperor, Aurangzeb, in 1687, he conferred the title of Nizam on his viceroy in Hyderabad and the no longer invincible Golconda gradually fell into ruin. But when the last Mogul in Delhi had died – a weak and senile old man controlled by the British – Golconda's traditions of refinement and courtesy could still be felt in the Nizam's court of Hyderabad. One day I sat like a medieval scribe at the feet of the art collector Jagdish Mittal, copying out his translation of a verse recipe written in 1688 by the blind poet Hashmi: 'Fry parathas in lots of ghee until they become brittle,' Mittal read, 'then grind them with cardamom and sugar.' (Weeks later I was served this same delicacy in the home of a Rajasthani noble – proof that India's past exists concurrent with its present.) Hashmi goes on to say that whenever an invitation to a feast is sent, cardamom should be enclosed with it, to prove the invitation is serious. 'This is a tradition which survived until very recently,' Mir Hussein's wife told me. 'I remember invitations being sent out covered in silver ribbons, with crystallized sugar, spices and fine nuts.'

The culture of this region is unique in its interweaving of South Indian and Muslim traditions. Hindu friends used to send their cardamom and sesame sweets to Mir Hussein's grandfather's household during Islamic religious feasts and every year on the joyous Hindu festival of Holi, the ladies of his court would indulge in the custom of splashing coloured water – so enthusiastically that the whole palace had to be whitewashed afterwards.

'Although we have many northern-style Moglai dishes here,' said Mumtaz Khan, a well-known Hyderabadi hostess, 'we use twice the quantity of green cardamom as the North, and we add southern touches – red chillies, curry leaves, mustard seeds, coconut. Most important of all on the Deccan plateau is the strong, sour note of tamarind – never used in the North.' I was Mumtaz's guest at a *chowki* dinner, a traditional Hyderabadi meal eaten sitting on the floor around low tables. 'You see these tables in Persian miniatures,' said another guest. 'It was how Muslims ate, sharing their food, as opposed to Hindus, who ate in a long row, divided by caste.'

Coconut and red chillies.

The meal Mumtaz served would have seemed quite familiar to the Middle Eastern merchants who traded horses and spices for the diamonds of fourteenth century Golconda. We had the square Arabic pastries called *lukmi*, with layers as crisp and papery as new bank notes. We had Baghdadi *haleem*, a medieval dish of lamb, wheat and saffron which is beaten to the texture of clotted cream. We had the sweetish brioche, *sheermal*, traditional with *haleem*, and a purée of apricots flavoured with their own cracked kernels. The conversation over the meal was typical of Hyderabad. Are gold or silver dishes preferable for serving food? How should chicken be cut for the best flavour? (From the joint only, not in small pieces, as cooks do in the rest of the South.) Had the son of the last Nizam squandered his father's hoarded wealth? Lakshmi Raj, whose father had been the last Nizam's doctor, said the dishes we ate, like much classical Hyderabadi food, had been culled from distant lands, some as far away as Abyssinia – anywhere the

Pomegranates and roses, the flavours of Old Hyderabad.

Nizams had recruited troops. The link can be tasted in Hyderabad's rich legacy of Persian fruit drinks called *sharbets*, in its rice pulaos and biryanis, and in its fondness for creamy sesame seed pastes, so similar to Middle Eastern *tahini*, though ground here with red chillies and tamarind.

Three cities – Lucknow, Delhi and Hyderabad – once each laid claim to being India's capital of court cooking. Of the three, Hyderabad came closest to an ideal blend of Lucknow's refinement and Delhi's robustness and preserved its traditions longest. Further than Delhi from a predatory neighbour like Afghanistan, it was free to absorb cosmopolitan influences.

This culinary supremacy was proved, Mir Hussein said, in Kashmir in 1934, when he was opening batsman against the British for a cricket team captained by the Maharaja of Jaipur. The Nizam of Hyderabad's heir was there, with his wife and a staff of a hundred, including his favourite chefs, who had come up by special train and stayed in houseboats on the lakes. Before leaving, the Nizam's heir threw a party.

'I will not forget it,' said Mir Hussein. 'Everyone was there – Lakshmi's father, the chief ministers and maharajas of several states, the British. And both Kashmir and Jaipur said they had never seen such variety and quality of food in all their lives. Mark you, this was Hyderabad in Kashmir – Hyderabad *sur place* was something out of this world. I remember my grandmother sending the Nizam forty or fifty different kinds of fruit *murabba* (our version of jams) in cut-glass jars.'

Murabbas were part delicacy and part prescription, used in the ancient form of medicine, known as Unani (Persian for 'Greek'), the Muslim equivalent of Hindu's Ayurvedics. A Persian translation based on the theories of Hippocrates (460–377 BC) and Galen (AD 130–210) was introduced into India in the tenth century, and its practitioners found such favour in Golconda that the city's rulers established a Unani hospital (still in existence) in Hyderabad.

The Venetian adventurer Niccolao Manucci, travelling in India in the 1600s, was not impressed by the Unani doctors in Delhi's Mogul court. 'All the physicians are Persians by race…. They follow the ancient books of medicine, which say a great deal but tell very little.' As practised in old Hyderabad, Unani developed into a unique form akin to gastronomy. Because so many of their prescriptions involved sugar, honey and spices, Unani doctors, the *hakim*, became known as fine confectioners and spice blenders, whose masalas were flavourful as well as medicinally beneficial. Clearly, a prescription that tasted good was more likely to be popular with patients. The best *hakim* worked for noble families and kept their valuable recipes and prescriptions secret, although the concepts were widely known. To them are attributed many of modern Hyderabad's delicious *sharbets* and *murabbas* made of such ingredients as tamarind and ginger, violets, mangoes and moonflowers.

If the idea that milk and fish cause cholera when eaten together (as I was told by one modern *hakim*) seems a little far-fetched, most of the traditional Unani suggestions make good culinary sense: mutton with pomegranates, red chillies in ghee, quail in lime juice, shrimp with black cumin, rabbit with fennel seeds, raisins and ginger. As with yin and yang, the theory is to balance opposites – foods with 'hot' and 'cold' qualities – a way of cooking that has become part of most Hyderabadi cooks' folk memory, even after they have forgotten the original theories behind it. When Raazia, a friend from an old Hyderabadi family, gave me her recipe for lamb biryani, she stressed that it was to be eaten with gingery *burani* (a classic Unani combination recommended to prevent any constipation caused by the rich meat and rice biryani). 'I don't know why,' she said, 'it's just tradition.'

Lakshmi's grandmother always made her eat sesame seeds during January, the season of kite flying, because she said the sun was changing positions then – an idea Lakshmi felt must have stemmed from Unani or Ayurvedic principles. Sesame went into baths and spice masalas (as in the aubergine dish, *Baighare Baingan*, on page 77), and were ground with coriander seeds, onions and tamarind to season green beans. During that period the family would go from house to house visiting friends. 'It was considered good manners to offer sweets made with jaggery [a raw brown sugar] and sesame.'

Among the Unani medical and culinary treatises in the state museum is one dealing with the manners expected of a perfect Hyderabadi gentleman, from how to choose a horse or a cook to the definition of a perfect menu. Good manners are the sign of a refined society. They can also be a barrier isolating us from the barbarians, the invaders or simply those who do not share our beliefs.

'Our legendary courtly manners are preserved by only a few of the old families now,' said Lakshmi, sipping tea flavoured with lemon grass and a sprig of mint, 'as is inevitable with all this exposure to the outside world.' Her old china rattled as a jet flew low over the roof. 'In North India, daughters-in-law used to be judged on how they peeled potatoes. Here, it was by how delicately they folded betel leaf to enclose the spices for pa'an.'

Old Hyderabad, the city that grew out of Golconda's ashes, is falling down; all its best buildings are tombs. Charminar, the old town's enormous Indo-Saracenic gate, is a traffic island now, held hostage by a thousand screeching mopeds, and a modern suburb of the Flintstones' ferroconcrete school of architecture eats like dry rot into Golconda's old walls.

Hyderabad's strongest images are of enclosure and isolation, even on a domestic scale: the *tink tink tink* of the last smithy in a street now devoted almost entirely to video shops, hammering metallic silver ribbons into fine sheets of edible foil for rich people's sweets; a silver filigree pa'an box, each of its decorative betel leaf packages fastened by a silver clove; the white cloth on a chowki table, a setting for elaborately spiced dishes that no one has the time to prepare any more.

Once, chowki dinners were held under the stars, in courtyards or tented pavilions or in the walled gardens of great houses, a celebration of exterior as well as interior space. 'Now they are held indoors, behind old screens,' said the art collector Jagdish Mittal. 'The gardens have been flattened to make way for high-rise apartments and cinemas. The last time I saw a yellow cobra crossing the green grass of a garden was about eight years ago. We killed it as it shed its skin under the car. Like the gardens, the snakes exist only in paintings.' Early Deccani painters preferred the horizontal viewpoint, one artist told me, 'You could call it lack of perspective'.

When Mumtaz Khan gave a chowki dinner for 800 guests recently, it was the Hyderabadis who stood. 'They said they were too stiff to sit cross-legged at the chowkis. They said it was impractical. They asked who would look after their shoes, for one does not sit cross-legged with one's shoes on. In the end, it was the new culture who sat at the chowkis. It was the people from Bombay.'

*T*he Persian court's kormas and rice biryanis reached the old princely state of Hyderabad (modern Andhra Pradesh) to be transformed over the centuries into dishes that are a culinary family tree – from Turkish to Persian and Mogul and then to South Indian spicing: local cashews and coconut replace Turkish walnuts and Persian almonds (Muslims here use dried coconut, *copra*, Hindus use fresh); sweet paprika becomes the fiery Andhra red chilli; popular vegetarian spices such as black mustard seeds, curry leaves and fenugreek give Mogul masalas a warm southern aroma.

CARDAMOM, Green: *choti (small), elaichi*
BOT: *Elettaria cardamomum*
•

Used almost exclusively in sweets in its native Kerala and Sri Lanka, green cardamom indicates a savoury dish's Persian provenance. It has a particular affinity with creams, tropical or dried fruit and rice – sweet or savoury, hence the pulao- and biryani-eating Hyderabadi's love of it (they double the quantity used by northern cooks).

The seeds, which possess most of the sweet, highly-perfumed citrus fragrance (straying to medical eucalyptus when overused), should at their best be black and sticky with essential oil. Never buy them ground – this aromatic oil is fugitive. Prized in the Middle East for scenting coffee, in Northeast India, Pakistan and Kashmir – wherever there were Moguls or Persians – it is brewed with other spices in tea.

The scholar, Push Pesh Panth, described an old tradition of offering cardamom with your palm facing skywards, as a kind of supplication.

The guest who picks a seed up when offered it shows that he accepts your gesture of intimacy.

'It is astringent; if you keep it in your mouth it scents every breath you breathe. It is considered a touch of elegance, and, by implication, affluence; people even now carry small trinkets in their pockets with cardamoms in them. And it is an ingredient of most *pa'an* sold on street corners, but what you get inside is the worst farm rejects. They call it a "one-eyed *elaichi*" because there may be just one seed inside the leaf. Go instead to a fine old tobacconist in Lucknow, and he has the seeds from green cardamoms wrapped in edible silver and dipped in mild tobacco water, the ultimate delicate consumption of tobacco, part addiction but also a sign of sophistication.'

CARDAMOM MASALA

A highly scented masala recommended by a Hyderabadi cook for lamb stews and meat pulaos. Make smaller quantities using the same proportions: one to three-quarters to two.

25 g (1 oz) each coriander seeds, cinnamon sticks, dried red chillies, black cumin seeds
20 g (¾ oz) each whole cloves and desiccated coconut
seeds from 50 g (2 oz) green cardamom pods

Over medium heat in a dry frying pan, toast coriander and cinnamon until their colour darkens and they start to crackle. Add chillies, cumin, cloves and coconut and cook until they are lightly toasted and aromatic. Grind together finely with cardamom seeds and store in an air-tight jar.

——————— *Uses* ———————
• Gently simmer 1 tablespoon of masala in sauces for 15 minutes for an aromatic finish. Or brush roasting poultry with butter and sprinkle the skin with a light dusting of the masala for a crisp,

aromatic skin (a process known as 'frothing' in medieval English cookery books).

• For a lamb korma for 4, fry 1 large onion, finely sliced, until browning around edges in 2 tablespoons of peanut oil or ghee. Add 3 crushed garlic cloves and 5 cm (2 inches) of root ginger, grated, and cook until soft. Stir in 450 ml (15 fl oz) of Greek-style yoghurt mixed with 4 teaspoons Cardamom Masala and salt to taste. Add 2–4 green chillies, split lengthwise, and 450–750 g (1–1½ lb) of lamb cut in chunks. Simmer gently until lamb is tender and serve with wedges of lime and fresh coriander.

• For a summer rice pulao, fry onions, garlic and ginger as previous recipe for lamb sauce, stir in 1 tablespoon Cardamom Masala, 2 big handfuls of freshly shelled baby peas, the juice of 2 limes and salt to taste. Simmer until peas are just cooked and stir with a handful of fresh mint into enough cooked rice for four.

CHILLIES, *dried red: lal mirch*

·

Originally introduced into India by the Portuguese, Hyderabad's chillies are potent and famous. Their use can seem excessive to Western palates but the culinary scientist, Harold McGee, notes that they contain six to nine times the vitamin C of tomatoes, and the alkaloid *capsaicin* responsible for their pungency helps digestion and may have antibacterial effects as well. *Capsaicin* is strongest in the white membrane that binds seeds to flesh, not, as is widely believed, in the seeds themselves. The seeds are often used as a separate spice in India, when the whiteness of a dish is desirable. For every four parts *capsaicin* found in the seeds, 100 parts are present in the membrane and six in the remaining fruit.

The smokiest-flavoured chilli powder is made by roasting dried red chillies in a pan until they darken, become crisp and smoke slightly, then grinding them seeds and all. If you are unsure of how much pungency you can take, try tempering the chillies in oil or ghee and drizzling this oil over at the end, a process known as *baghar* in Hyderabad. In the court of the Nizam, I was told, an added elusive flavour was created by throwing a gold coin into this tempering – a tip for the chef.

RED CHILLI TEMPERING

A good finish to a side dish of stewed beans or lentils or steamed sour greens for four.

25 ml (1 fl oz) peanut or light sesame oil or melted ghee

5 garlic cloves, shredded lengthwise

4 dried red chillies, crumbled

The method, as for most temperings, is to heat fat until smoking, then reduce heat to medium and add spices (in this case, garlic and chillies), stirring constantly until they change colour and smell aromatic. This happens almost immediately. Watch they do not burn, pour into or over dish and stir well.

GINGER, *fresh: adrak*
BOT: *Zingiber officinale*

·

High in vitamin C – Chinese sailors used it to stave off scurvy – the hand-shaped rhizomes remain fresh for a long time, producing shoots like potatoes if kept dry and cool in brown paper. In early Indian culinary/medical texts, ginger is called *Mahabheshaj*, literally 'the great cure, the great medicine', a fact appreciated by Unani and Ayurvedic doctors, who recommend it for digestive disorders – hence its use in pulse dishes, where it is believed to relieve flatulence. Putting 25 g (1 oz) of fresh ginger grated at the last moment into beans or lentils does seem to have this effect, as well as imparting a fresh, mildly hot and sour taste quite unlike the dried spice.

Fresh ginger's greatest use is in ginger and garlic paste, the Indian equivalent of an Italian soffritto – 2.5–5 cm (1–2 inch) piece of root ginger ground with 4–6 garlic cloves, simmered until soft in ghee or good olive oil, with finely chopped onion – the starting point for many dishes. Unlike the North, where it identifies meat dishes of Mogul ancestry, in Hyderabad it serves as the aromatic base note and thickening for both Hindu vegetarian and Muslim meat sauces.

GINGER TEA

Serves 4

A homeopathic alternative to Western par-acetamol-based lemon flu remedies, this has a similar effect in providing added vitamin C and promoting perspiration. It also tastes good.

50–75 g (2–3 oz) piece root ginger, grated
2 glasses cold water
3 tablespoons honey, or to taste
1 teaspoon mild aromatic tea

Bring ginger, water and honey to a low boil and simmer 5 minutes. Add tea, steep another 5 minutes. Strain and serve hot.

GINGER SHERBET

Serves 4

A refreshing summer version of the previous drink, sometimes turned into a fruit punch called *falsa* with the addition of sliced oranges, apples and bananas.

10 cm (4 inch) piece root ginger
4 glasses of water
4 green cardamom pods

8–12 tablespoons jaggery, muscovado or dark brown sugar
juice of 2 big limes
8 sprigs fresh mint

Grate ginger into water, bring to a boil with carda-mom and sugar and boil 5 minutes. Mix with 4 mint sprigs and leave to infuse overnight (or for several hours). Strain and mix with lime, crushed ice and remaining mint.

GINGER BUTTER

Whenever I buy a 'hand' of ginger, I wind up with a lot of leftover knobs of it too small to use. High-caste brahmins, eschewing garlic and onions, treasure fresh ginger. A Hindu friend rec-ommended this: peel as much skin as you can from a collection of these knobs, chop ginger roughly and heat gently with ghee for about 10–15 minutes. Strain ghee into a jar and seal tightly. Use as a delicious basting for steamed vegetables or grilled fish and chicken. A good thing to do with butter while clarifying it.

ROSE PETALS: *gul*

•

A reflection of Persian gardens, rose petals (*gul*) can be bought dried from health food shops and Middle Eastern grocers. The powdered petals are used to add a sweet scented flavour to the deliciously cooling ground seed and nut drink called Thandai, popular at the Hindu spring fes-tival of Holi, and to masalas for delicate Hyd-erabadi sauces. More surprisingly, dried rose buds, along with sandalwood, cassia buds and pandanus, form part of the masala for old Hyd-erabad's favourite New Year dish, the earthy, medieval-tasting *nihari* (see page 76), in which goats' forelegs, tongues and other oddments are stewed overnight on a wood fire. Steep 4–6 table-spoons of petals for 1 hour in 275 ml (9 fl oz) of boiling water to produce rose water that is a lot less cloying than commercial brands. Macerate some dried apricots in it or fresh mangoes.

ROSE PETAL MASALA

*Makes 10–12 tablespoons, enough for
15 dishes*

Two to three teaspoons of this highly aromatic masala will give an instant scented Persian quality to roast chicken or game, even if just simply warmed in 3–4 tablespoons of butter or ghee (or in 8 tablespoons Greek-style yoghurt for a creamy sauce) until fragrant and poured over before serving. It is a delicate masala to be added at the end of cooking, then heated for no more than 10–15 minutes in sauce.

*6 Indian bay leaves (or 1 cm (½ inch)
cinnamon stick, roughly crushed)*

¾ teaspoon cloves

1 tablespoon black peppercorns

2 teaspoons black cumin seeds

2 tablespoons desiccated coconut

2 teaspoons green cardamom seeds

4 tablespoons dried rose petals

In a dry frying pan, toast bay leaves or cinnamon, cloves, pepper, cumin and coconut until they crackle and smell aromatic. Add cardamom, just to warm it, then grind everything to a powder.

SOURING

The most typical Hyderabadi fingerprint on food is *katha* – a sour acidic note. In humble dishes this comes from tamarind, lime, tomatoes, sour mangoes or tart greens (sorrel, purslane, amaranth), in grander ones it is from sour grapes, green apples, sour oranges and pomegranates. This may be inherited from pre-Mogul Persian, Turkish and Arabic traders, with their love of pomegranates and vinegar. Or the reverse may be

Copy of an early Deccani citrus orchard. The Persian-influenced cooking here has always had an acidic note: the sixth Nizam of Hyderabad liked his sauces flavoured with tart orange.

true, as both tamarind (its name in Persian, *tamr-e-hind*: Indian date), and the sour orange popular in old Hyderabadi court food, travelled from India to Persia over 2000 years ago.

Should you be unable to find any of the souring ingredients in this chapter, the following ingredients are roughly interchangeable, although each will give its own particular acidity – and colour, of course: tamarind is deep brown and will also thicken dishes slightly as it is a paste.

juice of 3 limes or
juice of 2 lemons or
50–75 (2–3 oz) tamarind paste, just covered in boiling water, soaked 30 minutes, then sieved or
150 ml (5 fl oz) pomegranate juice squeezed from 1–2 fresh pomegranates or
2–3 tablespoons canned pomegranate concentrate (available from Middle Eastern stores) made up to 150 ml (5 fl oz) with water or
150 ml (5 fl oz) tart green grape juice squeezed from fresh grapes

RICE

Hyderabad's Persian ties and its location in the rice-eating South have given it India's richest legacy of *pulaos* (greater proportion of rice to meat or vegetables) and *biryanis*, in which rice is cooked briefly, layered with an equal or greater proportion of meat, each layer drizzled with aromatic oil or ghee, and nuts, dried fruit and fresh herbs, then sealed tightly and steamed to finish.

Basmati rice is graded by length and fineness of grain and by its heady, cashew-like aroma. The finest is aged up to two years to intensify this fragrance. Vinod Nagpal (who played the Unani doctor in the television film *The Far Pavilions*) was once taken to the cellar of a famous musician who kept a collection of different rices there, ageing like fine wines.

Rice is used in the South like a spice. Try toasting 2 tablespoons until brown, then grinding it coarsely and sprinkling over food for a nutty flavour. Stirred into sauces instead of sprinkled over, it will thicken and enrich them.

To cook plain basmati rice, rinse it first under running water (until water runs clear) to remove starch that would make it sticky. Then soak it for 30 minutes in twice its volume water, to relax and expand it into a long thin grain less likely to break during cooking. Drain rice, bring its soaking water to the boil with ½ teaspoon of salt, add rice and stir gently so it does not stick. When water returns to the boil, immediately reduce heat to very low, place a damp cloth over pot and cover tightly. After 12 minutes, remove lid. If steam holes have formed in rice, cover again, remove from heat and leave to cook in its own steam for 10 minutes. This stops it getting mushy. If there is still water after 12 minutes, drain it, cover rice and finish off the heat as above.

Six fast things
to do with boiled rice

• To give plain boiled rice a scented Persian quality, add 2 Indian bay leaves, a stick of cinnamon, 4 cloves and 4 cardamom pods to water before boiling the rice.

• Boil rice for 10 minutes, drain and fold gently into 450 ml (15 fl oz) plain yoghurt warmed with 1 tablespoon of Cardamom or Rose Petal Masala (page 69). Chill and serve with lots of fresh mint and sweet baby peas.

• *Cucumber rice* A summery addition to cooked rice is 1 large cucumber, quartered lengthwise, cored, finely chopped and lightly salted, then left to drain off excess liquid for 30 minutes. Mix this with the juice of 1 lime, 2–3 tablespoons of sesame oil, 3–4 tablespoons of Peanut Chutney Powder (page 80), or a mixture of roughly crushed dry-roasted peanuts and 3–4 toasted and crumbled dried red chillies, and cooked rice for 4.

• *Screwpine or vanilla-scented rice* Pandanus or screwpine (Bot: *Pandanus odorus* and *P. tectorius*) resemble palm leaves more than pine when fresh, and the hypnotic, flowery aroma – somewhere between new-mown hay and vanilla – has been popular in South India from Vedic times. In the West, pandanus is available as a distilled essence called *kewra*, worth searching out in Asian stores. Although the rest of India uses this primarily in sweetmeats, Hyderbadis, with their love of perfumed flavours, add 1–2 teaspoons of it to rice pulaos, *pa'an* mixtures and fruit *murabbas*. If you can't find it, a vanilla pod added to rice while it cooks will give a hint of what they intended.

• *Rose petal rice* Rice boiled with 4 tablespoons petals will be gently fragrant and turn palest pink.
• *Coconut rice* (serves 4–6 as a side dish)

A good, simple and nutty rice with a light fluffy texture. You can use creamed instead of fresh coconut but the rice will be heavier, less attractive. To fry leftover rice, boil it early enough to spread it out in a thinnish layer and let it cool: hot rice becomes sticky when fried.

25 g (1 oz) ghee, or 2 tablespoons peanut or light sesame oil
1 teaspoon black mustard seeds
handful of cashew nuts
handful of raisins
2 teaspoons cumin seeds
1 tablespoons split red lentils
handful of fresh or dried curry leaves or fresh coriander
3 dried red chillies, crumbled
225 g (8 oz) basmati rice, cooked, spread out and cooled
½ teaspoon salt, or to taste
175–225 g (6–8 oz) freshly grated coconut

Over medium-high heat, melt ghee and fry mustard seeds until they finish popping (keep a lid handy), shaking pan occasionally. Lower heat to medium and add cashews, raisins, cumin and lentils. Cook until lightly browned. Remove from heat and stir in curry leaves and chillies until they sizzle and crisp. Toss with rice, salt and coconut. Excellent with grilled poultry, game or lamb.

AUBERGINE AND TAMARIND PULAO

Serves 6 as a vegetarian main course with other dishes

A dry spicy dish to eat with Fresh Ginger Pachadi (page 56) and Tomato Kut (page 77). Hyderabadis use small and pleasantly bitter egg-shaped aubergines, but larger ones cut in 2.5 cm (1 inch) triangles take on the meaty consistency of good dark mushrooms.

350 g (12 oz) basmati rice, cooked, spread out and cooled
175 g (6 oz) tamarind paste
550 g (1¼ lb) aubergines
salt

SPICE MIXTURE
2 teaspoons black mustard seeds
2 tablespoons channa dal (yellow split peas)
2 tablespoons white urad dal
1 teaspoon cumin seeds
2 teaspoons coriander seeds
¼ teaspoon black peppercorns
3–5 dried red chillies, broken in pieces and dry-roasted
¼ teaspoon asafoetida powder
¼ teaspoon ground turmeric
3 tablespoons peanut or light sesame oil
handful of fresh coriander or mint, chopped

Soak tamarind 30 minutes in 175 ml (6 fl oz) boiling water. Cut aubergines into quarters if using small ones, or into 2.5 cm (1 inch) chunks if large. Salt them lightly and leave for 30 minutes (unnecessary with small aubergines).

To cook spices, dry-roast mustard seeds in a small frying pan over medium-high heat until they pop (keep a lid handy to stop splattering). Set aside. Reduce heat to medium and dry-roast channa dal, stirring constantly. After 3 minutes, add urad dal and continue roasting. After another

3 minutes, add cumin, coriander and pepper, then roast, stirring occasionally, until dal is light golden and spices are fragrant. Allow to cool, grind to a powder with ¾ teaspoon of salt and mix with mustard seeds, chillies, asafoetida and turmeric.

Sieve tamarind, discard seeds. Pat aubergines dry. In a large wok over medium-high heat, stir-fry aubergines in oil until golden brown. Lower heat to medium, add spices, and stir for 15–20 seconds. Add tamarind, stir until absorbed, then add 275 ml (9 fl oz) hot water. Simmer until liquid is reduced by half. Toss rice in this to coat it with sauce. It will stay warm for about 20 minutes if left tightly covered off heat. Scatter with fresh herbs before serving.

FIVE SEED AND TWO NUT MANGO PULAO

Serves 4 as side dish

Sweet and nutty flavoured; excellent with a spicy, vividly-coloured Green Coconut and Coriander Chutney (page 92).

225 g (8 oz) raw basmati rice or equivalent leftover cooked rice
1½ teaspoons coriander seeds
2 teaspoons sesame seeds
3 tablespoons light sesame or other vegetable oil
½ teaspoon black mustard seeds
½ teaspoon fenugreek seeds
½ teaspoon turmeric powder
¼ teaspoon asafoetida powder
¾ teaspoon salt
juice of 2 limes (about 60 ml (2½ fl oz))
1 large semi-ripe mango, peeled, cut in slices 1 cm (½ inch)
2 tablespoons each raw cashews, peanuts and melon seeds (if you can't find melon seeds, double cashews or peanuts)
3–5 dried red chillies, crumbled

If starting from scratch with raw rice, rinse it well under running water, cover with 600 ml (1 pint) water and soak 30 minutes. Dry-roast coriander and sesame seeds in a small frying pan until browned and fragrant. Crush roughly. Over medium-high heat in a frying pan, cook mustard seeds in 2 tablespoons oil until they pop, keeping a lid handy to prevent splattering. Off the heat, stir in fenugreek, turmeric, asafoetida, and salt, return to very low heat and fry until fenugreek is lightly browned. Add lime juice and mango and immediately remove from heat.

Drain soaked rice and bring soaking water to a boil. Add rice and stir gently (to stop it sticking) until it returns to the boil. Turn heat very low, cover and cook for 12 minutes, until air 'dimples' form in surface of rice. If there is any water left, drain this and gently spread rice out in a non-stick wok or large frying pan to dry. Then add coriander and sesame seeds and mango sauce and stir gently over high heat until well mixed, allowing rice to sit for a minute or two occasionally without turning so it browns.

In remaining oil over medium heat, fry nuts and melon seeds until lightly browned, stir in chillies and pour sizzling oil over rice.

DRY-FRIED LAMB WITH WHEAT

Serves 4 as a main course

A mixture of aromatic lamb and beautiful, earthy-tasting wholewheat in which the wheat grain retains its delicious 'bite' and shine, and is matched by a grain of crunchy lamb (see photograph on page 73). All it needs is a salad of bitter greens – chicory, endive, dandelion, rocket – on the side.

Western cooks have access to an enormous range of grains and cereals which they seldom consider except at breakfast. Wholewheat was popular in medieval Baghdad and, through Golconda's ancient Baghdadi connections, in

An aromatic blend of glossy wholewheat grains and spiced lamb, based on a medieval dish.

something I can imagine modern Western cooks doing. The following recipe retains the medieval flavour without the time-consuming method. (The Arabic scholar and ex-Rolling Stone magazine editor, Charles Perry, once sent me a recipe for *mulahwaja* – literally, 'a hasty dish' – from the tenth century Baghdadi *Book of Dishes*. It was almost a blueprint for this recipe, although his version included a generous dose of the carcinogenic medieval barley condiment, *murri*. *Murri* never caught on in Hyderabad.)

225 g (8 oz) wholewheat grains
4 cloves
2 Indian bay leaves (or 1 ordinary bay leaf with 2.5 cm (1 inch) piece cinnamom stick)
4 green cardamom pods
2 big onions, finely sliced
1–2 tablespoons light sesame or olive oil
3–4 garlic cloves, crushed
2.5 cm (1 inch) piece fresh root ginger, grated
2–3 dried red chillies, crumbled
salt, to taste
225 g (8 oz) lean minced lamb
1½ teaspoons Cardamom or Rose Petal Masala (page 69) or garam masala
1 teaspoon vinegar
big pinch of saffron, soaked in a little hot water
275 ml (9 fl oz) yoghurt
fresh coriander, chopped

Hyderabad as well. It is still prepared all over the old city (where cooks add saffron and whole garam masala to the basic Arabic recipe) in a dish called *haleem* eaten to break the Muslim fast of Ramadan. *Haleem* has an exotic medieval texture, a result of soaking the wheat overnight, then cooking it slowly in aromatic stock and pounding it to a smooth cream with a wooden masher – not

Boil wheat gently for 1 hour with cloves, bay leaves and cardamom in 4 times its volume cold water. Drain.

Fry onions in oil until they are caramely-brown, reserve one-third for garnish. Add garlic, ginger, chillies and salt to pan, and cook until garlic is soft and aromatic. Stir in lamb, masala, vinegar and saffron. Turn up heat and stir-fry lamb until crunchy on edges, breaking up any lumps that form. Lower heat, stir in yoghurt, then wheat, mixing well to ensure all grains are covered with sauce. Remove from heat and stir in coriander. Serve heaped up with reserved onions on top.

--------- *Variations* ---------

• An excellent vegetarian version of the same dish: add cooked wheat to pan where you would have added meat, with an extra tablespoon oil, and continue as original recipe. Top with strips of peeled grilled red pepper.

• Another version of the dry-cooked meat is mixed with rice scented with bitter orange zest, a flavouring popular with the sixth Nizam. To make it, cook 225 g (8 oz) basmati rice (try it with wheat as well) with the juice of 2 oranges and water, then mix with the spiced lamb in this recipe, the grated zest of 1 of the oranges and fresh coriander. Very good topped with a few tablespoons of Dry Curry Leaf Masala (page 48).

'RAW' LAMB BIRYANI/KACHI YAKHNI

Serves 4–6 as a main course

The lamb here is only raw in the sense that the meat is marinated (in India, the meat would be mutton marinated first in the natural tenderizer, papaya) and then lightly steamed rather than stewed first, as is more usual. It gives the meat a superb, almost gamey taste. A grand dish served at Old Hyderabad dinners with Tomato Kut (page 77) and Stuffed Aubergines in Sesame Sauce (page 77). An elegant Hyderabadi matron advised me sternly that it must always be eaten with a 'chutney' of yoghurt beaten with finely chopped onion, salt, 2.5 cm (1 inch) piece freshly grated root ginger, 2 crushed garlic cloves and a handful of fresh mint and coriander, and a salad of chopped tomatoes and green chillies with lime juice on the side.

7.5 cm (3 inch) piece fresh root ginger, chopped
6–8 garlic cloves
4 dried red chillies, seeded
½–¾ teaspoon sea salt
300 ml (10 fl oz) Greek-style yoghurt
900 g (2 lb) lean boneless lamb (not stewing lamb – ask butcher for a tender cut)
50 g (2 oz) ghee or butter
3 onions, finely sliced
4 tablespoons milk
big pinch of saffron threads
450 g (1 lb) basmati rice
10 whole green cardamom
1½ teaspoons black cumin seeds
5 cm (2 inch) piece cinnamon stick
3–4 Indian bay leaves (or ordinary bay with an extra 1 cm (½ inch) cinnamon)
¾ teaspoon salt
6 cloves
handful each of fresh coriander and mint, finely chopped
4 green chillies
juice of 3 limes

Grind together ginger, garlic, red chillies and salt and beat into yoghurt. Cut lamb into 2.5 cm (1 inch) chunks, cover with yoghurt mixture and leave to marinate at least 3 hours, preferably 6.

Over medium heat, fry onions in ghee until light brown. Bring milk to a boil, add saffron and leave to soak.

Rinse rice under cold running water until water runs clear, then cover in 1.4 litres (2⅓ pints) cold water and leave to soak for 30 minutes. Drain rice and bring its soaking water to a boil with cardamom, cumin, cinnamon, bay leaves, salt and cloves. When boiling, add rice, bring back to boil, and cook for 2 minutes. Drain (use the water for soup or stock – it is highly flavoured and delicious).

Pre-heat oven to 180°C/350°F/Gas 4. Grease a heavy-bottomed saucepan or casserole very well and spread half the meat over it. Cover in half the fresh herbs and chillies and half the rice, fried onions and lime juice. Spoon remaining meat on top. Cover with remaining herbs, rice and lime juice and top with remaining onions and chillies. Poke a few holes in the top and sprinkle over saffron milk.

Lay a wet cloth over top of pan to seal in steam and press lid on firmly. Cook in oven for 30 minutes.

─────── *Variations* ───────

- This is made with chicken in Hyderabad, not something to be recommended, but a tender cut of beef is excellent.
- For a very southern 'korma' taste, grate 25–50 g (1–2 oz) creamed coconut into yoghurt, and fry a handful of cashews and raisins with onions.

PARTRIDGE AND COCONUT BIRYANI

Serves 6 as a main dish

Six plump birds in a nest of scented rice, a dish from a Persian miniature, described to me in loving and nostalgic detail at a dinner in Old Hyderabad. The coconut is almost undetectable, just a mild background sweetness, and the spicing is subtle – added first in the spice-scented water for cooking the rice (so individual grains absorb it) and then again whole in the sauce. Hyderbadis use a lot of melted ghee; this moistens game birds and adds a nutty roundness. You can cut down on it – although this dish is no richer than a classic French partridge in cabbage. Serve it with fresh mango and ginger chutney (see Take Three Mangoes, page 120), Almond and Cardamon Cranberries (page 81) and sourish buttered greens – try spinach with lemon juice. Can be doubled as a feast dish for 12.

450 g/1 lb basmati rice
8 green cardamom pods
6 cloves
5 cm (2 inch) piece cinnamon stick, roughly crushed
¾ teaspoon black cumin seeds (or ordinary cumin)
2 Indian (or ordinary) bay leaves
big pinch of saffron threads
4 cm (1½ inch) fresh root ginger, roughly chopped
4–6 garlic cloves, roughly chopped
2–4 green chillies, seeded and roughly chopped
3 medium onions, 1 roughly chopped, 2 finely sliced
1×400 ml (14 fl oz) can coconut milk
150 ml (5 fl oz) Greek-style yoghurt
¾–1 teaspoon salt, or to taste
about 50–75 g (2–3 oz) ghee or butter, melted
6 partridges, pigeons or quail
blade of mace (or ¼ teaspoon ground)
½ teaspoon cayenne pepper
handful each of fresh coriander and mint, chopped (save some for garnish)
juice of 2 large limes
2 tablespoons each melon seeds and cashews (or just cashews), toasted, to garnish

Rinse rice well, cover with water by 7.5 cm (3 inches) and soak 30 minutes. Drain water into saucepan and add half the cardamom, cloves, cinnamon, cumin and bay. Bring to a boil, add rice, bring back to boil for 3 minutes. Drain, run cold water through rice in sieve slowly, and set aside.

Soak saffron in 2 tablespoons hot water. Purée ginger, garlic, chillies and chopped onion.

Whisk together coconut milk, yoghurt, saffron and salt.

Pre-heat oven to 180°C/350°F/Gas 4. In one-third of the ghee, brown birds well on all sides over medium-high heat (about 7–8 minutes). Remove and set aside. Fry sliced onions until brown and crisp (add more ghee if necessary). Lift out with slotted spoon and drain on kitchen paper. Fry remaining whole spices, mace and cayenne until cumin starts popping. Pour in coconut milk mixture and half fresh herbs. Bring to boil, add birds and gently simmer 10 minutes. (Dish can be prepared ahead to this point.)

Spoon half rice into an ovenproof casserole. Nestle birds into it and spoon over half sauce and lime juice and one-third herbs. Drizzle over half remaining melted ghee. Add remaining rice, sauce and lime juice and ½ remaining herbs. Poke holes in the surface of rice and drizzle over remaining ghee and saffron. Lay a wet towel across top of pot to prevent steam escaping, cover tightly and cook 30 minutes. To serve, spoon rice onto a dish, nestle birds on top and scatter over fried onions, seeds, nuts and remaining fresh herbs.

SLOW-COOKED LAMB SHANKS NIHARI

Serves 4

A rustic dish (despite the exotic rose petal masala) based on nihari, the stew of goats' forelegs made in Old Hyderabad and favoured for New Year's breakfast. Goats' forelegs are not easy to come by so I make this with lean and succulent lamb shanks, a cut of meat that becomes melting and creamy when subjected to slow cooking. In Hyderabad it would be scented with sandalwood and pandanus leaf (a vanilla pod gives some of this exotic quality) as well as rose petals. I serve it with the rice-shaped pasta, orzo, tossed with fresh mint and some of the aromatic sauce – a modern play on rice.

4 lamb shanks
25–40 g (1–1½ oz) ghee or butter or 2–3 tablespoons good oil (sesame or olive)
6 green cardamom pods
5 cloves
1 teaspoon black peppercorns
8 dried red chillies
5 cm (2 inch) piece cinnamon stick
2 Indian bay leaves (or 2 ordinary bay with extra 1 cm (½ inch) cinnamon)
1 large onion (about 225 g/8 oz), chopped
8 garlic cloves, chopped
40 g (1½ oz) fresh root ginger, chopped
275 ml (9 fl oz) Greek-style strained yoghurt
¾ teaspoon salt, or to taste
½ vanilla pod or 1 teaspoon kewra essence
2 teaspoons Rose Petal Masala (page 69) or Garam Masala (page 158)
juice of 2 limes
handful of fresh mint, chopped

Make sure you have a pot big enough to cook lamb in one layer. If not, have your butcher cut shanks in half.

Over medium-high heat, brown meat all over in ghee with whole spices. Remove, add onions to pan and fry to a golden brown. Add garlic and ginger and stir-fry until everything is toast-coloured. Purée and return to the pan with lamb, yoghurt (whisked with 1 litre (1¾ pints) warm water), salt and vanilla pod, if not using kewra. Bring to a boil, cover tightly, reduce heat to very low and simmer for an hour, or until meat is tender.

Remove lid, skim off surface fat (a very un-Indian thing to do), stir in rose petal masala (and kewra, if using), raise heat to a low boil and simmer 10–12 minutes. Sauce should be the consistency of thin cream; if not, simmer longer.

Stir in lime juice and serve in big soup plates with rice or orzo tossed with fresh mint.

TOMATO KUT

Serves 6 as side dish or sauce

A thick and spicy tomato purée usually served with dry rice dishes. It also makes a fine sauce for vermicelli, with lots of fresh coriander or basil and toasted flaked almonds. Tomatoes are often used as a souring agent in India, but because even good Western tomatoes are less acidic than Indian ones, this needs lime juice to give it a typically Hyderabadi tartness.

3×400 g (14 oz) cans Italian plum tomatoes or 900 g (2 lb) fresh tomatoes

3 tablespoons light sesame or peanut oil

2–3 garlic cloves, finely chopped

½ teaspoon ground cumin

½ teaspoon ground coriander

2 teaspoons chickpea (besan/gram) flour

½ teaspoon cayenne pepper

½ teaspoon salt, or to taste

1–2 green chillies, split lengthwise

juice of 1 lime

TEMPERING

1 teaspoon black mustard seeds

handful of fresh or dried curry leaves, or fresh coriander

If using fresh tomatoes (only use if they are very good and tart), drop in boiling water until skin splits. Skin, seed and purée.

Heat 2 tablespoons of oil over medium heat, add garlic, cumin and coriander and cook until garlic is golden. Stir in flour, and when it starts to colour, add tomatoes, cayenne, salt and chillies, stirring well. Cook to a sauce the consistency of thick cream, sieve and mix with lime juice.

Over medium-high heat cook mustard seeds in remaining oil until they finish popping. Remove from heat, stir in curry leaves for a few seconds and pour into tomatoes.

STUFFED AUBERGINES IN SESAME SAUCE/BAIGHARE BAINGAN

Serves 6 as a side dish or 4 as a vegetarian main course

A beautiful dish (especially if you can find small, pretty aubergines with big green 'caps'), with all the classic nutty and sourish flavours of Hyderabad. The stuffing is good with any lightly-cooked vegetables. Try it in small onions and courgettes: drop them whole into boiling water and cook until just tender when prodded with a sharp knife. Scoop out the flesh, mix with the stuffing, fill the vegetables and finish under a hot grill, an Indian version of Provençal *petits farcis*.

SPICE PASTE

100 g (4 oz) tamarind paste

1½ teaspoons coriander seeds

3 tablespoons sesame seeds

6 green cardamom pods, seeds only

3–6 dried red chillies, seeds removed, crumbled

25 g (1 oz) creamed coconut

4 tablespoons toasted raw or dry roasted peanuts

1½ tablespoons muscovado or dark brown sugar

¾–1 teaspoon salt, or to taste

1 teaspoon turmeric

4–6 garlic cloves

2.5 cm (1 inch) piece fresh root ginger, chopped

12 small round or oval aubergines (about 900 g/2 lb)

8 tablespoons vegetable oil

2 onions, finely chopped

handful of fresh coriander, chopped

Cover tamarind with 175 ml (6 fl oz) boiling water. Soak at least 30 minutes, then sieve out seeds.

Ginger and garlic ground to a paste, base note of Hyderbadi cooking (the equivalent of Italy's soffritto), flavours both Hindu and Muslim dishes in this area where the two religions cross over.

Toast coriander seeds in a dry pan over medium heat until you can smell them. Add sesame seeds, cardamom and chillies and continue heating until sesame seeds and chillies have changed colour and the kitchen is full of the scent of cardamom. Grind to a coarse paste (reserving a tablespoon of sesame seeds for garnish) with remaining spice paste ingredients.

Slice aubergines lengthwise in quarters from round base to stem, without cutting through stem and green 'hat'. Keeping aside 1 tablespoon of paste, stuff a spoonful of it into each aubergine and press firmly together (if the aubergines are biggish, you may have to tie string around their middle).

Heat oil in a heavy-bottomed frying pan and fry aubergines over medium heat until lightly browned on a few sides. Drain off all but 2–3 tablespoons of oil and cook onions until they are soft and golden. Stir in remaining paste and tamarind. Finish cooking aubergines in this until sauce is thick and aubergines are tender when prodded with a sharp knife. Serve garnished with sesame seeds and fresh coriander.

--------- *Variations* ---------

• For a main course vegetarian dish, mix 2 tablespoons of toasted and ground red lentils into the ground spice paste for additional protein, and cook a couple of chopped tomatoes with the onions.

• Instead of fresh coriander, a garnish more typical of Hyderabad is 1 teaspoon of popped black mustard seeds and a handful of curry leaves crisped in a hot pan.

SORREL MUSTARD

Serves 4–6 as a condiment

Hyderabadis are fond of sour green leaves, known under the portmanteau title of *bhaji*. This smoky, lemony, khaki-green 'chutney' is what Western cooks would call mustard. Use as you would mustard – with grilled meats, in sandwiches, under grilled cheese – and with rich meaty fish such as salmon, tuna, halibut.

1 teaspoon black mustard seeds
1 tablespoon urad dal or red lentils
½ teaspoon fenugreek seeds
2–4 dried red chillies, seeded and crumbled
½ teaspoon salt, or to taste
2 tablespoons light sesame or peanut oil
¼ teaspoon ground turmeric
pinch of asafoetida powder
225 g (8 oz) sorrel or purslane (including stalks)

In a dry frying pan, toast mustard seeds over medium-high heat until they finish popping. Remove, lower heat to medium and toast dal until lightly coloured. Add fenugreek and chillies and continue cooking until they change colour as well (do not allow to burn or the fenugreek will turn bitter). Grind to a fine powder with salt. Heat oil, stir in turmeric and cook over medium heat until it loses its raw smell. Add asafoetida, cook for a second or two then add sorrel and cook just until it wilts. Stir in ground spices.

--------- *Variations* ---------

• To serve as a vegetable rather than a mustard, double the quantity of sorrel.

• You can make this with spinach instead of sorrel, in which case add the juice of 1 lemon or lime to taste, to achieve the sourish taste favoured by Hyderabadi cooks.

Mung Beans and Greens

Serves 4–6 as a side dish

Another example of Hyderabad's love for sour greens. The original recipe, made with the leaves of amaranth (a seed brought from Aztec Mexico), was an Unani doctor's 'prescription' called *kholamba masala*. I came across a similar dish – *shula kalambar* – in Claudia Roden's *Middle Eastern Food*, with spinach and lentils prepared, she said, 'in medieval Persia to heal the sick'. Serve for lunch with tart mangoes and yoghurt (see Take Three Mangoes, page 120) and a sprinkling of crunchy Peanut Chutney Powder (page 80).

225 g (8 oz) sorrel (including stalks) chopped
½ teaspoon cumin seeds
2–3 dried red chillies, seeded and crumbled
1 tablespoon grated fresh or creamed coconut
½ teaspoon salt, or to taste
100 g (4 oz) mung dal, cooked and drained
3 tablespoons light sesame or peanut oil
½ teaspoon black mustard seeds
2 medium onions, finely chopped
1 teaspoon white urad dal or split red lentils
2 green chillies, slit lengthwise
¼ teaspoon asafoetida powder

Drop sorrel into boiling water, cook for 5–7 minutes until tender and drain well (do not squeeze out water). Lightly toast cumin seeds and red chillies and grind together with coconut and salt. Stir into cooked beans with sorrel and cook for several minutes to blend flavours.

Over medium-high heat, cook mustard seeds in oil until they have finished popping. Add onions, urad dal and chillies and cook until onions are browning around edges. Stir in asafoetida and sizzle it for a few seconds. Add to vegetables and warm through for 2 minutes.

Note – Cooking time can vary depending on brand of beans. Some, notably those produced for supermarkets in the West, require only 20–25 minutes cooking and no soaking. If you buy mung beans without cooking instructions printed on the package, bring to a boil in plenty of cold water, boil rapidly for 10 minutes, then leave to soak for 1 hour. Finish cooking for 20–25 minutes, or until beans are tender but still whole.

Variations

- Use spinach instead of sorrel and add the juice of 1 lemon.
- Instead of mung beans, substitute cooked rice – the sorrel will colour it a deep green.

Peanut Chutney Powder

Serves 6–8 as an accompaniment, fills 2 jam jars

Another link with the Middle East, reminiscent of the Egyptian spiced nut mixture, *dukkah*. But whether this went West or *dukkah* came East, who knows? Use it like *dukkah*, dipping hard-boiled eggs or chunks of bread first in olive or sesame oil and then in the nuts. Sprinkle it on noodles, rice or stir-fried vegetables, or dip fish in stiffly beaten egg whites, then into the powder and fry or grill for a spicy crust.

1 tablespoon white urad dal or split red lentils
1 teaspoon light sesame or peanut oil
1 tablespoon sesame seeds
5–6 dried red chillies, seeded and crumbled
½ teaspoon asafoetida powder
165 g (5½ oz) dry-roasted salted peanuts
1–1½ tablespoons muscovado or dark brown sugar
coarse sea salt, to taste

Over medium-low heat, cook dal in oil until light brown, then add sesame seeds and chillies and continue cooking until they darken in colour. Sizzle asafoetida in the oil for a few seconds at the end and grind everything to a coarse crumbly mixture – it should not form a paste. The mix should be quite salty and sweetish as it is meant as a contrast to blander foods but be careful adding salt as nuts are already salty.

──────── *Variation* ────────

• For a hotter, fruitier paste, double quantity of red chillies and add 50–75 g (2–3 oz) tamarind paste, barely covered in boiling water for 30 minutes, then sieved.

ALMOND AND CARDAMOM CRANBERRIES

Makes 6–7 jam jars

In the past, every 'good' Hyderabadi family had a bowl of *murabba* (fruit preserves), which had been prescribed by its Unani doctor, sitting on the table next to the English marmalade. The most popular preserve, because of its high vitamin C content, was made with *amla*, known as the Indian gooseberry. Cranberries make a good vividly-coloured substitute, and like gooseberries and *amla*, go well with oily or rich food. This is a preserve for the dinner table rather than breakfast. I like to chew on whole cardamom – if you don't, remove pods and crush seeds first.

900 g (2 lb) fresh cranberries
1 tablespoon green cardamom pods (or just seeds, crushed)
5 cm (2 inch) piece cinnamon stick, roughly broken
6 cloves
450 g (1 lb) caster sugar
1 tablespoon red wine vinegar
25 g (1 oz) blanched almonds and shelled pistachios (skins roughly rubbed off), halved

few drops rose or kewra essence or 2 teaspoons Rose Petal Masala (page 69)

Place berries in a pan. Add enough cold water so that you can see it but it doesn't float the berries. Push spices into middle and bring to a low boil. When about half the berries have popped, stir in remaining ingredients until sugar dissolves. Spoon into hot clean jars, cover with kitchen wrap and press it down well so there is no air above berries. Cover tightly.

TAMARIND AND GINGER SORBET

Serves 6

A romantic flavour of the past turned into a fruity sour-sweet sorbet. It is based on a tamarind sherbet prescribed by Unani doctors (although it would clearly not have had alcohol in the original). To serve as a refreshing drink, leave out cream, add lots of crushed ice and serve, as recommended by an old Hyderabadi doctor, with fresh flower petals floating in it.

5–7.5 cm (2–3 inch) piece root ginger, grated into saucepan (so as not to lose ginger juice)
225 g (8 oz) jaggery, or dark brown sugar
100 g (4 oz) tamarind paste
8 green cardamom pods
175 ml (6 fl oz) single cream
4 tablespoons rum (optional)

Boil ginger with sugar, tamarind, cardamom and 600 ml (1 pint) water for 5 minutes. Leave to infuse overnight (or at least 3 hours). Strain through sieve, rubbing tamarind well to obtain maximum pulp, and beat in cream and rum. Either use an ice-cream maker or freeze until almost firm, beat mixture to break down ice crystals, and re-freeze until firm.

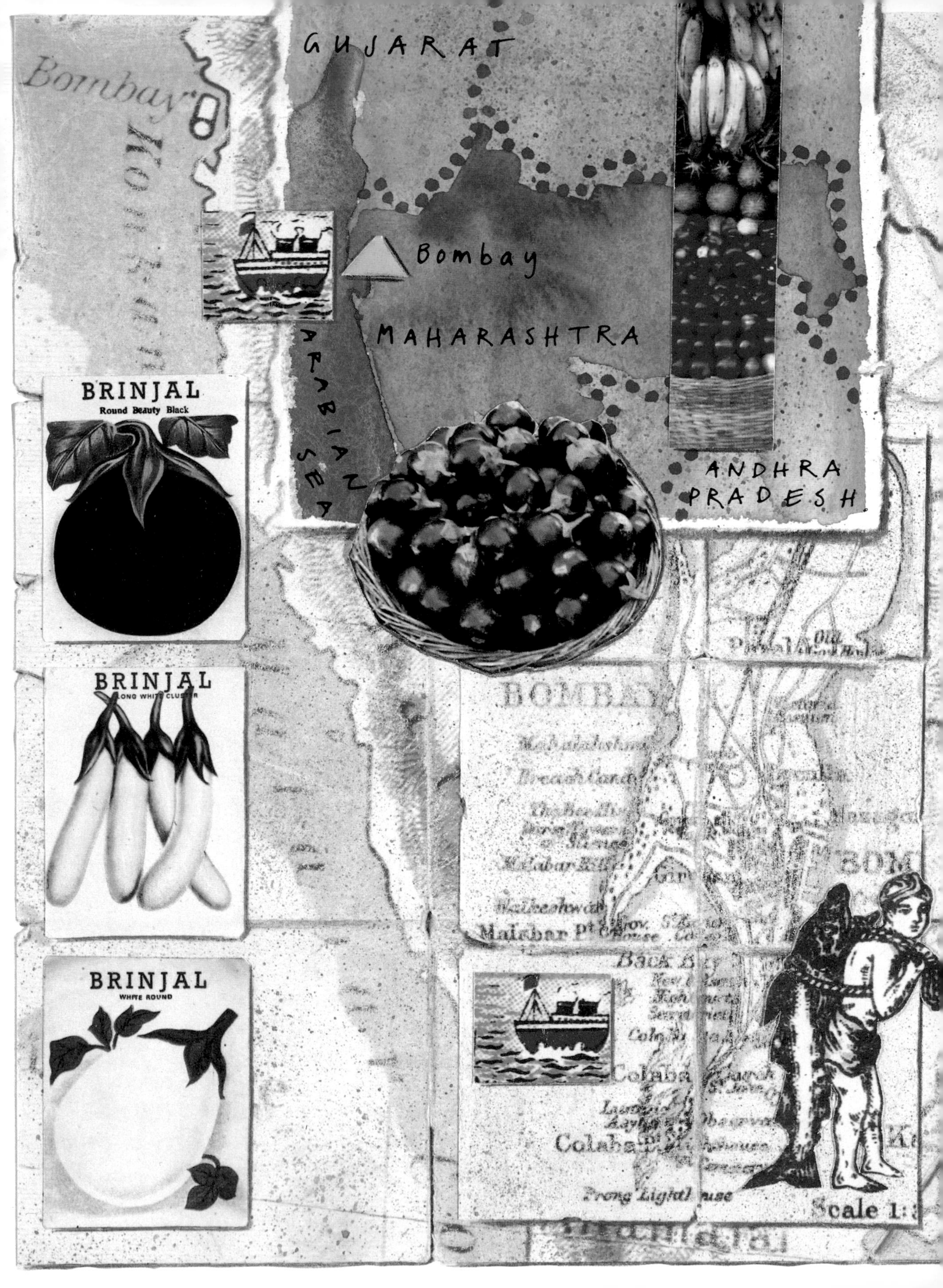

GUJARAT

Bombay

MAHARASHTRA

ARABIAN
SEA

ANDHRA
PRADESH

BRINJAL
Round Beauty Black

BRINJAL
LONG WHITE CLUSTER

BRINJAL
WHITE ROUND

BOMBAY

Mahabaleshwar
Breach Candy
The Bee Hive
Parsi Tower of Silence
Malabar Hill
Walkeshwar
Malabar Pt. Gov. House Colaba
Back Bay
Colaba

Colaba

Prong Light House

Scale 1:

CHAPTER FOUR

THE LEFT-HAND SIDE OF THE THALI

•

Bombay is a city of leftovers.

TRIPTI PANDEY, RAJASTHAN

Movies are Bombay's masala, and the street people of India's Hollywood are the movies' biggest consumers. 'What they like,' said the film producer Gul Anand, 'are what we call masala films, where a director throws in all kinds of spicy ingredients. The classic movie masala is: eight songs, four fights, one rape and a mother-in-law/daughter-in-law confrontation.' For one rupee the poor can buy three hours of air-conditioned comfort and dreams, and for a couple more, dinner from one of the thousands of stalls that turn the city into an enormous open-air kitchen. As a friend said, 'You can eat in all of India by walking through Bombay for a day.'

Bombay is not interested in who your grandfather is, I was told by the gossip-writer Shoba De; and it doesn't want to know the provenance of the meal you serve. It is a city created for and by entrepreneurs who believe in fast cars, technology and capitalism. The traffic moves at a pedestrian pace, the phone system is, at best, like shouting underwater and the original British entrepreneurs' colonial mansions on Malabar Hill grow piebald with damp and are replaced by even more ephemeral high-rises, giving Bombay the unreliable skyline of a film set. Still, when people in the West tell me, 'Nothing works in India,' I think of Bombay's *dabbawalla* connection, so complex, ingenious and baroque it could only have been invented here.

A *dabba* is a three-tiered aluminium lunchbox enclosed in an outer shell to keep food warm and prevent it from splashing. This is an important consideration for the *dabbawallas*, some 2000 men in white Gandhi caps who every day transport about thirty-nine dabbas each from Bombay's remotest suburban kitchens through a Mobius strip of urban railways so that

100,000 office workers can have hot, home-cooked meals. For Bacchi Karkaria, senior editor at the *Times of India*, the dabba connection is a symbol of her adopted city.

'Do any lunches go missing?'

'Of course,' said Bacchi. 'Twelve to fifteen of the 100,000 every day.'

It would be a remarkable feat anywhere in the world. Performed by a group of illiterate men in a country of rigid food taboos and intermittent electricity, it's a miracle.

To prevent a Parsi's garlicky mutton *dhansak* from winding up on the desk of a garlic-eschewing, vegetarian Gujarati, an elaborate system of hieroglyphics is used. 'Say you are a typist at the *Times*,' Bacchi said. 'The only lunch you could afford normally would be street food. Instead, at 10 a.m. every morning, dabbawalla No. 1 appears at your family's home, collects your lunchbox and adds it to his consignment. Each box has a mysterious mark (in addition to your own name, which the dabbawalla cannot read) indicating its destination. At 10.20 a.m. dabbawalla No. 2 takes over and cycles with the boxes to the nearest train station.

There, dabbawalla No. 3, with all the other dabbawallas who have arrived at the station, looks for boxes with his identifying mark, gets into the carriage reserved for dabbawallas and heads for Victoria Terminus, the city's business core, where dabbawalla No. 4 picks out the boxes with his symbol, the white cross. Your box will have an extra mark, the *Times of India*'s black circle. At 12.30 p.m., dabbawalla No. 4 carries his boxes up four flights of stairs to our canteen, you find your name and eat lunch. At 2 p.m., the procedure goes into reverse.'

ABOVE: A dabbawallah takes time out for his own lunch of tangy poha (spiced, flattened rice flavoured with lime and curry leaves) wrapped in the Times of India.

ABOVE RIGHT: The ultimate Bombay snack is Chowpatty Beach's bhel-puri – savoury, tangy bits and pieces, an edible symbol of this flirtatious city of exiles and pioneers.

The service charge for hot lunch delivered daily in monsoon and summer heat wave is determined by how far the dabbawallas walk or cycle between stations. They are not infallible; still that old Broadway spirit of 'the show must go on' does prevail. Bacchi knew of one dabbawalla who had been killed in an accident on his bicycle. Within minutes the news reached his guild, The Bombay Tiffinbox Suppliers Association, who orchestrate the system, and they managed to get someone else to deliver his lunches.

For the dabbawallas themselves, lunch is not home-cooked. More likely it will be *bhel-puri* eaten on Chowpatty Beach next to what looks like a casting call for an epic film set in a medieval Court of Miracles: naked holy men, sword-swallowers, sand sculptors of Ganesh, Bombay's favourite, elephant-headed god, eunuchs dressed as women, jugglers – and ragged urchins who may be this year's pickpockets or next year's film stars; Bombay is the city of overnight success.

Bhel-puri could be said to represent the city's food just as dabbawallas represent its entrepreneurial spirit. Like the city, it was created out of bits and pieces from elsewhere. The *bhel-puri-wallas*, originally from the northern state of Uttar Pradesh, probably first set up their little stalls on the sands of Chowpatty about 1904. Over the years their mixture of salted *sev* (chickpea flour noodles), *puris* (crisp-fried mini-chapattis) and *murmuras* (puffed rice) was given the Bombay sweet-sour flavour with tamarind chutney, lime juice and green mango sauce.

Just as social classes are levelled in Bombay's movie world, so culinary distinctions among the city's largely immigrant population have been washed away by the southwestern coastal tastes. In little Punjabi cafés opposite the General Post Office, the maize *roti* and spinach typical of that state are tempered with mustard seeds sizzled in coconut oil, unthinkable in the Punjab; in Bombay's Muslim quarter, among the raw Northwest Frontier smells of goat, black cardamom, drains and rosewater, a Kashmiri *sherbetwalla* gives his luscious tropical fruit drinks the Mogul aroma of saffron from the Himalayas, while his neighbours, grilling Delhi-style kebabs over portable charcoal braziers, serve a typically southern chutney of coriander, coconut and curry leaves.

The cooks of Maharashtra – the state of which Bombay is the capital – are particularly proud of their mastery of the left-hand side of the *thali* (India's equivalent of a TV dinner, an entire meal served on a tray), where one finds the chutneys, pestos, pickles, sweet and savoury snacks. It is an apt metaphor for Bombay, which in 1862 was turned, by a massive land reclamation, from a series of seven malarial mudflats into this booming port on the left-hand side of the subcontinent, now home to many of the country's minorities – Sikhs, Gujaratis, Sindhis, Jews, Parsis and Catholic Goans of Portuguese descent.

The function of Portuguese Goa in the sixteenth century was to supervise the Malabar Coast and break the Arabs' monopoly of the spice trade through Egypt to Europe. The function of Bombay, a city built by British East India Company money, was to supervise the Portuguese. Encouraged by the Moguls, who disliked Catholic Portugal's persecution of other religions, the East India Company leased Bombay from the British government in 1668, at a yearly cost of £10 in gold. India was then, at best, a consolation prize for the British, who had lost their chance of a foothold in the Dutch Spice Islands. Indian spices were confined to Kerala, and there the British had to compete with Dutch, Portuguese and French for the European market. The East India Company concentrated instead on a less versatile but infinitely more valuable spice: opium. By 1859 40 per cent of the company profits came from opium (traded in China for tea) and 30 per cent from cotton. Not until 1863, when the railway connected Bombay to the cotton-growing Deccan plains, did opium begin to lose its ascendency.

Fast food and the quick buck go together. Bombay's most inveterate snack-eaters are Gujaratis, many of whom came seeking to make their fortunes in the new textile industries created by the British in the nineteenth century. So diverse are Gujarati snacks that they are divided in two categories, *nasto* and *farsan*. *Nasto* includes anything insubstantial like crunchy chickpea noodles in all different widths and lengths, roasted peanuts, fried lentils and sun-dried potatoes. Tossed together with citric acid crystals (lemon would destroy the essential crispness), grated jaggery and cayenne pepper, they become a 'Bombay mix'. The components are prepared in advance, stored separately and combined to taste at the last minute; the result is a popular breakfast with spiced tea. The poor settle for *bhoosoo*, literally 'sawdust' – broken crumbs at the bottom of the *nasto* container.

Farsan are to *nasto* what buttered corn-on-the-cob is to popcorn. Prepared to order, usually fried (Gujaratis are the highest per capita consumers of cooking oil in India) and eaten hot, they vary from spicy chickpea flour crispbreads spread with ground fenugreek chutney to leaves of the aloe plant rolled with spiced lentil paste, steamed, then sliced like miniature green Swiss rolls. A Maharashtrian cook said derogatorily of the Gujaratis, 'Their food improved when they came to Bombay. Unlike Maharashtrians, who respect the rhythm of the seasons and do not overprocess their food, in Gujarat, everything is either dried, liquid or puréed.'

Maharashtra was far enough removed geographically from the Mogul empire not to feel the impact of that elaborately ornamental cuisine. Maharashtrians tend to add spices only at the final stage of tempering, and these will be the lighter southern ones such as mustard seeds, curry leaves and cumin. Their vegetables have a bite to them (unusual in India), as well as visual appeal and a play of colours – especially greens – but they are invariably cooked with an almost Italian simplicity which has earned the cuisine scorn as well as loyalty among gastronomes, just as Mediterranean peasant food did for many years in the West.

Maharashtrians along the coast from Bombay, a working-class caste of farmers, once Hindu India's best warriors (in the seventeenth century their leader, Shiva-ji, had an empire that challenged the Moguls' and, later, the British), have a strong chauvinistic streak. They have retained their peasant roots. 'We are not like those people in the North,' I was told, 'whose traditions were buried under layer after layer of invaders until the best they could do was try to ape the Moguls' overuse of garam masala.'

The films of Shyam Benegal, a Bombay director, have something of the earthy elegance of this Maharashtrian food. He comes from a family of Saraswati brahmin scholars and teachers whose traditions prohibited them from owning property. 'They have a history of wandering,' he said, 'and in a feudal agrarian society this meant making do with what they were given or could find. They became adept at using things like the stalks, even the peel of vegetables – things that other people thought of as leftovers or animal fodder. As the Buddha taught, if you have to traverse the road, you must become the road itself.'

'Were spices important?' I asked.

'Of course: with a few mustard seeds and some red chillies, the mundane is transformed. A Saraswati recipe called *saung* is no

Fresh and tart tamarind pods (bottom) are sun-dried to make a commercial paste for cooking.

more than chopped potatoes fried with half their weight in onions, to which the simplest masala of ground tamarind, red chillies and salt is added. Yet it is the essence of potatoes.'

Another group of immigrants were to create two of Bombay's landmarks: the Taj Hotel, facing the harbour, for almost a century a symbol of luxury and arrival (in both the social and the geographical sense); and the Towers of Silence, symbol of departure, where Parsi Zoroastrians leave their dead, not wishing to let corpses pollute the sacred fire.

The Parsis arrived on the coast of Gujarat in the eighth century AD, fleeing Muslim persecution in Persia. They began moving to Bombay not long after the East India Company transferred its headquarters to this city in 1687. Unlike Hindus, Parsis have no caste or food restrictions and they rapidly became go-betweens, clerks, lawyers and even butlers for the British. Their golden age, when the Taj Hotel was built by India's greatest entrepreneurs, the Tatas, coincided with the height of the Raj. The rapport still exists. There are Parsi tea shops with interiors reminiscent of a British seaside boarding house and famous Parsi clubs, such as the Ripon, modelled along London lines, with dark wood and a membership as ancient as its yellowing copies of *Punch*. Parsi food, however, enriched with aromatic spices and quantities of dried fruit, reveals its Persian ancestry.

'Although we use some of the Persian spices, our cuisine lacks Persian finesse,' said Bacchi Karkaria, a Parsi whose family moved here from Calcutta. 'All our dishes are variations on the stew: meat and veg cooked together until quite dry with an egg poached on top. We put eggs in everything.' There are two basic spice mixtures, she told me: cumin seeds, red chillies and garlic, pounded to a paste for prawns or fish, and ground ginger and garlic fried with onion for meat dishes – rustic preparations that Bacchi felt stemmed from her sect's having fled their home so hurriedly that elaborate cooking traditions were lost or survived only as vague memories.

Time in India is like a wall plastered with movie posters that peel away to reveal, still intact, the familiar stars of a previous generation – what Shyam Benegal calls 'India's perennial present'. The best place to buy spices in Bombay is in the market area known as Mandvi, near the city's Muslim quarter. Mandvi, I learned, was once a great trading post on an old caravan route across the Gujarati desert of Kutch. The market was named after the Mandvi Jain merchants who came here centuries ago and now dominate its trade.

A stream of Jains, from wealthy grain and spice dealers to humble vendors of *sev*, flows into the area's seven temples, each penitent anointing the diamond-encrusted deities with a paste of sandalwood and saffron, ground in vast mortars in the temples and provided free of charge. On one side of the temples are the sellers of diamonds, on the other side is the spice market. All spice roads in India lead back to the Jains.

'It's the only street in Bombay that is cleaned six times a day,' said one trader. 'And you can be sure the cleaners aren't looking for cloves.'

Flavours of Bombay & Maharashtra

·

CHUTNEYS, PESTOS, PICKLES AND STREET FOOD

*I*n a monsoon country like India, where refrigerators are still a luxury and mangoes are more easily bought by the bushel than the bag, preserves are a necessity. There are literally thousands of Bombay chutneys and pickles but many require a team of aunties to help bottle them. The recipes in this chapter have been adapted to suit a faster pace of life.

Up to a point, cultural origins of the Bombay mix could be defined by the spices they use to flavour chutneys and pickles. Sindhis add fennel and dill seeds to their dry-fried aubergines and okra, Gujarati dry chutneys are soured with citric acid crystals or green mango powder, the Parsis have a preference for star anise and Persian spices – cinnamon, clove and cardamom – while local Maharashtrians prefer lighter southern spices such as mustard seeds, curry leaves and cumin. One of my favourite chutneys for grilled vegetables marries Kashmir with Maharashtra: two handfuls of walnuts are ground with salt, red chillies and lime juice, tempered with toasted mustard seeds.

STAR ANISE: *badayan*
BOT: *Illicium verum*

·

Although it probably arrived in India with the first Chinese traders a few thousand years ago, star anise is used rarely, perhaps because its fascinating musky aroma can overwhelm delicate dishes: try a little before you use a lot. It identifies many Parsi pilafs and stews in Bombay. One 'star' boiled with even the most flavourless chicken carcass will give a fine pheasanty flavour to stock.

ROASTED ONION AND COCONUT CHUTNEY WITH STAR ANISE
Serves 6–8, lasts about 2 weeks in sealed jar

A carnivores' chutney from a Parsi friend: the roasted onions and star anise give this a strong smoky, musky aroma good with game or with meaty fish such as tuna and swordfish.

100 g (4 oz) tamarind paste
450 g (1 lb) onions, unpeeled
light sesame or peanut oil
2.5 cm (1 inch) cinnamon stick, roughly crushed
½ teaspoon coriander seeds
½ teaspoon cumin seeds
½ star anise
3–5 5 cm (2 inch) dried red chillies, seeded and crumbled
½ teaspoon sea salt, or to taste
150 g (5 oz) fresh or creamed coconut

Pour just enough boiling water onto tamarind to cover and leave to soak for 30 minutes. Sieve and discard seeds.

Halve onions lengthwise, lay in 1 layer skin side up in a greased pan and brush skins with oil. Put under hot grill until skins are black, then turn over and grill flesh until it is blackened in spots. Discard skin and roots.

In a dry frying pan, toast first cinnamon, then coriander, then cumin, and finally star anise and chillies until lightly coloured and fragrant. Grind to a powder, add onions and other ingredients and grind coarsely with 1 tablespoon of oil.

——————— *Variations* ———————
- Toast a handful of cashew nut pieces in the oil and stir in at end.
- Parsis add raisins to this, or even finely sliced dates instead of coconut – I prefer 6–8 roughly chopped sun-dried tomatoes for colour and tang.

PARSI PICKLED SHRIMP (OR PRAWNS)

Makes enough to fill 1 400 ml (15 fl oz) jar
or 4–6 little ramekins

Mango pickles require a lot of salt and time but this spicy, tangy Parsi version of potted shrimp takes only a few minutes. It should be eaten in small quantities with crisp pappadums or roti. I like to serve it as a summer starter or snack, packed into little ramekins like potted shrimp, with brown toast and lots of butter. Or you could serve a spoonful of it with sliced mangoes on the side, a good balance of sweet and spice. 'Between February and May, people think so much about mangoes they begin to acquire the look of them,' the *Times* editor Bacchi Karkaria told me. 'Sharp, hard and green or luscious, orange and squishy. I have one aunt so fond of them that every year from the beginning of March until the end of May her ears would be pricked for the sound of the street vendor and she would put her clothes into storage to make room for crates of fruit.'

Like the Gujaratis, Parsis make a lot of mango pickles, using every part of the fruit including skin and kernel, enjoyed for its chewiness. There are women in Bombay's food markets who have specially sharpened knives for slicing the mango kernels into bite-size pieces for pickles.

Mangoes, the flavour of spring in Bombay and Gujarat.

'Across the road from those women is the spice merchant,' Bacchi told me, 'and he's got packets of whatever kind of spice masala you want. You just mix it with your mangoes, bung it in jars on your terrace and leave it for the sun to cook.' Unfortunately, markets in the West are not so geared up for pickle-makers.

---
4 tablespoons light sesame oil
---
1 medium large onion, finely chopped
---
1 tablespoon cumin seeds

4–6 garlic cloves, finely chopped
---
*450 g (1 lb) small raw shrimps or prawns,
peeled and cleaned**
---
1 teaspoon salt, or to taste

1.5–2.5 teaspoons cayenne pepper
---
8 tablespoons white wine vinegar

In medium-hot oil, fry onions and cumin seeds until caramely brown. Stir in garlic and let it soften, then add shrimps or prawns, salt and cayenne, stir to take the rawness off the cayenne and add the vinegar. Stir-fry until vinegar has evaporated and pack into ramekins. Keep refrigerated and eat within 5 days.

*This recipe will make even the most boring pre-frozen cooked shrimp or prawns taste like a trip to Goa.

FRESH PUMPKIN AND COCONUT PICKLE
Serves 8 as a condiment

A very pretty pickle with strips of bright orange pumpkin peel, remarkably similar to one made in modern Sicily that dates from Roman times. It is typical of the Saraswat community in Bombay (did that sect of wandering scholars ever travel to Rome?), who make it using crisply fried pumpkin skin alone – a good idea if you are using the flesh for something else. Adding most of the spices at the end with minimal cooking preserves the flavours' individuality: explosions of orangey

coriander and toasted sesame, mellow sweet pumpkin and garlic. Try it with Christmas turkey and game.

---
*90 g (3½ oz) tamarind paste
(or juice of 2 limes)*
---
50 g (2 oz) muscovado or dark brown sugar

¾ teaspoon salt
---
2 green chillies, finely sliced lenthwise
---
*450 g (1 lb) pumpkin or orange American
squash, pulp and seeds removed*
---
1 teaspoon coriander seeds
---
25 g (1 oz) desiccated coconut

2–4 dried red chillies, seeded and crumbled

4–6 garlic cloves
---
1 tablespoon light sesame or peanut oil
---
1 tablespoon sesame seeds

Cover tamarind in boiling water and soak for 30 minutes.

Slice pumpkin with its skin into rough 5×2.5 cm (2×1 inch) strips – skin should be no more than 3–5 mm (⅛–¼ inch) thick. Boil 150 ml (5 fl oz) of water with sugar, salt and green chillies. Add pumpkin, reduce heat and simmer just until pumpkin skin can be easily pierced with a sharp knife (about 10 minutes).

Over medium-high heat in a dry frying pan, toast coriander seeds until they change colour and smell aromatic. Add coconut and red chillies and stir until lightly browned.

Sieve tamarind, discard seeds, then grind coarsely in a processor with coconut, chillies, coriander and 2 garlic cloves. Stir into pumpkin and simmer gently while making tempering: heat oil and fry remaining garlic, finely sliced in julienne, and sesame seeds. When golden, pour into pumpkin and stir. Serve warm or cool.

'Fresh' implies this belongs in the fridge rather than the store cupboard – in India, it would be eaten on the same day. Keeps about 10 days in an airtight container in fridge.

● Punjabis in Bombay make a similar pickle substituting 450 g (1 lb) carrots, finely sliced lengthwise in long flat strips, for the pumpkin. Fresh ginger is ground in the masala instead of coconut and to the final garlic tempering they add 1 teaspoon each of cumin and black mustard seeds. Very good with rare roast beef.

GREEN COCONUT AND CORIANDER CHUTNEY

Serves 6–8 as a condiment

A stiff pistachio-green paste to use as a chutney with grilled duck, chicken or fish (or as a surprise filling inside a baked potato or a kebab – see also next recipe); as a sauce, thinned with lime or lemon juice; or as a pesto. Stirred into risottos, soups, pasta or lentil stews at the last minute, it adds a taste as bright and fresh as its colour.

50 g (2 oz) fresh coriander (including stalks) roughly chopped
90 g (3½ oz) fresh or creamed coconut
½ teaspoon ground cumin
1 cm (½ inch) piece fresh root ginger, chopped
2 garlic cloves, chopped
2–4 green chillies, seeded and chopped
juice and grated zest of 1 lime
½ teaspoon sea salt, or to taste

Grind all ingredients to a fine paste and serve at room temperature (it stiffens to a solid mass when chilled). Refrigerated, it lasts about a week.

COCONUT CHUTNEY-STUFFED POTATO FRITTERS

Makes 8 fritters

Bright green chutney and creamy potatoes inside a crisp crust: a snack for 8 or light lunch for 4 with a ripe tomato or cucumber salad. These fritters can either be shallow-fried in a little butter or olive oil (try them as a vegetarian alternative to fishcakes, served in a puddle of good tomato sauce) or deep-fry them (even better) for extra crunch.

550 g (1¼ lb) potatoes
¼ teaspoon turmeric
4 spring onions with a bit of green top, finely chopped
1 teaspoon cumin seeds, toasted and coarsely ground
5–6 tablespoons Green Coconut and Coriander Chutney (left) or
40 g (1½ oz) creamed or fresh coconut
3 green chillies
1 cm (½ inch) piece fresh root ginger, chopped
large handful of fresh coriander (about 15 g (½ oz))
¾ teaspoon salt
1 small tomato or 3 cherry tomatoes, finely chopped
vegetable oil for frying
flour (rice flour for preference)
2 eggs, beaten
fresh breadcrumbs

Boil potatoes until tender then mash with turmeric, onions and cumin.

Grind together coconut, chillies, ginger, coriander and salt, then add just enough tomatoes to dampen mixture to a smooth paste without making it wet. Roll potato mixture into 8 balls, stuff each with about a 2-teaspoon nugget of chutney, press to seal well and flatten into 1 cm (½ inch) fritters.

To deep-fry, fill a deep saucepan with 1 cm (½ inch) oil, and heat until a crumb dropped into it sizzles immediately and browns in about 30 seconds. When hot, dip each fritter in flour, then in egg, then in breadcrumbs and slide into oil. Do not crowd pan. When fritters have browned on one side, turn over with a slotted spoon and finish browning on reverse. Remove and drain on kitchen paper. Good hot or at room temperature. To re-heat, put in an oven pre-heated to 220°C/425°F/Gas 7 until crisp.

POTATO ROTI

Serves 4 as a light lunch or starter,
6 as bread or a snack

The most fashionable snack when I was in Bombay was a modern version of Gujarat's savoury *dhokla*, in which a two-coloured lentil dough was separated by a thin layer of coriander chutney, then steamed and sliced to reveal a tri-coloured interior. Traditional *dhokla* is laborious enough. To make that one you needed an Indian pedigree as long as the *Mahabharata*. You can give this gingery Gujarati potato cake the Bombay sandwich treatment in a fraction of the time (see variations). Serve it for lunch, cut in thick wedges with grated fresh coconut on top and Bombay Ketchup (page 100) on the side, or slice it thinly as an alternative to bread served with smoky ham.

1 tablespoon light sesame or peanut oil plus extra for greasing pan
1 tablespoon yoghurt
2.5 cm (1 inch) piece fresh root ginger, grated
3–4 green chillies, seeded and shredded
4 tablespoons chopped fresh coriander (1 small bunch)
salt to taste

¼ teaspoon turmeric
450 g (1 lb) cooked potatoes, mashed
70 g (2¾ oz) rice flour
juice and grated zest of ½ lime

TEMPERING

1½ teaspoons black mustard seeds
1 tablespoon sesame seeds
¼ teaspoon asafoetida powder

Pre-heat oven to 220°C/425°F/Gas 7. Grease a 25–30 cm (10–12 inch) shallow metal pan (I use a small paella pan but a cast iron frying pan is better) and heat in oven. This will give roti a crisp base.

Whisk together 135 ml (4½ fl oz) water, yoghurt, ginger, chillies, coriander, salt and turmeric and slowly beat into potato. Stir in flour and lime juice.

Spread potato mixture in hot pan and smooth the top. Bake for 20–25 minutes until starting to brown. Just before serving, prepare tempering: heat 1 tablespoon of oil to hot, pour in mustard seeds (keep a lid handy to prevent splattering) and when they stop popping, immediately stir in sesame seeds and asafoetida and pour over roti.

———— *Variation* ————

• *Chutney layered potato roti* Smooth half the potato mixture into pan, spread over it a 5 cm (¼ inch) thick layer of Green Coconut and Coriander Chutney (page 92) or one of the aubergine chutnies (see Three Fast Smoky Chutneys to make with Two Aubergines, page 100), then top with another layer of potatoes. Continue as in the main recipe.

SPICE BATTER

A crisp spicy crust for deep-frying 4 small whole fish or fillets or the florets from 1 small cauliflower. For coating larger quantities, double the ingredients.

5 tablespoons chickpea (besan/gram) flour
¼ teaspoon ground turmeric
¼ teaspoon sugar
¼ teaspoon salt
1 cm (½ inch) piece fresh root ginger, grated

Mix together all ingredients, whisk in 50 ml (2 fl oz) of water and leave for 30 minutes.

—————— *Uses* ——————

● *Spicy cauliflower fritters* Mix 1 teaspoon of cayenne pepper and 1 teaspoon of toasted cumin seeds into batter. Break a small cauliflower into little florets, dip them in batter and deep-fry until brown in 1 cm (½ inch) sizzling peanut or sunflower oil.

● *Fresh-tasting carrot or courgette fritters* Slice 225 g (8 oz) baby courgettes or small scrubbed carrots into thin strips lengthwise. Salt lightly and leave 30 minutes to remove excess moisture. Pat dry. Mix a handful of finely chopped mint and juice of 1 lime into batter, dip carrots into it and deep-fry until brown.

AUBERGINE AND CORIANDER CHUTNEY SANDWICH

Serves 2 as a snack

Parboiling aubergine stops it absorbing oil and gives it a creamy melting texture, a good contrast to the fresh clean chutney and crisp batter. I usually fill it with the spiced Drained Yoghurt Cheese but paneer, Middle Eastern yoghurt cheese (available under oil in delicatessens and health food stores) or even ricotta are just as good. A good lunch for two with stewed greens.

1 big aubergine (about 225 g (8 oz))
3 tablespoons paneer, Middle Eastern
yoghurt cheese, Drained Yoghurt Cheese
(page 123) or Greek-style yoghurt
handful of fresh coriander, finely chopped
2 green chillies
1–2 garlic cloves, crushed
¼ teaspoon salt
1 quantity Spice Batter (left)
peanut or sunflower oil for frying

Halve aubergine crosswise, then quarter lengthwise into 8 pieces. Drop in boiling water for 3 minutes and drain.

Mix together paneer, coriander, chillies, garlic and salt (if yoghurt is not salted). It must be a very thick paste (add a little more coriander if it is too thin). Spread a quarter of this between each 2 pieces of aubergine and press together firmly to make little sandwiches.

Heat enough oil to cover a heavy saucepan or wok by 2.5 cm (1 inch). When a bit of batter dropped in sizzles instantly and crisps after about 30 seconds, dip each 'sandwich' into batter and slip into oil. Fry 3 minutes each side or until golden brown.

DOUBLE CORIANDER FISH AND CHIPS

Serves 4 as a light main course

I was served a version of this made with very small boned mackerel, but fillets are easier if you worry about bones. I did. For Bombay fish and chips, cook this with Potato Ribbons (page 96).

juice of 1–2 limes
1 tablespoon coriander seeds, toasted and
roughly crushed

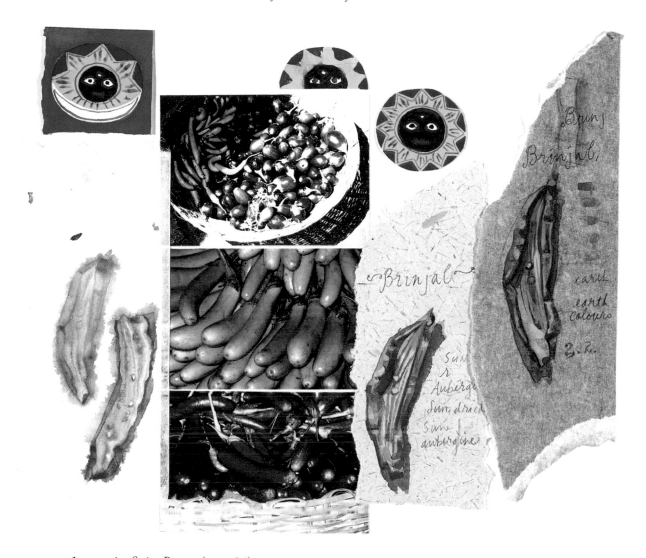

1 quantity Spice Batter (page 94)

4–6 tablespoons yoghurt mixture from previous recipe or Green Coconut and Coriander Chutney (page 92)

550–750 g (1¼–1½ lb) fish e.g. 4 small boned mackerel or 8 thin white fish fillets (cod, haddock etc.)

flour (rice flour for preference)

peanut or sunflower oil for deep-frying

Mix lime juice and coriander seeds into batter and set aside. Spread 1 rounded tablespoon of chutney inside fish or between 2 fillets. Press together. I use a chef's trick for getting really crisp deep-fried fish. You will need a thermometer for this: heat 2.5 cm (1 inch) oil to 170°C/340°F in deep saucepan. Dip fish first in flour, then in batter and fry 2 minutes in oil. Lift out with a slotted spoon and drain on kitchen paper. Remove any stray bits of batter from oil, raise temperature to 190°C/375°F and fry fish again until crisp and brown. Drain on kitchen paper.

ABOVE: *Aubergines in all shapes and sizes in a Bombay street market – some Gujaratis even sundry them, to grind in pickles later with tamarind and fresh coconut.*

POTATO RIBBONS

Ribbons of potato skin, deep-fried until golden and curled, then sprinkled with spice – from an extraordinary book on Indian food, *Ras-achandrika*, published by the Saraswat community in Bombay in 1947. Among such useful tips as how to alleviate gas ('Put a little asafoetida in water or buttermilk and drink it. It feels better after belching.') and what kind of food and oil baths are to be given cattle in festivals, is a collection of recipes so uncomplicated they seem hardly recognizable as Indian. In one, the sliced stems of 'any leafy vegetable' are simmered until tender with salt, sugar, green chillies, tamarind and garlic, then seasoned with crushed garlic cloves fried in ghee. Another describes a simple chutney of cooked leaves ground with 4 garlic cloves, 2–3 green chillies, a little tamarind and salt and sugar to taste.

Prepare crunchy potato ribbons to munch while cooking one of the other potato recipes in this chapter: peel potatoes, trying as much as possible to keep skin in one piece (or at least in long pieces), and drop peel into cold water until ready to use.

Heat 1 cm (½ inch) vegetable oil in a deep saucepan until a crumb dropped into it sizzles instantly and browns in about 30 seconds. Drain potato skins and pat dry, drop in oil and when brown around edges but just creamy yellow in middle (about 1 minute), lift out with slotted spoon and drain on kitchen towel. Sprinkle with sea salt and cayenne pepper to taste and 1 teaspoon cumin seeds, toasted and coarsely ground. In Bombay, these are eaten with the Tamarind Sweet and Sour Sauce (page 120).

COCONUT CRUST POTATOES

Serves 4–6 as a side dish

I like these with grilled or barbecued chicken and Bombay Ketchup (page 100) – or just on their own with a big dollop of yoghurt to mop up the crunchy brown crumbs.

750 g (1¼ lb) potatoes (about 4 medium), cut in eighths lengthwise
2–3 tablespoons light sesame or peanut oil
¼ teaspoon black mustard seeds
½ teaspoon cumin seeds
¼ teaspoon asafoetida powder
¼ teaspoon ground turmeric
1 teaspoon coriander seeds, toasted and roughly crushed
3–4 green chillies, seeded and finely sliced crosswise
5–6 curry leaves (or few tablespoons chopped fresh coriander)
½ teaspoon salt, or to taste
1 teaspoon muscovado or dark brown sugar (optional)
2 tablespoons desiccated coconut
juice of 1 lime
cayenne pepper to taste

Drop potatoes in boiling water and cook until just tender but not soft when a sharp knife is pushed in. Drain well.

Cook mustard seeds in medium-hot oil. When they finish popping, stir in cumin and asafoetida for a few seconds and then remaining spices, salt and sugar. Stir well and add potatoes and coconut. When potatoes start to brown, squeeze on lime and cook until juice is absorbed and potatoes are crisp. Sprinkle with cayenne.

BOMBAY HASH BROWNS

Serves 4–6 as a side dish or snack

A Maharashtrian speciality. Its slightly candied nutty quality marries well with roast duck and green coriander chutney.

If using fresh coconut, add at end of cooking with coriander. This preserves the flavour more and adds a light soft texture to the dish.

750 g (1¼ lb) potatoes
2 tablespoons light sesame or peanut oil
1 teaspoon cumin seeds
2.5 cm (1 inch) piece fresh root ginger, shredded
1 teaspoon muscovado or dark brown sugar
2–4 green chillies, finely sliced crosswise
40 g (1½ oz) grated fresh or creamed coconut
4 tablespoons dry roasted peanuts, coarsely crushed
juice and grated zest of 1 lime
sea salt, to taste
handful of fresh coriander, chopped

Peel potatoes and grate coarsely (or leave skins on if they are unblemished and thin-skinned). Put them in a thin tea towel and squeeze out as much liquid as possible.

Cook cumin seeds in medium-hot oil until lightly coloured. Add potatoes and ginger and when they start to brown, stir in remaining ingredients except fresh coriander. Keep stirring and tossing potatoes until they are well browned and crisp. Serve garnished with coriander.

PARSI CARAMELIZED RICE

Serves 6 as a side dish

When the first Parsis arrived on the Gujarati coast in the eighth century, fleeing persecution in Persia, the local prince was worried they would disturb his small community. The Parsi leader asked for a glass, filled it to the brim with milk, and added a pinch of sugar. 'Even though you occupy this place fully,' he said, 'we can merge with you like sugar, causing no spillage, but, on the contrary, sweetening the mixture.' An appropriate fable for Gujaratis and Parsis who are both fond of adding a pinch of sugar to their food – just as Italians do with tomato sauce – to enhance the flavour. Traditional with a Parsi stew called *dhansak*, this rice is good with any spicy dishes, like the Rajasthani Grilled Lamb Fillet with Fiery Chilli Sauce (page 143).

350 g (12 oz) basmati rice
40 g (1½ oz) ghee or butter or 3 tablespoons light sesame oil
2.5 cm (1 inch) piece cinnamon stick, roughly crushed
1½ teaspoons cumin seeds
5 cloves
3 tablespoons sugar
1½ teaspoons salt
2 Indian bay leaves (or ordinary bay leaves with an extra 1 cm (½ inch) cinnamon)

Rinse rice well under water, then soak 30 minutes in twice its volume cold water. Fry spices in oil over medium heat until they smell aromatic. Stir in sugar and cook until it melts and turns caramel brown. Add drained rice (reserve soaking water) and stir to coat well with caramel.

Pour in reserved soaking water, add salt and bay leaves, bring to a boil, cover tightly and lower heat immediately. Cook 12 minutes, then check to see if steam holes have formed in top of rice. If they have, cover again, turn off heat and leave to steam a further 10 minutes. If they haven't, leave another minute on heat before steaming.

To turn this into a Persian pulao, cook the shredded zest of a Seville orange and a handful of almonds and raisins with the sugar.

SPICED RICE SALAD/POHA

Serves 4–6 as a side dish or light lunch

Bhel-puri, a savoury mixture of fried titbits that could be said to represent Bombay style, used to be served wrapped in newspaper and eaten with the fingers like British fish and chips. One street food still sold in newspapers is *poha*, a flattened rice (it looks as if it has been steam-rolled) popular for pilgrimages. Every afternoon, a huge tray of newsprint-wrapped packages of *poha* (see photograph on page 84) is delivered, appropriately, to the *Times of India*, what the journalists call 'collective poisoning time', while admitting that the mixture – rice equivalent of *bhel-puri*, sweetish and sourish, flecked with mustard seeds and coloured yellow with turmeric – is irresistible. If you can't find *poha*, this recipe works just as well for cooked basmati rice.

225 g (8 oz) flaked rice or poha (available from Asian markets and many supermarkets)

juice of 2 limes

3 tablespoons light sesame oil

2 onions, finely chopped

¼ teaspoon asafoetida powder

¼ teaspoon ground turmeric

2–3 green chillies, finely sliced crosswise

handful of fresh or dried curry leaves (optional)

1 teaspoon black mustard seeds, toasted

handful of fresh coriander, chopped

handful or two of roasted peanuts

¾ teaspoon salt, or to taste

½ teaspoon muscovado or dark brown sugar, or to taste

Rinse rice well under running water, drain and mix with lime juice (you can use any souring ingredient like tamarind, bitter orange, lemon juice). Cover and leave to absorb flavour.

Cook onions in oil over medium heat until golden. Stir in asafoetida and turmeric, then chillies and curry leaves. When onions are starting to brown on edges, separate rice with a fork (it will have formed small clumps) and add with mustard seeds to onions. Stir-fry until rice is lightly coloured and dryish. When cool, add coriander and peanuts and season to taste with salt and sugar.

——————— *Variations* ———————

• To the basic *poha* may be added any or all of the following:

½ teaspoon or more cayenne pepper

2–3 garlic cloves, finely chopped

½ teaspoon each cumin and coriander seeds, toasted and coarsely ground

50 g (2 oz) grated fresh or creamed coconut or 25 g (1 oz) toasted desiccated coconut

1 cm (½ inch) piece fresh root ginger, grated

a few cooked new potatoes or cauliflower, chopped and stir-fried with onions

a handful of cooked fresh peas or ½ cucumber, finely chopped

• Should you feel like offering a present to Krishna on his birthday, the basic *poha* mix (minus onions and lime but with more green chillies and ginger) should be mixed while still hot with equal volume thick yoghurt, allowed to soak and then formed into small plum-shaped balls.

WARM BEETROOT SALAD

Serves 4–6 as a side dish or starter

The Saraswats can make a feast out of vegetables that other communities disdain. This is one of their most beautiful salads – deep magenta beetroots against a pale green sauce. It is even prettier if you can get baby beetroots still with their stalks.

8 small beetroot (about 900 g (2 lb))

550 ml (18 fl oz) yoghurt

2–4 green chillies, ground
½ teaspoon cumin seeds, toasted and ground
handful of fresh coriander (about 25 g (1 oz))
1 teaspoon black mustard seeds, toasted
salt to taste
3 spring onions, finely sliced

Pre-heat oven to 180°C/350°F/Gas 4. Wash beetroot, being sure not to tear skin. Dry them and wrap loosely in foil, then bake until skin splits easily when pressed (about 1–1½ hours). Grind together yoghurt, chillies, cumin, coriander and salt and mix with onions. Halve beetroots lengthwise and serve with dollops of yoghurt and a sprinkling of black mustard seeds.

chUkAndAR

Three Fast and Smoky Chutneys to Make with Two Aubergines

1 Sourish and Fresh

Serves 4 as a condiment or sauce

2 aubergines (about 750 g (1½ lb)), rubbed with oil
2–4 green chillies, seeded
2.5 cm (1 inch) piece fresh root ginger
50 g (2 oz) creamed coconut or big handful of freshly grated
¾ teaspoon salt, or to taste
juice of 1 lime
handful of fresh coriander, finely chopped

Put aubergines under a medium-hot grill, turn frequently until they are soft and black all over. Grind together chillies, ginger, coconut, salt and lime. Peel aubergines and mash flesh with spice paste and coriander.

2 Fruity and Pungent

100 g (4 oz) tamarind paste
50 g (2 oz) creamed coconut or big handful freshly grated
2 green chillies, seeded and chopped
¾ teaspoon salt, or to taste
2 aubergines, grilled as previous recipe
2 tablespoons light sesame or peanut oil
½ teaspoon black mustard seeds
4 dried red chillies, seeded and crumbled
handful of fresh or dried curry leaves (optional)

Cover tamarind in boiling water, soak 30 minutes and sieve. Grind with coconut, green chillies, salt and peeled aubergines. Fry mustard seeds in medium-hot sesame oil until they pop. Stir in red chillies and curry leaves just until they crisp and change colour slightly and pour this tempering into peeled mashed aubergines.

3 Sweet and Nutty

2 tablespoons light sesame or peanut oil
1 tablespoon urad dal or split red lentils
1 tablespoon sesame seeds
¼ teaspoon asafoetida powder
2 dried red chillies, seeded and crumbled
2 green chillies, seeded and chopped
1–2 tablespoons muscovado or dark brown sugar
¾ teaspoon salt, or to taste
2 tablespoons creamy yoghurt
2 aubergines, grilled as first recipe

Stir-fry dal in oil over medium-low heat until toasted, adding sesame seeds at the end so they brown but do not burn. Stir in asafoetida for a few seconds just to release flavour. Grind with chillies, sugar and salt to a coarse paste. Mix with yoghurt and peeled, mashed aubergines.

Bombay Ketchup

Makes 1 large jar or 2–3 average jam jars

Real Bombay ketchup, in the sense of a sauce that is served with everything from chips to *bhel-puri*, is a thick sweet tamarind syrup with lots of cumin. This tangier, more aromatic spiced chutney has tamarind as a tart, fruity base, and is twice enriched with tomatoes – once in the sauce, to give it a burnished chestnut colour, and again in slices at the end, to preserve the fruit's fresh taste and shape (the freshness means that it must be kept in the fridge). I had this first in Bombay with a slice of Tibetan yak cheese. At home, I like it with oatcakes (Scotland's answer to the *roti*) and cold butter, with melted Cheddar cheese on toast, in rare roast beef sandwiches (beef being more easily available than yaks outside India) or rolled up in thin chapattis with creamy yoghurt.

180 g (6 oz) tamarind paste
900 g (2 lb) firm, tart tomatoes e.g.
Italian plum tomatoes
3 tablespoons light sesame oil
2 teaspoons black mustard seeds
½ teaspoon asafoetida powder or 4 garlic
cloves, crushed
crushed seeds from 6 cardamom pods
1 cm (½ inch) piece cinnamon stick,
roughly crushed
3 cloves
1–1½ teaspoons cayenne pepper
½–¾ teaspoon salt
100 g (4 oz) jaggery, muscovado or dark
brown sugar

Pour just enough boiling water onto tamarind to cover and leave to soak 30 minutes. Sieve and discard seeds. Drop one-third of the tomatoes into boiling water until skins split. Drain and peel. Quarter all tomatoes and discard cores and seeds.

Over medium heat pop mustard seeds in oil (keep lid handy to avoid a kitchen full of seeds). Off heat, stir in asafoetida, then spices, salt and sugar. Put back over medium-high heat and when sugar has melted, add tamarind and peeled tomatoes. Simmer for about 10 minutes until thick, stir in remaining tomatoes and remove from heat after 5 minutes. Use immediately or bottle in warm, dry jam jars with a piece of plastic kitchen film between metal lid and sauce.

———————— *Variation* ————————

• If you cannot get good sharp tomatoes, substitute 2×400 g (14 oz) cans Italian plum tomatoes

instead and simmer them 30 minutes until thick, then continue as for the fresh tomato recipe, popping mustard seeds etc. The result will be more like a real tomato ketchup and will last considerably longer than the fresh version (which lasts about a week in the fridge).

HOT AND SOUR CHUTNEY

Serves 4–6 as a condiment

The twin sauce that comes with Bombay ketchup on *bhel-puri*. For a change try it instead over fried potatoes, or stirred into plain boiled rice or vegetables.

½ teaspoon coriander seeds
¼ teaspoon cumin seeds
¼ teaspoon asafoetida powder
25 g (1 oz) fresh coriander, chopped
25 g (1 oz) fresh mint leaves, chopped
3–4 green chillies, seeded and chopped
½ teaspoon cayenne pepper
1 teaspoon mango powder (amchur)
(optional)
½ teaspoon salt, or to taste
juice of 1 lime

Toast seeds in a dry frying pan over medium heat until you can smell them, stir asafoetida into hot pan for a few seconds, then grind with remaining ingredients, adding lime juice at end. If you are not using mango powder, you may want to add some more lime juice – this should have a quite sour tang.

———————— *Variation* ————————

• For a fresher, greener-tasting sauce, excellent with salmon or grilled lamb, omit cumin and asafoetida from previous recipe, double the mint and grind with 1 green tomato, 2.5 cm (1 inch) piece fresh root ginger and ½ teaspoon of lightly toasted dill or fennel seeds.

CLIMBING BEANS
DALICHO OF INDIAS

CLUSTER BEANS
BIG BEANS VARIETY

ASPARGUS BEANS

COW BRAND
PRICE RE 0.0.6

G U J A R A T

Bhuj

Mandvi

Ahmedabad

Lothial

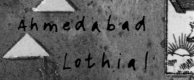

BHARAT
PRICE RE 0.0.6

PRICE Re 0.0.6

Palitana

KISAN PRICE Re 0.0.6 कीसान

GULF OF
CAMBAY

PUMPKIN
GIANT

CHAPTER FIVE

CLIMBING
THE
SPICE
MOUNTAIN

•

The heathen of Gujarat held they must never kill anyone,
nor must they have armed men in their company. If they were captured
and their captors wanted to kill them all, they did not resist.
This is the Gujarat law.

TOMES PIRES, EARLY SIXTEENTH CENTURY

High above the small town of Palitana, a walled complex of white marble temples obscures the twin summits of Mount Shatrunjaya like a cumulous cloud. On a clear day from the highest of the temples you can see as far as the Gulf of Cambay. With a little imagination, you can see even farther. One of the oldest spice routes by sea ran through Cambay, from Petra, around the Persian Gulf to ancient Barygaza (modern Broach) on the coast of Gujarat. To the west is Mandvi, on the caravan route by land to the Mediterranean. To the north is Lothal whose ancient dockyard, archaeologists believe, built ships that sailed to Mesopotamia and to Egypt.

A landscape defined by trade, then; a map whose boundaries are limited by the profit margin. A place where I might make sense of something I had been told by a young Jain businessman on the plane to Bombay: 'Although Jains constitute only 5 per cent of India's 900 million population, we pay 25 per cent of the income tax.'

'Where did all the money come from?'

'In the past, I suppose, from trading spices, jewels and cotton as far away as Zanzibar. Gujaratis have always been the merchants of India, and its bravest sailors.' To their pacifist traditions may be attributed the Indian Ocean's history of peaceful trade. It seems more than

coincidence that Gandhi was born and lived in this region. Although not a follower of Jainism, he possessed that religion's twin preoccupations with non-violence and renunciation.

Mount Shatrunjaya is the supreme Jain shrine to renunciation. At least once in a lifetime, members of the 'White-clad' sect must climb it. Yet the ideas supporting Shatrunjaya's temples like pillars are the antithesis of everything represented by spices and the spice trade.

'Unlike Buddha, who believed in following the Middle Path,' I was told by the scholar and film-maker Dr Push Pesh Panth, who is a high-caste Hindu, 'Mahavira, the Great Hero, most enlightened of all the Enlightened Ones whose teachings Jains follow, was an extremist. If you are true to his teachings, you deny yourself not only meat, wine and spices, you deny yourself taste.'

The classical Hindu treatises have three classifications of food, corresponding to the human temperament: *satvik, rajasik* and *tamsik*. These translate as respectively, noble/pure (milk,

Henna hand patterns seen on the way to the Jain temple of Shatrunjaya. The controlling hand of Jainism is evident everywhere in Gujarat, even on this remote mountain-top high above the Gulf of Cambay, on the old spice route to Egypt.

yoghurt, clarified butter, leafy greens and lighter vegetables, rice, wheat, sprouts and pulses – these are considered to be calming foods for scholars, celibates and priestly types); passionate/energetic (the food of heroes and kings, or those with passionate temperaments, food that arouses desire and charges the metabolism in winter: wine, some spices, urad dal – and any foods that are bitter, sour, hot, salty, pungent, like pickles and chutneys); and demonic/ignorant (foods that keep individuals shackled to the baser instincts: onions, garlic, potatoes, meat and aubergines).

Jainism, like Buddhism, began as a reaction against brahmin Hindus' wealth, elitism and animal sacrifice (at about the same period, the sixth century BC). While accepting some of the Hindu food classifications, it carried them much further. 'More than any religion in the civilized world,' a Jain religious leader said, 'we have always been concerned with conservation of the environment – and not just for man's sake. One could as easily say we are concerned for the air's sake. We believe that everything possesses life.' Jains will eat no green vegetables during the four monsoon months (considering greens to be rich in bacterial life at this time) and the more orthodox exclude spices and chillies as well. For five days in those months they will not even have salt or ghee. And all roots (with their potential to grow), such as garlic, onions, carrots, ginger, are completely excluded from their diet. Once dried, however, ginger is acceptable – one of many contradictions, not least that out of such austerity, Jain cooks have created a fascinating and sensually pleasing cuisine.

Shrenik Lalbhai, trustee of the sect that manages Shatrunjaya, believes it was the Jains' austere life and charitable works that lead to their prosperity. His ancestors were jewellers to the Mogul emperor Akbar, but he is now in textiles 'among other things'. He is sixty-seven, with the pallor and myopic eyes of someone who has never worked outdoors. He lives in a palatial house in a suburb of Ahmedabad, a place the seventeenth-century mogul emperor Jehangir called 'The City of Dust'. It hasn't changed much, although dust, heat and the pollution of Ahmedabad's modern industries have been excluded from Shrenik's home.

Shrenik himself ate garlic and ginger in his youth but he gradually gave them up as he learned more about his religion. Now he eats no prohibited foods and frequently practises 36-hour fasts in which he takes nothing but purified water. 'I have learned that to give up things is more enjoyable than to depend on them every day,' he said. Then he showed me his extensive collection of miniature paintings. His renunciation of food balanced his acquisition of art.

Jyotinder Jain, director of India's Craft Museum, had a more prosaic explanation for Jain financial success. 'They became merchants originally because their religion banned them practising crafts and agriculture (trades involving the taking of life) and they prospered, I believe, because of the extreme self-discipline inherent in our religion.'

'But surely the spice trade is the reverse of renunciation?' I said.

'Their link with spices may have come about because much of Gujarat is coastline, so they were in constant contact with ships on the great spice sea routes. Kutch, the Gujarati side of the great Thar Desert, was in the past populated almost entirely by Jains, and from Bhuj, Kutch's last trading post on the caravan route to Jaisalmer in Rajasthan, spices and grain were distributed throughout the whole of the Thar.'

Jains became experts at sun-drying fruit and vegetables for the four days each month when eating fresh produce was discouraged. 'Our households anywhere in India can be identified by their use of dried ingredients,' Jyotinder said. 'If you think of it, spices are just dried roots and seeds, so this old art of drying may be another link.'

Perhaps involvement in the spice trade was the ultimate act of self-sacrifice. Perhaps they simply liked the feeling that while they made millions, they were capable of denying themselves indulgence in the product. They deny themselves aubergines as well.

'Because in an aubergine you destroy all those seeds in one dish.' said Shrenik.

'But you eat cumin and coriander – they are seeds too?' I said. He dismissed with a smile my naive attempt at logic.

Shrenik's breakfast on non-fasting days was an example of how strict parameters can assist rather than suppress creativity. There was tea scented with cardamom, little pillows of deep-fried *puri* filled with chutney, two kinds of a deliciously papery crispbread reminiscent of the Sardinian bread *carta da musica*, spread with ghee and sprinkled with dry spiced masalas. The food of travelling merchants and pilgrims: light enough to carry to Canterbury and back – or to Shatrunjaya, which Shrenik climbs at least twice a year.

'What do you remember of Shatrunjaya from your boyhood visits?' I asked him.

'Fun,' he said. 'A great outing.'

Sixty years ago his extended family of thirty or forty used to go by train to Shatrunjaya; they have been making the pilgrimage since the days when Akbar had given them a pass that read 'Treat this family as my family.' To achieve enlightenment, I felt, even culinary enlightenment, I would have to follow in their footsteps.

My producer, Matt, and I arrived at dusk in Palitana, at the foot of Shatrunjaya. In the narrow streets, cars gave way to horse-drawn carts and the lights were coming on one by one to reveal a Lilliputian vision of India. It was as if someone had slid the front off a doll's house. There were no supermarkets or general stores as one finds in the West: the buildings were divided into 5-foot-wide cubicles and each cubicle was a separate shop, its function, the bones of commerce, laid bare. There was a barber. There was a man with a sewing machine. Then a man selling flour. Another selling ghee. Yet another selling spices. And at the end of this row of individual pursuits there was a woman making spiced breads of flour and ghee and spices.

Ghee, the gold of Gujarat, approved even by the austere 'white-clad' Jain sect (left)

107

Any building in Palitana that was not a shop was a pilgrims' guesthouse. Medieval Canterbury must have looked something like this, but without the neon; one guesthouse was as strung with neon lights and flashing Catherine wheels as a Las Vegas casino. To eat, we had to leave our guesthouse: Jains do not eat or cook after sunset (the street traders were not Jains). Later, our hosts at the Oswald Guesthouse gave us some of the special millet flour crispbread for which Palitana is famous and I lay under my mosquito net admiring the extraordinary selection of insects that flourish in every Jain sanctuary. Next door, Matt accidentally trod on a cockroach the size of a spaniel puppy.

'How do you feel?'

'Disloyal,' he said.

Shatrunjaya is a moral as well as a physical mountain. With each step uphill pilgrims are supposed to shed worldly attachments. No cooked food should be taken on the mountain and even water is forbidden within the complex at the top.

'Climb as a true pilgrim would,' Jyotinder Jain told me. 'He makes no distinction between temples built in the seventh century and those built yesterday; for him they are all timeless. Mahavira himself is said to have come to this hill a few million years ago, and true pilgrims believe that the essence of him is still there. Thus they relive their own mythology every time they climb.'

'Start before the sun comes up, take a hat, a walking stick and a handful of sweets,' said a less orthodox Jain friend. 'It is a long hot two hours to the top.'

We left at five. But before we had a chance to consider the effort of climbing over two miles of steps, we were met by the saviours of all old, infirm and weak-willed pilgrims: the *dolleywallas*. These were four small men carrying heavy bamboo poles from which dangled two primitive hammocks – and us, after negotiating the price. I folded myself in like a deckchair, my legs about five inches too long for either dignity or comfort.

At six, the sky turned the colour of pomegranates and in the distance a range of glacial temples became visible on the horizon. We passed several sets of carved stone footprints, said to indicate the locations where a monk or Enlightened One had attained nirvana. Some of them did this by fasting to death, a process which Jyotinder Jain had photographed in 1973.

'Within every Jain,' he said, 'from the crudest street trader to the wealthiest spice merchant, is always lurking this inbuilt potential. He may begin by renouncing ginger and garlic and end by renouncing life itself.'

'It's a long way from selling spices.'

'Yet I know examples of wealthy spice merchants who in one moment gave up their whole empire and fasted unto death.'

We entered the temple complex through a gate hung with creeping vines. It looked overdressed in Hollywood mystery, like the gate to Steven Spielberg's Temple of Doom. Inside, a white marble jungle of pillars and shrines stretched across the hills and hung over the edges of precipitous ravines. A thousand-year-old banyan tree grew out of an inner courtyard and enclosed one of the older shrines in an intimate embrace, and around the tree marched a family of pilgrims, chanting. They left rice, almonds and fruit for the deity (to be eaten later by the temple guardians). Green parrots flew out of Victorian ruby glass candelabras. The mirrored eyes of deities shone in the twilight of gloomy shrines. Stalactites of bats with lizard tails hung from temple ceilings like living chandeliers. A man in an orange loincloth lit a cigarette and tried to sell me some old coins. It was not very Scottish.

Some say there are 200 temples on Shatrunjaya, some say a thousand. There were a lot. It had taken an aeroplane, a train, an old car, a horse-drawn cart, a man-powered hammock and my own feet to get here, but I did not achieve Nirvana, or even enlightenment. Between the two temple complexes was a gulley and in the gulley was a man selling terracotta saucers of creamy buffalo milk yoghurt sprinkled with toasted cumin seeds. Even here, spices were inescapable. He saw that I liked his yoghurt and offered me chapattis and green chillies. Clearly, he was not a Jain. The *dolleywallas*, as non-Jains, were also enjoying chapattis and yoghurt. When they had finished, we set off at great speed down the mountain. Descent is always faster.

'If you had waited to eat until you got to the bottom,' Shrenik told me later, 'you would have been given free food and masala tea, as all true pilgrims are.' But at the bottom we had been kidnapped by a group of Jains and taken to the Las Vegas-style guesthouse. We were shown into a banqueting hall the size of an aircraft hanger where thousands of pilgrims are fed every day. We met two Enlightened Teachers and were blessed. We met four fat semi-naked businessmen on fasts. We were fed bowl after bowl of bland variations on the lentil: lumpy, smooth, gritty, lumpy. Too late, I spotted a dish of spices on the table. 'For those who cannot do without them', said the guide, reprovingly. 'One hundred days a year our monks eat *dal* that is not spiced or salted at all.'

Four hundred years ago, Shrenik's family had migrated to Gujarat from their home near Jodhpur on the edge of the Thar Desert in Rajasthan. 'There is a story, its origins obscure,' said his daughter-in-law, 'that we were once meat-eating Hindu Rajputs [warriors]. Then, seeing the killing of a deer on a hunt, we converted to Jainism.'

To time travel in India, all you need now is a train ticket. The train's internal noises banish external reality; and in the desert it passes through places where roads infrequently used are rapidly obliterated by sand.

LEFT: *Ways of achieving enlightenment on the climb to Mount Shatrunjaya; being carried up by the dolley wallas is less tiring but not so spiritually rewarding.*

Vegetarian cooking in India makes up for lack of meat by using a variety of textures, temperatures and colours. Fresh vegetables go into *raitas* (cool salads with yoghurt) and *pachadis*, the piquant appetizers of Indian meals, characterized in Gujarat by a sweet and sour taste, and the presence of peanut or sesame seeds, both widely grown in this region. But cooking without onions, garlic, potatoes and carrots is unimaginable to Western cooks; even Hindu brahmins, who eschew garlic and onions, add masses of fresh ginger to compensate, a solution denied to Jains. Still, there is always a way round the rules in India, I was told by the writer, Bill Aitkin. When he was in a Hindu ashram in the hill provinces, the brahmins found a high altitude shallot called *jambu*, dried it and used it instead of onions in their final tempering. The Jain solution is musky asafoetida, an alchemical ingredient which rescues their dishes from potential blandness.

ASAFOETIDA *heeng/hing, hingra*
BOT: *Ferula asafoetida, Asafoetida narthex*
•

Made of sap extracted from the living stems of a giant, evil-smelling fennel native to Iran, Afghanistan and northern India, asafoetida may be our last link with the antique tastes of Rome: the Romans' prized silphium (already extinct in Pliny's time) was also the product of a giant wild fennel. Don't be deterred by asafoetida's raw smell of mouldy onions; adding half a teaspoon of the powdered spice to some butter before you cook a sauce is the rough equivalent of stirring in a chopped onion, two garlic cloves and a handful of dried morels – the travelling merchant's ideal spice. The pure brown resin, if you can find it, is even more potent than the powder (which is usually adulterated with turmeric, hence its common English translation 'yellow powder'). In recipes in this book, half a teaspoon of asafoetida powder is equivalent to a pea-sized pellet of resin.

Bill Aitkin mentioned another use, 'A non-ecstatic one…. When there is a blocked pipe, instead of calling the plumber, the monks add a little *hing* to clear it.' Because of its oniony, truffly aroma and its reputation as a digestive to combat flatulence, asafoetida is always put in the pot with dried beans and lentils, just as French cooks would put in an onion stuck with cloves, and it gives the beans the same earthy base.

CAROM/AJOWAN SEEDS: *carom, ajwain*
BOT: *Carum ajowan (Carum copticum, Ptychotis ajowan)*
•

Spices prescribed by Ayurvedic doctors against wind (*vaya*) and flatulence (*badi*) are carom, black cardamom, pepper, fenugreek and both dried and fresh ginger. Do not disdain their prescription – Indians have more experience with windy foods than any other people on the planet. Sometimes it is almost impossible to distinguish whether ingredients are added for flavour or for digestive purposes; certainly, the wind-combatting spices are more popular amongst vegetarians (who eat a higher proportion of pulses) than among carnivores.

Carom, a seed high in thymol (found in thyme), is popular in Jain pulse dishes, and recommended with dried ginger in the making of anti-allergenic curries (for people suffering from food allergies); a spoonful with some rock salt is a common household cure for indigestion. Interestingly, a Provençal home remedy for stomach ache is a tisane of thyme. In cooking, I find carom lacks the subtlety of fresh thyme – in all these recipes I have substituted fresh thyme leaves for carom.

CITRIC ACID/LEMON CRYSTALS:
nimboo ka sat

This colourless crystalline souring agent (available from Asian stores) is popular in Gujarati dishes where lemon juice would destroy texture or crispness, or where, as a Gujarati friend said 'You can't afford or can't be bothered squeezing that many lemons.' It is very sour: half a teaspoon is the equivalent of about four fresh lemons.

MASALA SEEDS
To make 3 recipes in this chapter or sprinkle over 8 dishes

A hotter, more aromatic version of a dry chutney served at Palitana guesthouses. Their version was 65 g (2½ oz) dry roasted peanuts roughly crushed with 2 tablespoons of dark brown sugar, ½ teaspoon of salt and ¼ teaspoon of citric acid, sprinkled on buttered chapattis. Try this on buttered Sesame Masala Crispbreads (page 113) or melba toast, or sprinkled over a salad of sliced tomatoes and fresh coriander.

1 teaspoon sesame or peanut oil
50 g (2 oz) melon and pumpkin seeds or sunflower and sesame seeds
2 dried red chillies, crumbled
¼ teaspoon cumin seeds
½ teaspoon coriander seeds
¼ teaspoon fenugreek, lightly toasted and coarsely ground
leaves from several sprigs fresh thyme
¼ teaspoon black peppercorns, roughly crushed
½ teaspoon salt, or to taste
¼ teaspoon citric acid

Pre-heat oven to 180°C/350°F/Gas 4. Mix all ingredients except citric acid with your fingers and bake for 15 minutes, stirring a few times. Stir in citric acid and store in an air-tight jar.

OVEN-DRIED TOMATOES
Serves 4 as a side dish

Dried food – not just lentils, but leaves, cauliflower, okra, green mango – is a Jain speciality. The food is finely sliced, left several days to sun-dry outside the home, then stored or cooked as fresh. In the Bombay shop of film producer and food writer, Gul Anand, I saw my first Indian sun-dried tomatoes – from Gujarat. Tomatoes lose most of their bulk when dried (so use this recipe only when you have a glut), but the flavour of even bland fruit is intensified. The citric acid and sugar give a sweetness and tartness the tomatoes may never have had. These are not like the wizened dried tomatoes of Italy, but something to be stored in oil and eaten quickly.

900–1.5 kg (2–3 lb) tomatoes (plum for preference)
vegetable oil
1 teaspoon sea salt
¾ teaspoon citric acid
1 teaspoon muscovado or dark brown sugar
½ teaspoon fennel seeds

Pre-heat oven to 160°C/325°F/Gas 3. Halve tomatoes lengthwise, scoop out seeds and discard. Very lightly oil a heavy baking tray and a wire rack big enough to hold all tomatoes. Lay tomatoes on rack, cut sides up, with tray underneath. Sprinkle them slightly with salt, citric acid, sugar and fennel. Leave in oven for 1 hour – they will have shrunk to prune size – and turn over to drain off juices. They can be eaten now but if you switch off oven and leave them overnight they will be chewier and more intensely flavoured.

BUTTERY DRIED TOMATOES AND YOGHURT CHEESE SALAD

Serves 4 as a side salad or starter

15–25 g (½–1 oz) ghee or butter or
1–2 tablespoons sesame oil
½ teaspoon black mustard seeds
1–2 green chillies, finely sliced crosswise
handful of roasted peanuts, roughly crushed
½ teaspoon asafoetida powder
1 teaspoon muscovado or dark brown sugar
1 quantity Oven-dried Tomatoes (page 111)
1 quantity Drained Yoghurt Cheese
(page 123)

Over medium-high heat, melt ghee and cook mustard seeds until they finish popping. Add chillies and peanuts, remove from heat and stir in asafoetida and sugar, swirling around in hot oil until asafoetida loses its raw smell. Pour immediately over tomatoes and toss well. Slice yoghurt cheese, if drained for 6–8 hours, or spoon it if creamier, onto 4 plates with a little pile of spicy tomatoes on the side.

FENNEL SEEDS: *sonf/saunf*
BOT: *Foeniculum vulgare*

•

Anise-flavoured fennel seeds, native to the Mediterranean but cultivated in India since Vedic times, are the after-dinner mint of Gujarat – and of southern Italy. They have a long history of being used as a medicine both in Europe and in India and are in fact very good for the digestion. In Tuscany, they stud the sausage known as *finocchiona*; in Gujarat they appear in crêpes (see Honeycomb Popped Millet Crêpes page 122) and many masalas, to which they impart a strong citrus herbal flavour, not as sweet as aniseed, which becomes considerably less pronounced when they are toasted first.

FENNEL, MINT AND SESAME SEED AFTER-DINNER MASALA

This aromatic fennel-based spice mixture, based on one served in a Jain household in Ahmedabad, leaves a fresh taste in your mouth after a rich meal. I have never liked *pa'an* much (the mouthful of whole twigs and leaves makes me feel like a horse), but a pinch of this mixture wrapped in a fresh mint leaf and secured with a clove is better than peppermints.

4 teaspoons fennel seeds
1½ teaspoons desiccated coconut
5 mm (¼ inch) piece cinnamon stick
3–4 cloves
seeds from 3–4 green cardamom pods
1 tablespoon sesame seeds, toasted
1 teaspoon dried mint
muscovado or dark brown sugar, to taste
(optional)

Toast fennel, coconut, cinnamon and cloves together in a dry frying pan until lightly browned and aromatic, adding cardamom towards the end just to warm it through and release its oil slightly. Cool and grind coarsely – no smaller than the sesame seeds. Mix with sesame seeds, mint and sugar to taste and store in an air-tight jar.

MANGO POWDER, *dried green:*
amchoor/amchur
BOT: *Mangifera indica*

•

Sour, unripe mangoes are one of the most important fruits dried for Gujarati pickles, drinks, snacks and curries. And dried mango powder has a long history, understandably, as its light weight made it the perfect alternative to tomatoes, lemons and other souring ingredients during hot caravan journeys. It gives dishes a fruity sweetish sourness, very slightly reminiscent of pine. Add it towards the end of cooking. One or two teaspoons will give a pleasing tang to a dish for four people.

MANGO POWDER CHUTNEY

At Jain guesthouses in Palitana, a dry chutney (the proportions 1 tablespoon mango powder to 1 tablespoon muscovado/dark brown sugar and 1 dried red chilli) was served with sweet and crisp banana pakoras (fritters). To make them, slice firm semi-ripe bananas in 5 cm (2 inch) chunks, split each chunk halfway through lengthwise and stuff with ¼–½ teaspoon of this powder (if you increase quantity, use no more than 6 red chillies). Dip in Spice Batter (page 94) and deep-fry until golden brown.

SALT

Only recently, with the arrival of fashionable rock salt and coarse Sicilian sea salt, have modern cooks in the West begun to think of salt as a spice; Jains have always recognized its ability to enhance flavour – thus its prohibition on certain religious days. Some early Buddhist and Jain manuscripts mention six or more varieties: sea, black, rock, kitchen, red and earth salt. And modern Jains often include black salt (*kala namak*, available here from Asian stores) in their cooking, as it can be eaten in masalas when ordinary salt is prohibited.

Salt could be said to be the spice that launched Indian independence: Gandhi's salt march to the Gulf of Cambay in Gujarat on 6 April 1930 resulted in the repeal of the callous British salt laws in India. After signing the pact, Lord Irwin, Viceroy of India, toasted his rival with a cup of tea; Ghandi, ever attuned to the symbolic gesture, asked instead for a glass of lemon juice – and took it with a pinch of salt, Indian fashion, as he took most British offerings.

SESAME MASALA CRISPBREADS
Makes 8 large or 16 small pieces

These enormous, curled and brittle breads called *kakra* are like pappadums without the grease. Often made in Gujarat by Jain-supported co-ops of women who could not otherwise get any but the most menial work. The most famous version from Palitana is made with millet flour and eaten with cumin-scented yoghurt. This spicier *kakra* is usually served, broken in pieces like a rustic biscuit, spread with ghee and sprinkled with coarse sea salt (salt *in* bread is not an Indian concept). When made without chillies, it is eaten with a dry masala of roasted fenugreek seeds ground with red chillies, or with finely ground toasted coriander seeds, turmeric and salt. Not being a Jain, I like it brushed with olive oil, seasoned with fresh thyme or shavings of raw fennel and a papery slice of Parma ham – or spread with thick tomato sauce, like its Sardinian cousin, *carta da musica*, covered in a blizzard of grated Parmesan cheese and topped with a fried egg. Indians top it with Drained Yoghurt Cheese (page 123) and Bombay Ketchup (page 100).

100 g (4 oz) plain flour, plus a little for dusting
100 g (4 oz) wholemeal flour
¼ teaspoon ground turmeric
½ teaspoon cayenne pepper
2 tablespoons sesame seeds, toasted
½ teaspoon cumin seeds, toasted
¼ teaspoon black peppercorns, toasted and roughly crushed
150–175 ml (5–6 fl oz) lukewarm water

Sift together flours, turmeric and cayenne and stir in sesame and cumin seeds and peppercorns. Add just enough water to make a soft dough and knead for 10 minutes. Rub with a little oil, place in a plastic bag and leave to rest 30 minutes.

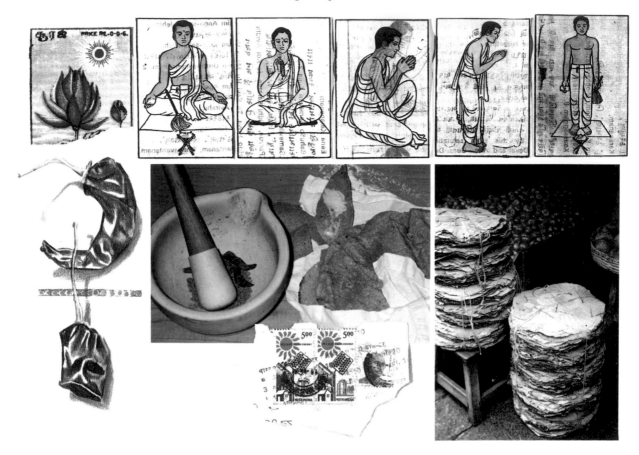

Pre-heat oven to 220°C/425°F/Gas 7 with a heavy metal baking tray. Divide dough into 8 balls and return 7 to bag. Press 1 ball into a flattish pillow, dip both sides lightly in flour and roll out very thinly (no thicker than 3 mm (⅛ inch), thinner if possible). It is a firm and forgiving dough so don't worry too much. Lift dough up and stretch a bit more (rather as pizza-makers do) until small holes appear in surface. Place on hot baking tray and bake until bubbled, curled at edges and light brown in spots (about 4 minutes), turning once. While it cooks, roll out next bread. Cool completely before storing.

ABOVE: Everyone from the greediest to the most austere can enjoy Gujarat's crisp, paper-thin sesame breads called kakra. They may be served on dried leaf plates (right) with a buttermilk curry, or on their own with chutney.

———————— *Variation* ————————

● *Masala tartlets* For little tart shells that crumble as soon as you bite into them (and are none the worse for that), divide dough into 32 balls, roll out very thinly and press into lightly oiled metal tart or fairy cake tins, leaving edges ragged. Bake until brown and crisp as above. Fill with Smoky Dry-Fried Red Peppers (page 117) or with Drained Yoghurt Cheese (page 123) and a teaspoon of Spicy Tomato Chutney (page 52), or Sour Mango Chutney (page 119) just before serving.

CHUTNEY-STUFFED MASALA ROTI

Makes 8 fresh breads

To turn *kakra* into plain rotis (chapattis), simply roll out dough a little thicker and fry over medium heat in a dry frying pan until bread is flecked with brown. I stuff this with Green Coconut and Coriander Chutney (page 92) before frying but you could make it with any other thick chutney.

1 quantity Sesame Masala Crispbread dough (page 113)

5 tablespoons firm chutney

Divide dough into 16 balls, and keep all but 2 balls in plastic bag. Make flattish pillows of the 2 balls, press lightly in flour on both sides and put about 2 teaspoons chutney between the 2 pieces of dough. Pinch edges together to seal and roll out to about 5 mm (¼ inch) thick. Over medium heat in non-stick frying pan lightly brushed with oil, cook bread on both sides until well spotted with brown. Remove and keep warm. While it cooks, continue with remaining dough balls.

———— *Uses* ————

• Make leftover rotis into Gujarati croutons for lentils stews and soups: slice in strips and fry in oil until crisp. Or gently warm through in butter and lemon juice and toss with fresh spinach and toasted sesame seeds.

• Gujaratis can make a curry out of the most unlikely ingredients. Leftover plain cooked rotis (i.e. without the stuffing) are sliced finely in strips like pasta and fried until well browned in butter or sesame oil; yoghurt is stirred in with ground green chillies, a handful of fresh coriander and a teaspoon of masala powder, and simmered until thickened. Sprinkled with Masala Seeds (page 111), it is worth having leftover rotis to make it.

GOURDS, BEANS AND LEAVES

Gujaratis are passionately fond of a wide variety of unusual fleshy gourds, beans and leaves, unfamiliar to any but Asian or East African grocers in the West. Narrow French green beans, pumpkin and savoy cabbage make good substitutes. The following three bean recipes work as well for okra, broccoli (or diagonal slices of broccoli stems), tender pea pods – shred pods lengthwise and add the peas themselves towards the end of cooking – and courgettes (sliced thinly lengthwise).

SWEET AND SOUR LIME AND MUSTARD SEED BEANS

Serves 4 as a side dish

1 tablespoon light sesame or peanut oil

½ teaspoon black mustard seeds

½ teaspoon asafoetida powder

½ teaspoon cayenne pepper

½ teaspoon ground turmeric

½ teaspoon salt, or to taste

2 teaspoons muscovado or dark brown sugar

juice of 1 lime

250 g (9 oz) runner beans, cut in 5 mm (¼ inch) slices crosswise

8 black peppercorns

½ teaspoon cumin seeds

Cook mustard seeds in medium-hot oil until they pop. Remove from heat and stir in asafoetida, cayenne and turmeric, let sizzle 15–20 seconds, return to heat and add everything except peppercorns and cumin. Cover, reduce heat to low and simmer until beans are tender (about 7 minutes, depending on beans). While beans cook, heat a small frying pan to medium-hot and dry roast cumin and peppercorns until they are fragrant and cumin seeds browned. Pound just enough to crack pepper, then sprinkle over cooked beans before serving.

French Beans in Coconut Milk

Serves 4 as a side dish

Mild sweetish beans that go well with hot, highly spiced foods.

scant 15 g (½ oz) ghee or butter, or
2 teaspoons light sesame or peanut oil
½ teaspoon cumin seeds
¼ teaspoon asafoetida powder
1–2 green chillies, finely chopped
250 g (9 oz) fine green beans, topped and tailed
3 tablespoons fresh or canned coconut milk or whole milk
½ teaspoon salt, or to taste

Over medium heat, fry cumin seeds until lightly browned and toasty smelling. Stir in asafoetida for a few seconds, then other ingredients. Cover and cook 5 minutes or until beans are just tender.

Coconut and Peanut Green Beans

Serves 4 as a side dish

A lovely buttery nutty smell from roasting spices, worth making for this alone. In southern India, the same dish is made with 2 cloves of shredded garlic instead of asafoetida.

250 g (9 oz) fine green beans
2 tablespoons peanuts
1 tablespoon desiccated coconut
2–4 dried red chillies, crumbled
¼ teaspoon ground turmeric
½ teaspoon asafoetida powder
3 tablespoons light sesame or vegetable oil
½ teaspoon black mustard seeds
½ teaspoon salt, or to taste

String beans, if necessary, and slice crosswise into 5 mm (¼ inch) pieces. Over medium-high heat in a dry frying pan, roast peanuts, coconut and chillies until lightly coloured, shaking pan occasionally. Stir in turmeric and asafoetida for a few seconds at the end. Cool and grind coarsely.

Cook mustard seeds in hot oil until they pop (keeping a lid handy). Stir in beans, cover, and reduce heat to low. Cook about 7 minutes, until just tender, turn up heat, stir in spices and salt. Stir-fry for a few minutes until beans are tender.

--------- *Variation* ---------

● Add chickpeas or black-eyed peas (popular in Gujarat), either canned or previously cooked, lime or lemon juice and a few shredded mint leaves. Serve with a tablespoon of sesame oil.

Spring Vegetable Peanut Raita

Serves 4–6 as a side dish or salad

A very mild yoghurt salad to serve with hot and spicy dishes.

400 ml (14 fl oz) Greek-style yoghurt
1–2 teaspoons muscovado or dark brown sugar (optional)
salt to taste
1 teaspoon black mustard seeds
1½ teaspoons light sesame oil
350 g (12 oz) baby vegetables (such as green beans cut in 5 mm (¼ inch) pieces, cauliflower or broccoli broken into small florets, mangetout, fresh peas)
big handful of fresh mint, chopped
4 tablespoons dry-roasted peanuts, roughly crushed

Beat together yoghurt, sugar and salt. Over medium-high heat, fry mustard seeds in oil until they finish popping. Pour, still sizzling, into yoghurt. Lightly cook vegetables in boiling water or steam until just tender. Stir into yoghurt and chill. To serve, stir in mint and top with nuts.

SMOKY DRY-FRIED RED PEPPERS

Serves 4–6 as a side dish

A Gujarati method for using chickpea flour to impart protein as well as bulk and earthy flavour to greens, gourds and capsicums. Instead of peppers and mustard seeds, try it with courgettes, finely sliced lengthwise, and the orangey taste of crushed coriander seeds, or with spinach and lemony sorrel (stirred until it wilts in the oil before adding flour).

> *3 large red peppers (about 450 g (1 lb))*
> *1 tablespoon chickpea (besan/gram) flour*
> *½ teaspoon salt, or to taste*
> *1 teaspoon cayenne pepper*
> *½ teaspoon ground turmeric*
> *1 teaspoon black mustard seeds*
> *3 tablespoons light sesame or peanut oil*
> *½ teaspoon asafoetida powder*
> *1 lemon or lime*

Halve peppers lengthwise, remove and discard anything that isn't red, then finely slice crosswise. Sift together flour, salt, cayenne and turmeric. Over medium-high heat, pop mustard seeds in oil. Stir in peppers and asafoetida and when peppers are well coated in oil, sprinkle them with flour mixture. Do not stir. Cover tightly, lower heat and cook 3 minutes. Remove lid, turn up heat and stir-fry peppers until they are slightly blackened in spots. Squeeze over lemon. To serve as a raita, mix with enough yoghurt to cover, and chill for 1 hour.

SWEET AND SOUR SESAME PUMPKIN

Serves 4 as a side dish

For a more substantial dish, a cheater's risotto, perfect partner for roasts, stir this into cooked rice or Fennel-Cooked Millet (page 121) and warm through with thick cream or Greek-style yoghurt. Top with a sprinkling of Masala Seeds (page 111).

> *750 g (1½ lb) pumpkin or American squash*
> *25 g (1 oz) ghee or butter or 2 tablespoons light sesame oil*
> *½ teaspoon fenugreek seeds*
> *¼ teaspoon asafoetida powder*
> *¼ teaspoon ground turmeric*
> *1 teaspoon cayenne pepper*
> *2 teaspoons coriander seeds, toasted and roughly crushed*
> *½ teaspoon salt, or to taste*
> *1 teaspoon mango powder (amchur)*
> *½ teaspoon muscovado or dark brown sugar (optional)*
> *2–3 tablespoons Masala Seeds (page 111) or 2 teaspoons roughly crushed dry-roasted peanuts*

Peel pumpkin, discard seeds and cut in rough 2.5 cm (1 inch) chunks.

Heat ghee in a frying pan, add fenugreek and stir over medium-low heat until it changes colour (watch it doesn't burn). Add remaining spices, then pumpkin, stirring well to coat with spiced fat. Pour over 135 ml (4½ fl oz) of hot water, cover and simmer 5 minutes on medium-high heat.

Remove lid, stir in mango powder and sugar and raise heat to high, tossing and stirring pumpkin until it begins to brown and is tender to a fork. Sprinkle with masala seeds.

——————— *Variation* ———————
• For a summer raita, mix with 3 tablespoons yoghurt, leave 1 hour and sprinkle with seeds.

ABOVE: Spiced Sesame Steamed Leaves.

SESAME PUMPKIN PURÉE

Serves 4 as a side dish

I serve this with roast turkey at Christmas.

750 g (1½ lb) pumpkin or American squash
8 tablespoons sesame seeds, toasted
1½ teaspoons coriander seeds, toasted
¾ teaspoon cumin seeds, toasted
3–4 dried red chillies, toasted and crumbled
salt to taste
1 teaspoon mango powder (amchur)
40 g (1½ oz) ghee or butter, or 3 tablespoons sesame oil
½ teaspoon asafoetida powder

Cut pumpkin in big chunks, remove pulp and seeds and steam pumpkin until tender. Peel and purée flesh. Stir half the sesame seeds into purée and grind all but 2 tablespoons of remaining seeds with coriander, cumin and chillies to a powder. Beat into pumpkin with salt and mango powder. Heat ghee until smoking, remove from heat and stir in asafoetida until its raw smell disappears. Stir into pumpkin, sprinkle with reserved seeds and serve.

SPICED SESAME STEAMED LEAVES

Serves 4 as a light main dish or more as a snack

A fascinating dish like a miniature Swiss roll in green and brick red (see photograph, left). I have made it as well with canned vine leaves instead of cabbage, rinsed well to get rid of vinegar. Serve with a chunky tomato sauce.

50 g (2 oz) tamarind paste
3 tablespoons light sesame oil
90 g (3½ oz) chickpea (besan/gram) flour
¾ teaspoon salt
¼ teaspoon ground turmeric
1 teaspoon coriander seeds, toasted and coarsely ground
¾ teaspoon cumin seeds, toasted
½ teaspoon cayenne pepper
½ teaspoon asafoetida powder
½ teaspoon ground ginger
3 teaspoons sesame seeds, toasted
¼ teaspoon bicarbonate of soda
4–6 leaves savoy cabbage
½ teaspoon black mustard seeds
handful of fresh coriander, chopped

Cover tamarind in 175 ml (6 fl oz) boiling water and soak 30 minutes. Sieve and discard seeds.

Rub 1 tablespoon of oil into flour, then beat to a smooth paste with everything except cabbage, mustard seeds, coriander and remaining oil. Blanch cabbage in boiling water for 1 minute, refresh under cold water and pat dry. Smear each leaf with a thin layer (about 5 mm (¼ inch) of the paste, leaving 1 cm (½ inch) free around edge. Roll up tightly and steam in a covered saucepan over boiling water for 30 minutes.

When ready to serve, cook mustard seeds in medium-hot oil until they pop. Slice cabbage rolls crosswise in 1 cm (½ inch) thick pieces, add to seeds in pan and fry on both sides until browned. Serve sprinkled with fresh coriander.

MANGOES

A beautiful, sad young woman from the tribal area on the mango coast of Gujarat married a merchant seaman and spent more time away from her home than in it. She wrote poems of mangoes when she could not eat them:

The May sky
after today's sunset
the colour of ripe mango

She was often homesick, she said, especially when she missed mango season in Gujarat. 'On the long train journey from Bombay, I know when I am nearly home because as you get close to Gujarat the scent of mango blossom invades your car.' April flowers, June fruit: mangoes are picked all day and night and loaded at 3.30 a.m. onto bullock carts (the big white bullocks that one sees on coins of the Harappan civilization, horns as long and curved as scimitars). 'You must pick them before the rains come. The tribal people say: throat of the iguana, tinting red; rain imminent rain.'

In India, the unripe green mango is a vegetable, the ripe mango a fruit. They call it 'the cherished seed', and it has been cultivated here for over 4000 years. There may be as many as 2000 varieties: some juicy, with fibrous flesh suitable only for pickles, others, like the famous Alphonso, so highly perfumed that they should be eaten simply, with reverence – and perhaps a squeeze of lime. Niccolao Manucci, a Venetian traveller of the seventeenth century, wrote of the mango 'the gentlemen…give them special names, taken from the first person to have good mangoes of that kind. Thus they speak of mangoes of Niculao Afonço, which are the largest and best; Melajassas mangoes and Carreynas mangoes…' He goes on to mention an Afghan ambassador who arranged that on arrival in Isfahan he received a shipment of mangoes from India.

Alphonso

SOUR MANGO CHUTNEY

Serves 4–6 as a condiment

This chutney would be made with green mango, which has a sour, fruity taste similar to green damsons. If green mangoes are unavailable, substitute sweet mango with citric acid or green mango powder (to prevent chutney becoming too liquid). Non-vegetarians could try it as an accompaniment to roast pork.

1 tablespoon light sesame oil
¼ teaspoon asafoetida powder
3–5 dried red chillies, crumbled
350 g (12 oz) green mango, grated or 1 large hard ripe mango, finely sliced and mixed with ¼ teaspoon citric acid or 1 teaspoon mango powder (amchur) or grated zest of ½ lime
¾ teaspoon cumin seeds, toasted and ground
salt to taste
handful of fresh coriander (about 15 g/½ oz), finely chopped

Heat oil, stir in asafoetida and chillies and cook over medium heat until chillies change colour. If using sour green mango, add to the pan and stir-fry for 2 minutes, then mix with remaining ingredients. If using sweet mango, mix all ingredients together over heat until blended, then remove immediately to a bowl so that mango does not cook. Leave to absorb flavours for a couple of hours, then serve chilled or at room temperature. To be eaten same day.

———————— *Variations* ————————

• For a refreshing summer raita, stir this chutney into equal volume cold yoghurt.
• For a spicier, more aromatic chutney, you may fry 3–4 cloves and 5 mm (¼ inch) crumbled cinnamon stick with chillies until they are aromatic and cloves are puffed, then grind to a fine paste and stir into the chutney.

TAKE THREE MANGOES

Serves 4 as a sauce, 2 as soup

Made with an additional 2 teaspoons of sugar, dried instead of fresh ginger and no chillies, this is considered a digestif in Gujarat. Stir in soured cream and chopped fresh coriander for a summery sauce for grilled chicken or fish, or as a chilled soup. For a sunset-coloured salad dressing, sharpen with a few drops of balsamic vinegar and serve over sliced avocado with a few fresh shrimps or prawns – a treat.

3 mangoes (skins and stones reserved)
135 ml (4½ fl oz) Greek-style yoghurt
2.5 cm (1 inch) piece fresh root ginger, grated
1 teaspoon ghee, butter or light sesame oil
1 teaspoon black mustard seeds
¾ teaspoon cumin seeds
2 dried red chillies, crumbled
¼ teaspoon asafoetida powder
6–10 fresh or dried curry leaves or small handful of fresh coriander
salt

Purée mango flesh with yoghurt and ginger. Pour about 550 ml (18 fl oz) boiling water over mango skins and stones and soak 30 minutes. Melt ghee over medium-high heat, and fry mustard seeds until they pop. Add cumin and chillies and when they have coloured slightly, stir in asafoetida for a few seconds. Add strained liquid from mango stones (press down well to extract juice) and remaining ingredients and simmer until thick (about 20 minutes), stirring often.

TAMARIND SWEET AND SOUR DIPPING SAUCE

Serves 6 as a light thin soup or 8–10 as a dipping sauce

A dark and tangy dipping sauce often served with the steamed savoury cake *dhokla*, or, in non-Jain households, with Potato Roti (page 93). If you have any left, boil it down to a syrupy sauce as a marinade for barbecued chicken, or use to brush on plantains before grilling.

175 g (6 oz) tamarind paste
100 g (4 oz) toor dal or split red lentils
2–3 tablespoons light sesame, peanut or vegetable oil
2 teaspoons coriander seeds
½ teaspoon cumin seeds
½ teaspoon fenugreek seeds
½ teaspoon ground turmeric
40 g (1½ oz) muscovado or dark brown sugar
½–¾ teaspoon salt
large handful of fresh coriander, coarsely chopped
SPICE TEMPERING
1 teaspoon black mustard seeds
3–5 dried red chillies, crumbled (and seeded, if you prefer)
½ teaspoon asafoetida powder

Cover tamarind in 175 ml (6 fl oz) boiling water and soak 30 minutes.

Put dal with 750 ml (1¼ pints) cold water in large saucepan, bring to the boil, lower heat and simmer, partly covered, for 30 minutes (20 for red lentils).

While dal cooks, heat 1 tablespoon of oil over medium-low heat and fry coriander, cumin, fenugreek and turmeric until fragrant and fenugreek has changed colour (watch it doesn't burn), then grind to a paste. Purée dal. Sieve tamarind, discard seeds and add liquid to dal purée with 1 litre (1¾ pints) cold water, sugar, salt, spice paste and two-thirds of the coriander. Bring back to the boil and while it heats, prepare the tempering: fry mustard seeds in 1–2 tablespoons of oil over medium-high heat until they pop. Reduce heat, add chillies and cook until they change colour. Stir in asafoetida for a few seconds at the end, pour over soup and garnish with coriander.

The steamed savoury cake called dhokla, seen here on a dried leaf plate (sun-drying is the great Gujarati art) is usually served with a dark and tangy dip – almost a soup – made with tamarind. The same sauce is served by non-Jains with a potato version of dhokla.

FENNEL-COOKED MILLET

Serves 4–6 as a side dish

Millet, used as bird seed in the West, is the rice of India's poor, cultivated in Asia for over 6000 years. High in protein, it flourishes in arid soil and has one of the lowest water requirements of any cereal. It also tastes good, as the Gujaratis, who grind it to flour for breads and cook it whole with sprouted beans in pulaos, are well aware. I like this mixture with cold shredded chicken or duck meat stirred in, and a spoonful of Tamarind Sweet and Sour Sauce (page 120), or a mango sauce (see Take Three Mangoes also page 120) drizzled over. Made with chicken or vegetable stock, it is even better. If you have no asafoetida, fry a small onion and a couple of crushed garlic cloves instead.

40–50 g (1½–2 oz) ghee or butter or 3–4 tablespoons light sesame oil
4 dried red chillies, crumbled
2 teaspoons fennel seeds
225 g (8 oz) millet
½ teaspoon asafoetida powder
about 750 ml (1¼ pt) stock or water
¾ teaspoon salt
2 tablespoons sesame seeds, toasted

Over medium-high heat in a heavy-based saucepan, melt ghee and fry chillies, fennel and millet until millet is toast-coloured. Stir in asafoetida, add stock and salt, bring to boil, then cover tightly and reduce heat to very low. Check millet after 15 minutes. If it is not cooked (it should be tender but not mushy), continue cooking, covered, another 5 minutes. If millet dries during cooking, add a few tablespoons hot water.

When cooked, drain, stir in a knob of butter and sprinkle sesame seeds over. Or serve as a vegetarian main dish with Sweet and Sour Sesame Pumpkin (page 117).

HONEYCOMB POPPED MILLET CRÊPES

Serves 4–6 as lunch or light main course

A Californian technique (popped millet) from Greens Restaurant in San Francisco, in what would otherwise be a classic Gujarati pancake of millet and chickpea flour. The little crêpes – golden with turmeric and freckled with pale green fennel seeds – have a crunchy texture and a subtle flavour of popcorn from the popped millet (see photograph, right). A good alternative to bread, brushed with melted butter or a spoonful of Drained Yoghurt Cheese (page 123) – or roll them up with bright green shreds of spicy cabbage, as suggested below.

90 g (3½ oz) millet
100 g (4 oz) chickpea (besan/gram) flour
¾ teaspoon cayenne pepper
½ teaspoon ground turmeric
½ teaspoon asafoetida powder
½ teaspoon salt
2 tablespoons yoghurt
1½ teaspoons fennel seeds
a little vegetable oil for frying
Spiced Cabbage, to serve (right)

Cover millet with hot water and leave to soak. Sift together flour, cayenne, turmeric, asafoetida and salt. Rub yoghurt in. Slowly beat in 400 ml (14 fl oz) water, whisking well to get rid of lumps, and stir in fennel. Rest for 45 minutes.

When ready to cook, drain millet and stir-fry over medium hat. It will start to crackle and pop like miniature popcorn. When it is browned and toasty smelling, stir into crêpe batter, pressing with a spoon to get rid of lumps.

Warm a non-stick frying pan over medium heat until a drop of water sizzles when sprinkled on it. Brush lightly with oil, pour on a ladleful of batter and swirl it out very thinly – either with the back of ladle or with magnificent wrist action by shaking pan. When crêpe sets on top, turn it and briefly cook reverse side. Keep warm while you cook remaining crêpes. If you are adept, you may be able to do several at once.

To serve, either fill each crêpe with cabbage and roll up with dark side in, or put a pile of crêpes and a bowl of spicy cabbage in the centre of the table and let everyone roll up their own. Eat with your fingers.

——————— *Serving suggestion* ———————

• *Spiced cabbage* Warm 1½ tablespoons of light sesame or peanut oil over medium heat, stir in ½ teaspoon of asafoetida powder for a few seconds, then half a savoy cabbage, finely shredded, tossing well to coat in flavoured oil. Add 3 tablespoons of warm water, cook just until water evaporates and mix with about 3 tablespoons of Masala Seeds (page 111). This method works equally well with bean sprouts instead of cabbage.

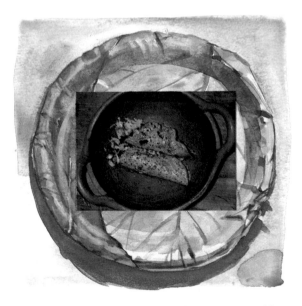

Spicy Honeycomb Popped Millet Crêpes, golden yellow with turmeric, filled with lightly cooked shredded Savoy cabbage and served on a dried leaf plate – a fusion of Gujarati flavours and ingredients with California technique: a good main course vegetarian meal.

MILLET, SPROUT AND PEANUT SALAD

Serves 4 as a main dish, 6 as a side dish

A dish that marries well with freshly boiled peeled shrimp or prawns – save the shrimp water and the shells to give that metallic taste of rock pools to the millet cooking liquid. Or, instead of shrimp, top it with ribbons of red pepper, grilled until their skins blacken, then peeled, Mediterranean fashion.

4 tablespoons light sesame oil
½ teaspoon asafoetida
225 g (8 oz) millet
1 cm (½ inch) piece cinnamon stick
1 teaspoon coriander seeds, roughly crushed
750 ml (1¼ pt) stock or water
salt
6 green cardamom pods
2 sprigs thyme
200 g (7 oz) bean sprouts
juice of 1 lemon
4 tablespoons raw skinned peanuts, roughly crushed
3–5 dried red chillies, crumbled
2 good tart tomatoes, diced, or 8 cherry tomatoes, halved

Warm 2 tablespoons of oil over medium heat, add asafoetida, millet, cinnamon and coriander seeds. Cook, stirring often, until millet smells toasty and starts to brown. Pour in stock, ½ teaspoon of salt, cardamom and thyme, and bring to the boil. Cover tightly (with a tea towel under lid to stop steam escaping) and simmer 15 minutes.

Fluff millet with a fork, stir in bean sprouts and lemon juice, cover again while you prepare tempering: warm remaining oil over medium heat and stir-fry peanuts and chillies until lightly browned. Toss with millet and tomatoes, season to taste with salt and serve it warm or at room temperature.

DRAINED YOGHURT CHEESE

Serves 4–6 as cheese

Yoghurt is the meat of Gujarat and pure clarified butter its gravy. Gujaratis are famous for the quality of their butter (a sign of opulence) and the frothiness of their buttermilk. Most of India's milk and butter comes from a co-op diary near Baroda. Hung yoghurt – drained of whey through muslin for several hours – is a Jain speciality, rich and dairy-tasting, not like the relatively tasteless *paneer* (Indian curd cheese made by curdling milk). I make it with Greek-style strained yoghurt. Put 450 g (1 lb) creamy yoghurt in a thin piece of muslin or cheesecloth and hang it up to drain off liquid. After 3–4 hours, it will be the consistency of soft cream cheese; after 6–8, more like firm cream cheese (wonderful in puddings), and after 12, it can be scooped up with a spoon, rolled into soft balls and kept for a week in spiced oil (try light sesame or olive oil with 4 crumbled dried red chillies, 1 teaspoon of crushed coriander seeds and 6 cloves).

Uses

- For a simple lunch with a green salad or a spicy spinach purée, spread it on toast or Sesame Masala Crispbreads (page 113) and sprinkle with either roasted and roughly crushed black peppercorns coriander seeds and coarse sea salt, or with a spoonful of Masala Seeds (page 111).
- Mix firm cheese (8–12 hours drained) with 3–4 ground green chillies, salt and a handful of finely chopped fresh coriander or mint. Scoop spoonfuls of it onto small plates and serve with peeled baby broad beans warmed in light sesame oil with 1 teaspoon toasted black mustard seeds.
- For a simple dessert, beat soft set yoghurt cheese (3–4 hours) with 2.5 cm (1 inch) grated fresh root ginger, a handful of finely chopped fresh mint and sugar to taste. Scoop onto sliced mangoes tossed in lime juice.

CARDAMOM AND SAFFRON YOGHURT CREAM

Serves 6 as a pudding

This is based on *srikhand*, sweet cream which is a symbol of hospitality in Gujarati homes. Serve it with caramel-brown dried hunza apricots from the Himalayan valleys, whose toffee flavour is best enhanced by simmering the apricots with a few shreds of lemon zest, a little dark brown sugar, a crushed cinnamon stick and just enough water to cover. When liquid is syrupy and fruit is tender but still chewy, fill china teacups with the sweetened cheese, spoon over some apricots and allow their juices to soak into the cream while it chills. Eat with chunks of buttery shortbread.

1.50 litres (2½ pints) Greek-style yoghurt
big pinch of saffron threads
1 tablespoon hot milk
100 g (4 oz) caster sugar
seeds from 8–12 green cardamom pods, crushed
2 tablespoons melon or chironji seeds or flaked almonds, toasted
2 tablespoons shelled pistachio nuts, roughly crushed

Put yoghurt in a thin piece of cloth or muslin and drain for at least 6 hours. Dissolve saffron in milk, then beat into yoghurt with sugar, cardamom and half seeds and nuts. Chill well and serve with a sprinkling of remaining seeds and nuts.

YOGHURT RICE PUDDING

Serves 6

In the tribal areas of Rajasthan and over the Gujarati border, rice is parboiled, then layered in an earthen pot with grated jaggery (raw cane sugar), saffron milk, raisins, cassia leaves, cloves fried in butter, and thick Indian cream. This is topped with fried cashews, sealed and cooked gently until the rice dries into the sweet equivalent of rice biryani. Further south, this alternative is made (see photograph, right). The yoghurt gives the nutty-flavoured rice a delicious tart backnote, and I add lemon zest, not at all traditional. If you do not like the medieval taste saffron gives to sweet puddings, leave it out. This quantity of yoghurt makes a creamy pudding – use one-third less for a firmer result.

225 g (8 oz) basmati rice
big pinch of saffron threads (optional)
handful of broken raw cashews
40 g (1½ oz) butter
75 g (3 oz) muscovado or dark brown sugar
¾ teaspoon ground cinnamon
¼ teaspoon ground cloves
¼ teaspoon ground ginger
handful of raisins
grated zest of ½ lemon
650 ml (22 fl oz) creamy yoghurt

Wash rice well, then soak it in 3 times its volume cold water for 30 minutes. Soak saffron (if using) in a little boiling water. Brown cashews in butter, lift out with a slotted spoon and drain. Add sugar, spices and raisins to butter in pan and cook, stirring often, until sugar has melted. Whisk this with saffron and lemon zest into yoghurt.

Drain rice and bring its soaking water to a boil. Add rice, stir so it doesn't stick and cook for 5 minutes after water returns to the boil. Drain and fold it immediately into yoghurt. Cover and leave to cool, then spoon into little cups (ideally, earthenware saucers) and chill well. Top with fried cashews and serve with cream, plain yoghurt or Orange Cardamom Custard on page 188.

RIGHT: Classic with a twist: Yoghurt Rice Pudding with spices, lemon zest and cashew nuts.

RAJPUTANA

Bhawalpur
Meerut
Delhi
Bikaner
Jaipur
Jodhpur
arabad
Thar or Indian Desert
Jaisalmir
Nagar
Didwana
Sambhar
Ajmer
Jodhpur
Dewair
Udaipura

RAJPUT

SUN
REGISTERED
TRADE MARK
GAPPA GOW

PHASES DE LA LUNE.

Nouvelle Lune
ou Conjonction
Croissant ou
1er octant
Déclinaison
ou 4e octant
la Terre
1er Quartier
Dernier Quartier
2e Octant
3e Octant
Pleine Lune
ou opposition

PAKISTAN

RAJASTHAN   Delhi
Jaisalmer
Jaipur
Jodhpur
Udaipur
GUJARAT

CHAPTER SIX

TRACKS
IN THE
DESERT

•

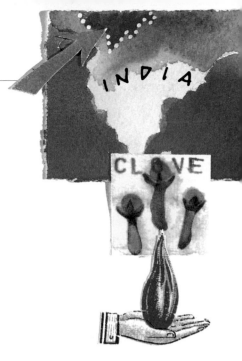

*Desert conditions of loose and shifting sand prevented the construction
of pukka roads. Maintenance is difficult and expensive because the
roads get buried under thick sand and lose their identity.*

MAJOR C.K.M. WALTER, RAJASTHAN
DISTRICT GAZETTEER, JAISALMER, 1877.

The Bombay Mail to Delhi still stops at Marwari Junction, where one of Kipling's characters was set down in the Great Indian Desert, but no man who would be king is waiting on the platform. Between Jodhpur and Jaisalmer, to the west, the landscape is a constant reminder that the word 'desert' is both verb and noun: empty, abandon, give up – to forsake.

When Bombay was opened as a port in the eighteenth century, the wild and hazardous desert spice route linking Gujarat with imperial Delhi and thence with China, lost importance, and one of the desert route's major staging posts – Jaisalmer, the twelfth-century citadel founded by a prince on the advice of a cave-dwelling hermit – was forsaken. Once, Jaisalmer had needed five huge caravanserais to cope with the traffic of camels carrying indigo from the Doab, opium of Kota and Malwar, the famed sugar candy of Bikaner, ivory, dates, coconut, spices, scented wood and dried fruits. With the shift of trade to Bombay, Jaisalmer lost its greatest source of income, from the forced levies by ruling Rajput families on those caravans. India's westernmost settlement of any significance was cut off from the outside world.

It is the nature of sand to slip and drift. The prophetic hermit, Eesul, had foretold that Prince Jaisal's fort would be sacked two and a half times. He failed to predict that its most devastating loss would come not through war or siege but from a displacement, a shifting of emphasis. By the Victorian era, Jaisalmer was the least known princely state in Rajasthan.

The total length of the metalled roads in 1909 was a mere six miles, all within the precincts of Jaisalmer town. The unmetalled roads amounted to 119 miles and served as camel or foot paths. Even these got buried under sand, sometimes leaving no trace at all. . . . Ibid

'If our poets had sung the Rajput forts', wrote the English principal of Madras School of Art in the 1890s, 'if our heroes had lived in them and our painters pictured them, their romantic beauty would be on every man's lips in Europe.' Instead, the tales of Jaisalmer and its sieges were left to the troubadours of Rajasthan, the hereditary balladeers who come from the region around its old rival, Jodhpur, and sing there still. It is as if the family of the Sheriff of Nottingham were alive to perform odes to Robin Hood. I went one evening to have dinner with a troupe of these musicians on their patron's rooftop. The men had the bold, fierce profiles of predatory birds and the arrogance of pop stars.

'What does the desert sound like?' I asked. They smiled and gave me *lal maas*, a dish that distils red chillies and garlic barely tainted by lamb into the essence of a desert's flavour and colour. After eating it, every internal space is seared and barren, devoid of life. Their patron, Himmat, said that the cooks had halved the number of chillies to make the dish less fiery for me. In a stew for eight they had used only sixty or seventy dried red chillies and a cupful of whole black peppercorns and cinnamon. With it, there was ground chilli and garlic chutney for those who found such a *lal maas* unpalatably mild. Himmat's eyes watered and his nose turned pink but he was a maharaja's grandson and did not admit pain easily.

Then the troupe played their strange vegetal flutes and wooden chapsticks and gourd-shaped drums. The fiddle howled and whistled like a wind full of sand and the lead singer cried out a hawk's scream in his raw, discordant voice. Behind them a full moon rose over a giant satellite dish. Television reception is bad in the desert.

The singer's ancestors had played at feasts for the Rajput rulers of Jodhpur. Now the singer and his troupe played for tourists at Jaipur's Rambaugh Palace Hotel. But at least their patron, Himmat, was a Rajput, a member of the old warrior caste, the sword arm of Hinduism. He was descended from men so heroic that the Moguls, rather than continuing to wage an endless series of battles and skirmishes against them, finally made peace and married into Rajput royalty – an alliance that was to be one of the most important foundations of Mogul power.

Jaisalmer's Rajputs had once been known as the 'desert wolves'. Himmat worked in the tourist industry organizing desert festivals called 'Romance of the Dunes'.

'Autumn full moon in the desert is so beautiful,' he told us, 'they say that heavenly honey showers from the sky. People make a special sweet *khir* in a silver pot and leave it out all night to let the moon's silver rays fall into it.'

He had the languid good manners and habit of command of a young prince. 'I am just a poor commoner,' he said. 'Merchants are the modern rulers of India.' Then he raised an eyebrow and the musicians instantly began again – a bantering, teasing tune this time, dating from the era when Himmat's family did not have to share their musicians with hotels.

Jaisalmer . Rajasthan

Jodhpur . Rajasthan

He remembered an evening at his father's house when the Maharaja of Jodhpur had come to dinner. The Maharaja was served a feast of the richest dishes and champagne in the best crystal glasses. But for him it was just another meal, one of many. In his palace he liked to throw champagne glasses over his shoulder to smash, Russian fashion, against the wall. 'By that time my family had fallen on harder times,' said Himmat. 'There was not such an excess of crystal champagne glasses.' His father gave instructions that a servant should stand behind the

Maharaja, fielding the glasses like cricket balls as he threw them. 'Then he refilled them with champagne, of course, and set them back on the table.'

Another Rajput noble, Mohan Singh, told a story of this same Maharaja. So expert were the cooks of Mohan Singh's uncle that when the Maharaja had hunted and killed a nice big boar, he used to send it from Jodhpur on a special aeroplane to be prepared at the uncle's palace. 'And the plane would be delayed while my uncle had the boar cooked and then sent it back.'

'About a two-hour flight?'

'About two hours, yes. But they would reheat it in the palace kitchen, naturally.'

Mohan Singh sat on the terrace of the Narain Niwas Palace and barked in a colonel's voice: Boy, bring some soda water with fresh lime. Boy, turn on the fan. Someone – shift the peacocks off the parking lot. Now, would you like to see the scar on my leg from a charging wild boar's tusk? Yes, very deep. No, you must never go pig-sticking on a camel. Camels will kneel and then lie down on the percussive beat of the drums but they are no good for pig-sticking. And elephants are only good for tigers and rabbits.

The biggest boar Mohan ever shot weighed 140 kilos and had a fan of tusks over its face like a deadly ivory muzzle. Its photograph hangs in the parlour with the other family pictures. To cook a boar, he said, remember this: first, you must pour boiling water over it and rub off the bristle to get to the skin. A wild boar's skin is often 5 or 6 inches thick. Very good for pickles, as is the fat. No one eats the liver, which is bitter. You must cook the meat in mustard oil with plenty of onions, garlic, whole garam masala (cinnamon, cloves, nutmeg, mace) and curd. When the oil rises to the surface, you add tomatoes, ginger/garlic paste and hot water – *never* cold water; that makes the meat tough. A hunter's dish. A real man's dish. He learned it from his uncle.

Mohan Singh's uncle was a minor Rajput feudal lord, the first Indian to get a king's commission in the British Army, in 1905. On his retirement he began to collect recipes from princely estates all over India. He had them copied out and bound into sixty enormous leather volumes. Every day he would order a couple of his officers (he was still commander in chief of the Jaipur state army) to choose some recipes from these books, and while he sat on the terrace smoking or writing in his diary, the officers would cook for him.

'That was his hobby. To have them cook his collected recipes – right there, where the parking lot is now.'

He would send one of these dishes to the Maharaja of Jaipur, whose wife said he waited impatiently for it and then pushed all other food away. One evening, Mohan Singh's uncle gave a big party at his palace for all the Indian and British officers. He chose the dishes himself and watched them being cooked. Then, when the party had dispersed, he drank a glass of milk, his usual cure for overeating, and died, a victim of his hobby. Since independence, his palace, like so many grand family homes in India, has been turned into a hotel to pay the bills. 'Democracy is always a mistake,' said Mohan Singh. 'Every country needs a strong master.'

A court cookery book of the 1890s gives some idea of the lifestyle the Rajput nobles

BELOW: A Rajasthani's fiery, potent chutney of chillies with garlic, shallots and salt.

Cumin and Pappadum Crumble (page 138): on the great desert route across Rajasthan, food was sun-dried to make it portable. Here, a musician's wife kneads bread dough.

lost with the accession of their territories to the Indian Union and the subsequent abolition in 1970 of their privy purses. A recipe for the little puffed breads called *puri* begins: 'Take fine wheat flour and lots of ghee, and when the bread puffs up, make an opening and insert a small live bird inside with a piece of ice. Then seal the bread and fry it so that only the upper limit is cooked. When the guest bites into it, the bird will fly out. For the experienced cook only.' Cooks were magicians then.

Yet the food most loved by the Rajputs is the elusive prey of *shikhara*, the hunt. 'You take with you the bare necessities for cooking,' Himmat said. 'You crush onions and garlic and chillies with your fist instead of chopping them. And somehow everything tastes much better.' They used to hunt on camel and horseback. It was the prerogative of a Rajput. Now they use a jeep and hunt rarely because wildlife, unlike royalty, is protected by the government.

Not all Rajasthanis lost ground when the British left. It has been estimated that more than half the assets of the modern Indian economy are controlled by Rajasthan's merchant castes, who prospered originally on the desert trade routes between Central Asia and China. But they are not Rajputs; many of them are Jains. They moved to Bombay and Calcutta when the desert route was made redundant, keeping only their hearts and their houses in Rajasthan. The frescoed walls of the merchants' mansions, or *havelis* (a Persian word meaning 'enclosed place'), record the history of desert trade: the camel supplanted – first by the horse-carriage, then by the train, boat, car and aeroplane. When Deepak Nowlakha, a wealthy Jain restaurateur, took us out for a traditional moonlit monsoon picnic, we went in his jeep. Conditions on the great trade routes determine means of transport.

He told us of the feast given by a Jain family for some English dignitaries sixty years ago. Being strict vegetarians, the Jains had prepared one of their laborious wheat gluten recipes, involving hours of work. We had eaten a similar dish the night before in the home of another Jain merchant. First, a simple flour and water dough was made and kneaded for ten minutes, as one would chapattis. This was rested for seven to eight hours to develop the flour's gluten and then the dough was washed in water until only wheat gluten, pure protein, remained. Pieces were pulled off and deep-fried (expanding to four times their original size); finally they were

boiled in water to soften them so they would absorb the spice-rich sauce while cooking. After frying, the gluten is light and easily portable, ideal for desert traders. When boiled, it is not dissimilar to tender pieces of chicken. Its use predates texturized vegetable protein by centuries.

'It is strange how many meat lookalikes go into our dishes,' Deepak said. 'Almost as if we were once non-vegetarian and changed.'

Wheat gluten forms the 'meat' in one of

133

Rajasthan's few rice dishes, an elaborate biryani that is the speciality of vegetarian Jodhpuri wedding feasts. For this dish the gluten is layered with rice, saffron yoghurt (heavily spiced to indicate the dish's festive nature) and lots of almonds and raisins. It is called *quabuli* – because it originated in rice-loving Kabul, I presumed, but Deepak was not sure. It is such an old dish, no one knows its origins. Its name may simply refer to the dried fruits and nuts which came from Kabul with the caravans.

'On this occasion years ago,' Deepak said, 'the Jains flavoured their food with all these things and the richest spices, but they wanted to prove they were as good as Rajput nobles. And although the gluten was like chicken in texture and taste, there were no bones.' To give the English something to chew on, they fashioned chicken bones out of solid silver.

After he had described the workmanship of these bones, Deepak picked up a cowpat and showed us how to make cow dung fuel. Mix the dung with straw. Pat it into a flat cake with your hands and slap it against the wall to dry – that is why you see all the handprints in it. It's ready to burn when it falls of the wall. In a book called *Cooking Delights of the Maharajas*, one item on its ingredients list is '20 cow dung cakes for fire'. 'A quick dish, then,' said Deepak. The bread we were to eat would need at least a hundred cowpats.

'Why cow dung?' I asked.

'Because it burns with the most intense heat. And there is no wood in the desert.'

The monsoon feast begins with *dal-batti-churma*. *Batti* are round breads of antique lineage and appearance. They emerge from the fire like cannonballs from an ancient battle, rock hard and covered in ashes. To make them edible they must be cleaned, cracked open and soaked in ghee. One eats them with spiced dal and *churma* – the same prehistoric baked bread, pounded to crumbs this time and mixed with sugar, saffron, almonds and pistachios. The spices and nuts are ground on a thick stone sill shaped like a fallen Mogul door.

'Or a tombstone,' my producer, Matt, says.

The craftsman who etched the stone to make it easier for grinding spices etched his name into it as well, but years of daily use have worn the name away, leaving only the faintest impression of an attempt at immortality, like a sand drawing after the sea has washed over it.

'Rajputs lost their kingdoms because the British made us lethargic,' said Mohan Singh. 'They told us – go on hunting; eat, drink and be merry. So we became useless and democracy set in. A slow poisoning. Our maharajas became circus lions and the British ringmasters. If we had realized our power, we would have eaten the ringmaster.'

'No more Rajputs making money by taxing spices on the old camel caravan routes, then?'

'Forget the old routes. Now we have made new routes through the desert. Not for camels – for tourists.'

> **Flavours of Rajasthan**
> •
> **CLOVE SMOKE AND
> CINNAMON FIRE**

*I*t may seem self-evident in a desert country like Rajasthan, but its strongest culinary identity is a lack of water. Food here is flavoured with garlic and dried red chillies, cinnamon, cumin, clove and cassia leaf, but its base notes, what the French would call its *fond*, are smoke and sun: wild desert game is roasted over cow- or camel-dung fires, bread is baked in the fire's ashes, while both rare fruits of the desert thorn and beans are sun-dried for portability and preservation, and other vegetables are cooked in milk or yoghurt rather than water. Grains such as millet, barley and maize are more common than wheat, since they can withstand the arid conditions – they are ground into flour for making pan-cooked breads instead of being used in water-prodigal pulaos, more common in greener Gujarat to the south.

Fresh produce was always rare in this region. A friend's ninety-one-year-old uncle said that until he began building roads across the desert for the British in the thirties, he had rarely seen vegetables for sale in Jodhpur. In experimenting with traditional desert recipes, without access to the plethora of sun-dried fruit and vegetables that are available only in Rajasthan (sometimes not even outside the state) I have looked at the roots of these flavour patterns and let those roots develop new branches in a modern kitchen.

BAY LEAF, *Indian: tejpat*
BOT: *Cinnamomum tamala*
•

Open a bag of European bay leaves and a citrussy, herbal, peppery scent hits your nose, quite unlike Indian bay – which is not surprising, because *tejpat* is actually the leaf of the cassia tree (known in some countries as Chinese cinnamon). It gives off a musky cinnamon scent and flavour, highly reminiscent of the bark of that tree, as do cassia buds and roots. Indian bay is widely available from Asian stores and is well worth a special reconnaissance to search out. A much wider range in size from European bay (some leaves are as big as rhododendron leaves), it is easily distinguished from European bay's regular 'tree-type' veining by its three long central spines (see illustration on page 136). Although Indian cookery books usually recommend substituting European bay for Indian, I think a piece of whole cassia bark gives a result much closer to the original intention.

CASSIA AND CINNAMON: *tejpat and dalchini*
BOT: *Cinnamomum cassia* (Indian cinnamon, bark of cassia tree), *Cinnamomum zelyanicum* (true cinnamon)
•

Thévenot, a French traveller in seventeenth century India, wrote of true cinnamon: 'It is this Isle of Ceylon which produces the best cinnamon; the tree (from which they have that bark) is straight, and pretty like to the Olive-Tree; it bears a white flower of an excellent scent, and the fruit of it is round. They take off the bark in the summer times and when they cut it the smell is so strong that the soldiers (who are to guard it) fall almost sick upon't. Towards Cochin there is wild cinnamon; but because it is weak, it is not much esteemed.' True cinnamon, native to Sri Lanka and Kerala, is a milder, sweeter and more delicate spice than cassia. It was known primarily by the peoples of these regions until discovered (and, in Kerala, subsequently destroyed) by the Dutch. Cassia, originating in Burma and the Eastern Himalayan foothills, has a longer history on the spice routes to the West and is the type preferred in Indian cooking. Pungent and peppery and less expensive than the tightly curled quills of true cinnamon, it is more suitable for savoury dishes than sweet. In fact, cinnamon is rarely if ever used in Indian sweets, although in Mexico and South America it is more popular than vanilla (which supplanted it in Europe). In Mexico, cinnamon's preservative effects are much appreciated in breads and cakes (like cloves, its essential oil contains the antibacterial phenol), and ancient heavily-spiced cakes such as the Tuscan panforte are living fossils of an era when spices were used to preserve as well as to flavour – as they are still in India.

There are references to cassia leaf and bark in early Ayurvedic literature, although they were more common in court dishes than in every day food. 'They were considered heating,' Push Pesh Panth said, 'not the right spices for a hot climate; so people of the South used them rarely.' Court circles and warrior castes like the Rajputs had no such inhibitions. 'They wanted to arouse their passions. They wanted to be lustful. They wanted their metabolisms souped up. The idea was that the garam masala spices like cinnamon, nutmeg and mace made you hot and randy – part aphrodisiac, part a reviver of lost vitality. Rich people, you see, were allowed to experiment with exotica and erotica.' In her book on spices, Elizabeth David noted that one of her favourite London Cypriot restaurants offered powdered cinnamon with their hot egg and lemon soup, avgolemono – a relic, perhaps, of garam masala?

CHICKEN BAKED IN CASSIA

An idea to try should you buy one of the enormous and inexpensive bags of cassia leaves or bark

European bay leaves differ both in size and flavour from Indian bay leaves (actually Cassia).

available in Asian markets: wash a clay chicken brick or unglazed earthenware baking dish and line base and sides with cassia leaves or bark – be generous; the spices can be re-used in savoury soups and stews. Brush chicken well with melted butter or ghee, lay on the nest of spice, cover tightly and bake in a pre-heated oven at 175°C/350°F/Gas 4 until tender, turning often. The steam from the drying clay will rise through the spices and give a subtle aroma to the beast. Finish off under a grill if you wish crisp skin. Eat with plain creamy yoghurt, a squeeze of lemon and Stuffed Carrot Pan Bread with Onion Seeds (page 168).

CLOVES: *lavaung, laung*
BOT: *Eugenia aromatica*

•

While the English name for this dried flower bud comes from the Latin for 'nail', the Indian word has more romantic associations. When the nose of a pubescent girl is pierced, a clove is inserted into the hole, partly for its powerful antiseptic ability to cauterize, partly so that the hole does not grow over. Even after reaching marriageable age and replacing the clove with a diamond, the jewel is still referred to as 'a clove in the nose'. The romantic association continues in Hindu folk music. One popular Hindi film song says that if you want to impress a girl, offer her a betel leaf with both clove and green cardamom in it. As folk music is a history of the poor, the song is an indication that not long ago these two spices must have been a rarity in the countryside – or only consumed by rich people. Push Pesh Panth sang me another version which dates from a time when there was less prudery and more equality in ordinary Indians' lives. It tells of a lady who makes the clove and cardamom *pa'an* for her lover, while her patient husband awaits his turn with her.

In folk medicine, cloves are one of the strong elements because of their antiseptic properties (used to preserve pickles and meat stocks), and their pungent taste and flowery aroma is essential to garam masala, Mogul meat dishes, pulaos and onion-tomato sauces, as well as for perfuming the tempering oil in Rajput dishes. Yet the spice is not considered a sinful, passion-exciting one like cinnamon: even the most puritanical brahmin can use it. Cloves are also used in sweet dishes – in one pastry dish, milk is simmered slowly until reduced to cheese, then wrapped in a triangle of filo and fastened with a clove before deep-frying.

When cooking with cloves, look for large, plump unbroken buds with an oily sheen, and remember that they can be overpoweringly medicinal if used with a heavy hand.

CLOVE TEMPERING
To flavour a dish for 4–6

Like most temperings, the process here is to heat fat almost to smoking in a small shallow pan, reduce heat to medium, add spices and as soon as they begin to change colour and crackle, remove them from heat – they will continue cooking in hot fat – then pour into cooked dish, thus disseminating the exotic flavour of half a teaspoon of expensive spices through a few tablespoons of inexpensive fat.

A very good flavouring for plain cooked lentils or beans to be served with lamb – try it with French haricots.

50 g (2 oz) ghee or butter
12 cloves

Heat ghee as described above, add cloves and when they turn dark brown and puffy, stir immediately into hot cooked pulses or rice.

CUMIN SEEDS, White: *zeera, jira*
BOT: *Cuminum cyminum*
•

Two flavours permeate all of India's dishes, one nutty, warm and pungent, the other fresh and green: toasted cumin seeds and fresh coriander leaves. Coriander is the basil of India and cumin seeds are almost as important on the subcontinent as salt. In the poorest households in Rajasthani desert villages, even the plainest bowl of yoghurt will come with a sprinkling of toasted cumin on it. The seeds should be bought whole, so that their aromatic oil does not escape into the shipper's grinders but into yours, then heated in a dry pan until their powerful scent fills your kitchen. I prefer to use cumin seeds whole or more coarsely ground than they would be in India. The white variety (actually sandy beige) is popular every-

where, while the black 'royal' cumin (*shahi jeera*), as its name implies, is more common in northern Mogul dishes.

CUMIN SEED TEMPERING
To flavour a dish for 4–6

Of this brick-red tempering or *chaunk* a Jain friend said 'It is to dal in Rajasthan what chocolate sauce is to vanilla ice-cream in America.' Rajasthanis use far more fat in their tempering than I do – and infinitely more cayenne – but this quantity gives a spicy, moderately fiery roundness to any plain dal (the usual in Rajasthan is a mixture of split urad, moong and toor dals). Very good in earthy winter root soups such as parsnip, Jerusalem artichoke, or leek and potato.

50–75 g (2–3 oz) ghee or butter (or, forsaking tradition, 4–6 tablespoons sesame, olive, even walnut oil)
½ teaspoon asafoetida powder
½ teaspoon ground cumin
1–2 teaspoons cayenne pepper

Melt ghee over medium-high heat (it is hot enough when a cumin seed dropped in boils up immediately), stir in asafoetida and cumin until they smell aromatic, then add cayenne and immediately remove from heat, stirring quickly to prevent it burning. Swirl into hot cooked dal and serve.

CUMIN AND PAPPADUM CRUMBLE WITH SMOKY ONIONS

An idea more than a recipe (see photograph page 132), offered by a maharaja's grandson under a desert moon. But I have eaten it in the less regal surroundings of my own kitchen with no less pleasure. Bought pappadums will do; they are simply the ballast. Fry or grill them as instructed on packet and crumble in big pieces into a bowl. Toss with 1 teaspoon or so of toasted cumin seeds, a few toasted and crumbled dried red chillies (or green chillies fried crisply) and lots of sea salt. Split 3 small onions lengthwise and grill skin-side up until skin is black. Turn and grill until blackening on flesh side. Peel, discard skin and chop roughly. Just before serving, mix with pappadums. You can add chopped tomatoes (seeded) and fresh coriander as well, but these tend to make the mixture soggy quickly. Chopped sun-dried tomatoes, on the other hand, do not, and toasted melon or pumpkin seeds are a good addition.

SPICE-SMOKING

One method of adding desert flavour is the process known as *dhungar* (smoking), in which a live coal is placed in a tiny iron sieve or an onion-skin cup in the middle of a dish of meat or vegetables. The coal is sprinkled with whole spices such as cloves, cinnamon or cumin and doused with butter so that it smokes. Then the dish is sealed tightly for up to 30 minutes to allow spiced smoke to permeate the food.

This is an excellent method if you happen to have a glowing charcoal handy. I seldom do. My solution is a blend of Rajasthani ingredients and Chinese ingenuity (loosely based on the northern Chinese method for tea-smoked duck) which gives a similar result. The smoked flavour is not the same as barbecueing (in fact, it is often done after preliminary grilling), as it is a combination of steam and smoke.

Do not use your best pan for the following recipes, nor any pan with a non-stick or coated finish – there is a certain amount of wear and tear. A large iron or steel pan or wok is ideal: there must be room for the smoke to circulate and it must have a tight lid. You can do the smoking a day ahead, as the flavour is even better when allowed to mature. Experiment with different ver-

sions of the following recipes. Try putting other vegetables (peeled and chopped first) in with the meat while it smokes – I find the most satisfactory results come from earthy or sweet vegetables such as aubergines, corn, onions and whole peeled garlic cloves, but a Jain friend did this with a snack of crisply fried chickpeas, and recommended a 10-minute smoking for fresh cucumber mixed with toasted cumin seeds for a mellow smoky salad.

SPICE-SMOKED SMALL BIRDS

Serves 4

A wild flavour. You can do this with partridge, wood pigeons, quail or small poussins. Eat the birds with your fingers, and use your fork for eating a mound of Gingery Spinach in Coconut Yoghurt (page 50) or some Red Hot Pan-Smoked Corn (page 142).

juice of 2 lemons
1½ teaspoons cayenne pepper
4 partridges, wood pigeons, poussins (halved through breast bone and back), or 8 quail
75 g (3 oz) sugar
3 tablespoons ground cinnamon or cloves
about 3 tablespoons melted ghee or mustard oil

Mix lemon juice and cayenne. Make 3 diagonal slashes on each side of birds' breasts. Rub peppery juice all over birds and into the cuts. Leave to marinate for at least 1 hour.

Line iron or steel wok or saucepan with foil. Mix sugar and cinnamon and spread evenly in pan. Place metal or steaming rack on top. Brush birds all over with ghee and lay on rack, breast side down. Put pan over high heat until sugar starts smoking, cover tightly, lower heat and cook 10 minutes. Temperature must be hot enough to keep sugar smoking but not so high that it blackens immediately and makes smoke acrid. Turn birds onto their backs, cover and smoke for another 10–15 minutes. The dish can be prepared to this point up to a day ahead.

Pre-heat oven to 240°C/475°F/Gas 9. Brush birds with melted ghee again and roast 3 minutes breasts down and 4 minutes breasts up. Check to make sure meat is cooked nearest the bone and give it another minute if not.

SPICED STUFFING FOR PARTRIDGE, QUAIL OR PIGEON

Fills 4 small birds

To elaborate on the previous dish, stuff birds first. Some cooks add 2 tablespoons of melon seeds or chopped almonds in place of some of the bread, an excellent idea. I often make the stuffing more Mediterranean by adding 6 chopped sun-dried tomatoes in oil, instead of raisins. Fresher tasting with coriander instead of bay, and zest of half a lemon instead of mango powder. Or make the stuffing even smokier by adding a few chopped dried morels (soaked first in boiling water for 30 minutes, then drained).

15 g (½ oz) ghee or butter
2–3 dried red chillies, crumbled
2 Indian bay leaves, crumbled, or ¼ teaspoon ground cinnamon
2 tablespoons raisins or chopped no-soak dried apricots
2–3 slices wholemeal bread, crusts removed, crumbled
1 teaspoon mango powder (amchur) or juice of ½ lemon
salt to taste

Melt ghee over medium heat and fry chillies and bay leaves until chillies turn brown. Stir in raisins and crumbled bread, let brown slightly, remove from heat and grind coarsely with mango powder and salt. Stuff birds and skewer them shut. After smoking and roasting, spoon stuffing out next to birds.

SPICE-SMOKED DUCK BREASTS WITH CARAMELIZED SHALLOTS

Serves 4–6

A Europe-meets-Rajasthan idea to serve with a smooth and fiery chickpea or lentil purée.

4–6 duck breasts
salt
75 g (3 oz) sugar
3 tablespoons ground cinnamon or cloves
25 g (1 oz) ghee or 2 tablespoons mustard oil (or other good oil such as olive, sesame)
8–16 shallots (enough to give each person 6 'cloves') or small onions or garlic
3 dried red chillies, crumbled
1–2 limes or lemons

Make 5–6 diagonal slashes in fatty skin of duck and rub in salt (this encourages excess fat to drain during smoking). Set up wok with sugar and spice as for Spice-Smoked Small Birds (page 139). Bring to smoking point over high heat and lay duck fatty-side up on metal steamer. Cover tightly, lower heat and smoke 15 minutes. Turn duck fatty-side down and smoke 10 minutes more. Dish can be prepared to this point up to a day ahead.

To finish dish, separate shallot cloves, bash them a few times with something heavy (to loosen the skin) and peel. Melt ghee over medium heat and cook shallots and chillies, stirring often, until onions are tender and caramel brown on edges. Lift out with slotted spoon and keep warm. Raise heat until fat splutters. Fry duck fatty-side down, until skin is dark and crisp. Serve with shallots and a squeeze of lime.

POMEGRANATE SEEDS: *anardana*
BOT: *Punica granatum*

•

Pomegranate (*anar*) is the apple of Eden in Arab mythology. Everywhere Persian and Turkish influence spread, so did their beloved pomegranate. Babur's first act after defeating the elephant armies of Delhi with his Turkish artillery was to lay out a garden at Agra in the Persian style, complete with the flame-coloured fruit. Ground, sun-dried pomegranate seed, the spice known as *anardana*, from a wild sour fruit common to the lower Himalayas, is popular in northern India, and its presence in a dish hints at Middle Eastern, especially Turkish, connections. *Anardana* often adds its mild, sweet and fruity note of acidity to the potato stuffing for parathas and naans and to Punjabi chickpea stews (whereas in the Middle East the seeds are sprinkled on the chickpea purée, hummus). Interesting and inexpensive, but not that useful. 2 teaspoons of ground seeds are roughly equivalent to 1 teaspoon of lemon juice. Try 4 teaspoons mixed into Gingery Chickpeas (page 163) instead of lemon juice, or 2 teaspoons in the Coconut Crust Potatoes (page 96) instead of the lime juice. Hyderabadi cooks use its sour-sweet juice in creamy Persian sauces (as do cooks in Iran and the Lebanon), and the people of the great northern desert grind its dried seeds to a powder to give their masalas, breads and dals a fruitier piquancy than can be achieved with mango powder.

POMEGRANATE SEED AND YOGHURT MARINADE

Marinates 900 g (2 lb) meat or 1 small chicken

Lamb kebabs, called *buthas* in Jodhpur, are marinated in a paste of garlic and ginger for two hours, then in a yoghurt masala soured with the desert fruit kachri, or with dried mango or pomegranate. The same technique is used with the wheat gluten mentioned on page 133 (vegetarians outside Rajasthan could use this marinade for barbecuing chunks of paneer or feta cheese with slices of red pepper). This is a faster version. Melon seeds, common in Rajasthani masalas (available from Asian stores), have a creamy flavour, somewhere between almond and pine nut.

1 cm (½ inch) piece cinnamon stick
1 teaspoon coriander seeds
½ teaspoon cumin seeds
1 black cardamom
3 cloves
1 tablespoon melon seeds or almonds
½ teaspoon salt
4 garlic cloves, crushed
2 tablespoons ground dried pomegranate seeds or 2.5 cm (1 inch) piece root ginger, grated
150 ml (5 fl oz) Greek-style yoghurt
1–2 teaspoons cayenne pepper

Toast cinnamon and coriander over medium heat until they change colour, then add cumin, cardamom, cloves and melon seeds, and roast until cloves are puffy. Grind finely with salt and mix with remaining ingredients.

To prepare chicken pieces for marinating, slash diagonally in several places to allow marinade to penetrate and soften the meat. Leave the chicken or chunks of lamb in the mixture for at least 1 hour, then grill or barbecue until well-browned and blackened around the edges.

RED-HOT PAN-SMOKED CORN

Serves 4 as a condiment or small salad

Rajasthanis are the masters of corn recipes, but their desert corn (like their lentils and beans, whose skins harden in the sun) takes longer cooking than the West's. This is a kitchen trick to give sweetcorn – even boring canned or frozen sweetcorn – the deliciously smoky-sweet character of corn eaten in Rajasthan which is roasted in its husk over a fire. Simply tossed with lime juice and fresh coriander, it makes a superb accompaniment to roasts and grills.

3 cobs sweetcorn, husk removed
4–8 dried red chillies, crumbled
¼ teaspoon coarse salt

Slice kernels off cobs and mix with chillies and salt. Heat a steel or uncoated iron saucepan over high heat until it smokes. (Do not use your best pan and do not use a non-stick pan – the corn must stick to get its flavour.) Pour in corn and leave for a few seconds to 'catch' on bottom. Scrape it up, stir and leave again. Continue to do this for about 4–5 minutes until corn is popping and covered in browny-black spots.

PAN-SMOKED CORN CHUTNEY

Serves 4–6 as a fresh chutney or salsa

Good with Grilled Lamb Chops Stuffed with Mint or Coriander Chutney (page 165) or sausages or as a stuffing for Spice-Smoked Small Birds (page 139).

½ teaspoon coriander seeds
½ teaspoon cumin seeds
3 tablespoons mustard oil
1 onion, finely chopped
4 garlic cloves, finely sliced lengthwise

5 cm (2 inch) piece root ginger, cut in fine julienne
2 cobs sweetcorn, husks removed
4–6 dried red chillies, crumbled
½ teaspoon salt
juice of 1–2 limes
handful of fresh coriander, chopped

Toast coriander and cumin over medium heat until fragrant and lightly browned. Roughly crush. Fry onions in oil over medium heat until light brown and starting to turn dark on edges, stirring often to prevent burning. Add garlic and ginger and stir-fry until well browned.

Slice kernels of corn cobs, mix with chillies and salt and pan-smoke as for previous recipe. Mix with onions, lime juice and coriander. Serve hot or at room temperature.

WARM PAN-SMOKED CORN AND BITTER GREENS SALAD

Serves 4

In northern Rajasthan and the Punjab, pungent stewed mustard greens are a popular farmers' dish, thickened with maize flour and eaten with maize flour *rotis* and frothy buttermilk. This is a Western alternative, a combination of bitter greens wilted in mustard oil and balanced with smoky sweetcorn, excellent with Grilled Lamb Fillet with Fiery Chilli Sauce (page 143) sliced on top.

3 tablespoons mustard oil
½ teaspoon coriander seeds, roughly crushed
½ teaspoon cumin seeds
1 large onion, finely sliced
4 garlic cloves, crushed
2.5 cm (1 inch) piece root ginger, grated
kernels from 2 sweetcorn, pan-smoked with chillies and salt (see Pan-Smoked Corn Chutney, left)

1 tablespoon melon, pumpkin or sunflower seeds, toasted
1 bunch (about 225 g (8 oz)) bitter greens such as frizzy endive, rocket, mustard greens
juice of 1–2 limes

Heat mustard oil to smoking, lower heat to medium and stir in coriander, cumin and onion, in that order. Stir-fry onion until light brown, add garlic and ginger and fry until soft. Stir in corn, seeds and greens, toss and stir just until greens wilt. Dress with lime juice (and a pinch of sugar, if greens are very bitter).

GRILLED LAMB FILLET WITH FIERY CHILLI SAUCE

Serves 4 as a main course

Lal maas, essentially red chillies and garlic with the faintest whiff of mutton, is one of Rajasthan's most fiery concoctions, not for the faint of heart or the delicate palate: the chillies in it make the heart race (literally) and the blood pound in your eyeballs. The following recipe is not *lal maas*, which anyway is too strong a brew for the delicate lamb we have in the West, but it has some of the original's fiery spirit, especially if the lamb is charred on a barbecue and eaten on a warm summer night.

Rather than grind fistfuls of red chillies and garlic on a stone, as the Rajasthanis do (often using 50 chillies and an equal amount of garlic cloves in a dish for 8–12), I use harissa (widely available in delicatessens), but any pure chilli/garlic paste will do – Italian delicatessens often stock their own version.

2 teaspoons coriander seeds
1½ teaspoons cumin seeds
2 black cardamom pods

3 Indian bay leaves (or 2.5 cm (1 inch) cinnamon stick and 2 ordinary bay leaves)
½ teaspoon salt
1 teaspoon black peppercorns
6–10 garlic cloves
3–4 tablespoons harissa (or other pure chilli paste)
175 ml (6 fl oz) Greek-style yoghurt
2 lamb neck fillets (about 550 g 1¼ lb)
3 tablespoons mustard or light sesame oil
3 onions, very finely chopped
big handful of fresh coriander, chopped

Toast coriander, cumin, cardamom and bay leaves in dry frying pan over medium heat until dark and aromatic. Grind coarsely with salt and pepper and mix with 4–6 crushed garlic cloves, harissa and yoghurt (add some more harissa if you prefer fiery food).

Make several 1 cm (½ inch) slashes diagonally across meat, rub spice sauce all over the fillets, then leave to marinate for at least 1 hour – overnight is even better.

When ready to cook, pre-heat grill or barbecue to very hot. Lift meat out of marinade. Fry onions in oil over medium-high heat until brown. Stir in remaining garlic until it softens, then add marinade, reduce heat and simmer gently.

Grill lamb 3–4 minutes each side – or until browned and starting to blacken on edges. Remove, and leave to rest 10 minutes. Slice lamb thickly crosswise and serve each person with a few slices of meat and a big spoonful of fiery sauce mixed with fresh coriander.

• You can identify a Jodhpuri kitchen by the smell of garlic and onion. The onion used is the little pink shallot, a gentler, drier and tastier creature (if more time-consuming to peel) than the West's watery giants, and thus used for thickening sauces as well as flavouring them.

143

BAJRA KI ROTI · KABAB · ELAIC
· GARA MASALA · DALCHINI
· ROTI · LAVANG · BHA

RUSTIC RABBIT PIE
Serves 4

Rajputs hunt as avidly as Tuscans, often cooking what they shoot on the spot – simply, with their favourite mustard oil or ghee, salt and whole red chillies (lacking a stone on which to grind). A cherished recipe of this school, using black buck (Indian antelope) is called *jungli mans* – literally, jungle meat. Rabbit or desert hare is a more likely catch. These furred beasties are simmered until tender in a little water, and the flesh separated from bones and prepared in a number of ways. A good method is to finely shred the cooked meat into long fibres and fry it in ghee with shredded onions until both are crisp and caramel brown. This is mixed with cayenne pepper and salt to taste, a teaspoon or more of toasted cumin seeds and a few crushed cardamom seeds, then rolled in a plain maize flour roti (try it with the Spiced Cornmeal Roti on page 166). I like it with a salad of papery thin slices of white mooli radish tossed with lime juice and fresh mint, although this, of course, is to feminize what is essentially a dish meant to bolster a warrior's machismo.

The following more elaborate version (essentially rabbit baked between two chapattis) was prepared by a Rajput hunter on his rooftop and baked in a shallow pan over a charcoal brazier (see photograph on page 147). A modern oven is a great improvement on method if not atmosphere. The pie smells sweetly of cinnamon while baking and the result is reminiscent of one of Italy's rustic pies of pizza bread dough. It is always made with rabbit or hare in Rajasthan but would be equally good with pheasant, chicken or duck.

1 teaspoon coriander seeds
2.5 cm (1 inch) piece cinnamon stick,
roughly crushed
2 Indian bay leaves, crumbled
5 cloves
1 teaspoon cumin seeds
2 dried red chillies, crumbled
450 ml (¾ pint) Greek-style yoghurt
½ teaspoon salt
1 teaspoon ground pomegranate seeds or
grated zest of ½ lemon
50 g (2 oz) ghee or butter
or 4 tablespoons mustard oil
2 onions, halved lengthwise, finely sliced
crosswise
8 garlic cloves, roughly crushed
5 cm (2 inch) piece root ginger, grated
900 g (2 lb) rabbit pieces
handful of fresh mint, chopped

PASTRY

100 g (4 oz) unbleached flour
100 g (4 oz) wholewheat or
chapatti (atta) flour
½ teaspoon salt
1 teaspoon baking powder
½ teaspoon bicarbonate of soda
2 tablespoons mustard or other
vegetable oil
milk, for brushing

Toast coriander and cinnamon over medium heat in a dry frying pan until they crackle. Add bay leaves and cloves and cook until cloves puff. Grind coarsely. Toast cumin and chillies until darkened and whisk into yoghurt with ground spices, salt, seeds, and 125 ml (4 fl oz) water.

Over medium heat, fry onions in ghee until golden brown, and stir in garlic and ginger until golden. Pour in spiced yoghurt, add rabbit, turning it in yoghurt to cover, and bring to a boil. Reduce heat and simmer, half-covered, for about 45 minutes or until rabbit is tender when prodded with a fork. Turn meat from time to time.

While rabbit cooks, make pastry. Mix dry ingredients and rub in oil until mixture resembles breadcrumbs. Trickle just enough water over to form a stiff dough and knead for a few minutes until pliable (this can also be done in a food processor). Rub oil over the dough and put in a plastic bag until ready to cook.

Pre-heat oven to 200°C/400°F/Gas 6 with a metal baking sheet to rest pie tin on. When rabbit is tender, lift it out and reduce sauce to consistency of thick cream. Shred meat off bones and mix with sauce and mint.

Divide pastry in two, one piece slightly bigger. Keep second piece covered while you roll out first very thinly – no thicker than 5 mm (¼ inch). Lay this in a shallow 20–23 cm (8–9 inch) greased pie tin but do not press into the tin. Prick all over with a fork and mound rabbit on top. Roll out remaining pastry and lay on top of rabbit, crimping pastry edges together. Aim for a flying saucer shape rather than a French flan. If you have a shallow wok or paella dish of the right size, these work even better. Brush pastry with milk, stand pie on the hot metal sheet (to crisp pastry) and bake 30–35 minutes until crust is brown and crisp. Serve cut in wedges with Warm Pan-Smoked Corn and Bitter Greens Salad (page 142).

——————— *Variations* ———————

• On the principal that Rajasthani cooks would not object to anything sun-dried, I often add a handful of sun-dried tomatoes or stoned prunes when I mix cooked rabbit with sauce.

• If you are in a hurry, this pie can be made with 450 g (1 lb) cooked, shredded meat. Simply cook the sauce separately until it thickens, then mix in meat and mint and continue.

The base notes of Rajasthan are smoke, fire and respect for water: traditional terracotta waterpots are made and decorated in the village of a potter caste in the Thar Desert, and (below), Jodhpuri musicians crush garlic with their fists for the tempering of dal, smoky from an open fire.

WATER MELON

BY AIR MAIL
PAR AVION
हवाई डाक से

QUTUB MINAR
ഖിനാർ
PRICE RE .0.06

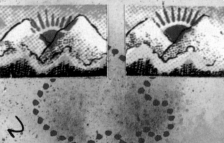

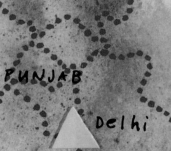

PAKISTAN

PUNJAB

Delhi

RAJASTHAN

UTTAR
PRADESH

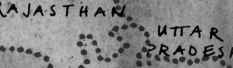

CHAPTER SEVEN

LAYERS
OF
INFLUENCE

•

From all that I have said, you may by the by see whether
a man ought to leave Paris to come to Delhi to make good cheer...
FRANÇOIS BERNIER, LATE PHYSICIAN TO THE GREAT MOGUL, 1655–61

Behind Chandni Chowk, the Moguls' Silver Street, in Old Delhi, there is a lane called the Street of Parathas (identified by its function, like the arteries of all antique towns) where sons, grandsons and great-grandsons have been making bread since Shah Jahan built his new city – not to become 'Old' Delhi until the time of the British Raj – on the site of fifteen or more infinitely older Delhis. This is the heart and stomach of Delhi, separated from its brain, Lutyens' pastiche Mogul parliament building in New Delhi, by a distance of five kilometres and some four hundred years

Old Delhi's tune is percussive, a clap-clap-clap of parathas, naans and chapattis being slapped from hand to hand. Through the bicycle bells and the street-vendors' lyrics, through goats' clarinet bleats and a cow's oboe and the trumpet squawks of chickens fated for the tandoor, this clapping is the city's metronome, proof of the durability of taste over transitory dominion.

Not far from the Street of Parathas is the seventeenth-century Jama Masjid mosque, whose negligée pink stone strikes a discordant feminine note in what is a predominantly masculine setting. 'When I was a boy,' said Satish Jacob, one of the BBC's Delhi correspondents, 'about thirty-five years ago, I used to play cricket here.' He dodged two converging horse-drawn tongas and narrowly avoided being hit by a moped on which sat: the driver, two small children (one asleep on the handlebars), a woman (in enveloping black *burqua*), holding a baby, and four chickens. Outside the old city walls New Delhi roared like a river approaching rapids.

'When I was a boy, my parents would not let me venture beyond these walls. They called that "the jungle area". Where you see a traffic jam now, we used to see fields and wild boar.'

149

Satish grew up in Old Delhi, a Christian in what is still mainly a Muslim city. He and his family moved to New Delhi a few years ago. But his school friends, his fellow cricketers, are here. 'Old Delhi has stayed more or less the same,' he said. 'I will take you now to the Street of Cooks, where there have been chefs for hire for three hundred years.'

We walked through Charvelli Bazaar, the old street of 'dancing girls', a local euphemism for prostitutes, although here they were more akin to Japanese geishas than to common whores. In Charvelli, before the British moved them to the outskirts of Delhi, the city's multi-talented courtesans trained some of the best classical singers in India. Satish remembers with fondness being allowed into their courtyards to listen – but *just* to listen. 'These women were only for rich men. The cream of Delhi society used to send its sons here in feudal times to learn etiquette and courtly language.' Now that business is poor the courtesans can no longer afford to employ the best chefs for their soirées. By contrast, Satish's friend the butcher still has plenty of business. He sits on the quartered tree trunk that is his chopping bock, holding a cleaver between his toes and slicing up bits of goat. You can tell it is goat because a goat's tail is draped next to him. 'There are many shops everywhere here that sell flesh,' wrote François Bernier in the 1650s, 'but you must take heed lest they give you mutton for kid…'

'The tail is proof for the customers,' said Satish. 'Indians like to eat goat, not sheep, and the sheep's tail doesn't have this black fringe.' Later I heard of a thriving business in Delhi selling goats' tails to butchers.

Satish's return to his old neighbourhood was greeted with friendly if somewhat uneasy smiles. His tall, well-fed body and English brogues looked out of place in this quarter of wiry men in white pyjamas and leather sandles. It was as if someone from the future had transcended time to visit a museum devoted to his ancestors' quaint and primitive customs.

It is said that he who builds a new city in Delhi will lose it, yet no victor has lost entirely until his taste too has been vanquished. The British have now been gone for nearly half a century. They left India a sense of itself as a nation, a labyrinthine system of bureaucracy, a unifying language and a rail network, but little of culinary significance. Gone too are the Turko-Agfhans and Moguls who, first with trade and then with sword, remade this city in their own image. Their fortresses are museums inhabited by ghosts and bad-tempered monkeys. But their culinary influence has outlived that of the British. The Moguls' rival, Sher Shah, who ruled in the mid-1600s, could still today indulge his Afghan passion for quick and portable pan breads, although in the old Street of Parathas there remain only two vendors.

A paratha is a bread of many layers, the meeting point of croissant and chapatti. Mogul chefs in the courts of Lucknow and Delhi became so adept at them that their parathas were said to have had a hundred layers. This stratification is made possible by the transparent film of ghee that both supports each crisp layer and separates it from its neighbour. You can see a similar layered effect in Old Delhi, where street signs are invisible and function – spice, silk, bread – defines each 'gully', as lanes are called here, reinforcing the impression given of an organic landscape created by some inevitable geological tension. In one such gully, the typical

Hindu farmers' breakfast of pooris and potato curry is cooked, very basic and simple. In the next, the most refined Moglai feast is prepared by Muslim chefs whose ancestors, so they claim, worked for Akbar. In a third lane, experts in the tandoor, the hive-shaped clay oven that once united Punjabi village women and now unites Indian restaurants, bake saffron naans and chickpea rotis.

Vinod Nagpal, an actor and musician who studied with one of India's greatest courtesan singers, lived most of his life at Kashmiri Gate in Old Delhi. He said of his home, 'Each lane, each layer, has to do with a certain kind of hunger, and there is not this movement between the layers one finds in Bombay, where in order to cater to the largest common denominator they have bastardized everything.'

A cook in the Street of Cooks brought me some warm bread containing shreds of red chilli, whole coriander seeds, fennel and black pepper. He held some of his own garam masala. Not as finely ground as Western varieties, the evidence of its origins in bark, root and seedpod still remained. Its scent in the airless heat of that narrow city canyon was as potent as whisky.

Vendors of poori in roadside stalls in Old Delhi.
(Below) spicy beetroot and spinach
balloon breads.

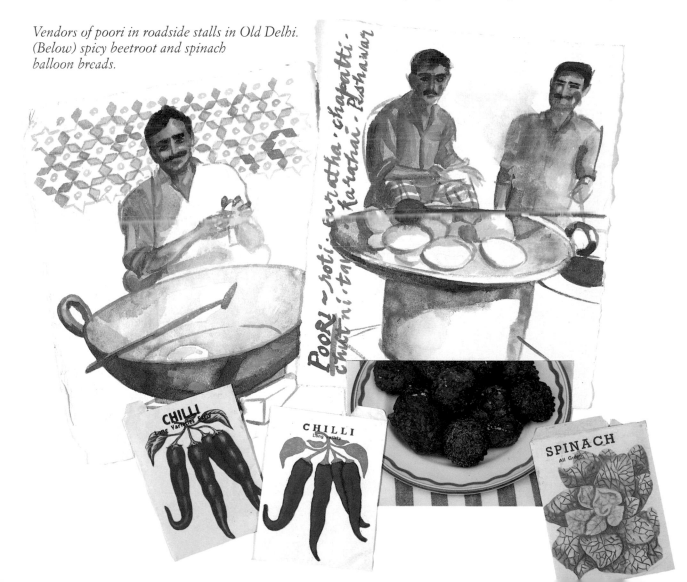

Delhi, crossroads of northern India, has always attracted immigrants. A Kashmiri Muslim pours out her traditional spiced tea.

This special 'masala' tea is brewed and flavoured with saffron, spices and ground almonds.

'In the evenings,' Satish said, 'people bring benches into the streets and listen to music and political discussions. And at two in the morning, when there is at least one tea shop open here, New Delhi will be deserted but for the jackals.' New Delhi is populated by those whose ancestors lived in the old city; even now, if there is an important occasion to celebrate, the new comes to the old for cooks.

Dishes in these streets match virtually every layer of Delhi's history – sweet chicken blancmanges of the twelfth-century Turks who built the Qutb Minar tower; Afghan-influenced tomato and black cardamom sauces; mild, deep-fried potato 'chops' (mashed potato patties dipped in batter and deep-fried to resemble meat chops), a legacy of the Raj, tea brewed with saffron and almonds by the most recent Kashmiri immigrants – although in a city that has been seventeen times capital of the subcontinent, some layers, inevitably, have been obscured.

When Sher Shah laid out the Grand Trunk Road in the sixteenth century, from Kabul to Calcutta via Delhi, he merely confirmed the city's already established position as the crossroads of Asia. Its key location left it open to so many influences and invasions that it never really developed its own distinct grand cuisine in the way that Lucknow or Hyderabad did. The old land trading route ran north from Gujarat across Rajasthan and along the Delhi road through Mathura (where 3500 years ago Krishna was born, to flirt with the dairy maids and later follow his nomadic cattle-herding family back into Gujarat). For thousands of years, spices and cultures overlapped in Delhi. The city was a distribution point for saffron from Kashmir, green cardamom from Kerala, Afghani asafoetida, opium and rice, and for diamond traders travelling from here down to Golconda.

Post-partition, it was the Punjabi refugees, with their onion seed breads from the tandoor and their plethora of *kanchas* – raw fresh ingredients like green chillies, onion rings and wedges of lime served with every dish – who most influenced Delhi. All around the city are small Punjabi *choli paturi* stalls selling the poor man's fast food. Five rupees buys him two *paturi* (breads), a small cupful of *choli* (dry-cooked channa dal) and a selection of pickles and *kanchas*, with a mug of tea to wash it down. 'A movable feast, literally,' said Push Pesh Panth, 'because the *choli paturi* vendors seldom have permission from the municipality, so when they see the inspector coming they must be mobile enough to pack up and run with their food stall to set up elsewhere.'

This is the humblest layer of Delhi cuisine. The top crust, I assumed, was represented by Moglai cooking. 'Not at all,' said Jigs Kalra, a journalist and culinary historian. 'What has come to be called Moglai food is in fact Persian, Arabic and Turkish from the traders of previous centuries who came in peace, not as conquerors. Refined, perhaps, by the later Mogul courts, but not original. The Moguls contributed very little to Indian cuisine. Genghis Khan was not a man who considered the subtle distinction between nutmeg and mace. Salt was the only spice he used.' If there are no recorded texts of Hindu cooks in the Mogul time, it is because the privileges of a master chef depended on the exclusivity of his knowledge; he would have vested interests in not giving out his recipes, so he alone could please the master.

'But in the Akbarama,' I said, 'an enormous list of dishes and the array of spices used in them is chronicled. Surely that suggests Akbar was a bit of a gourmet.'

The Moguls, foreign rulers whose flamboyant tastes overwhelmed subtle indigenous flavours, have a higher reputation outside India than within it. 'Embellishment is one of the characteristics of a *nouveau riche* trying to claim pedigree.' said Dr Panth. 'In the Akbarama you have a court writer wishing to further glorify a king who has attained great power in war and must also be seen to have great taste in food.' The Portuguese, from their distant capitals on the Malabar Coast, had far more effect than the Moguls, introducing tomatoes, capsicums, potatoes and a score of New World flavourings including the chilli. Levels of chilli use in Delhi corresponds to its social layers, the use rising in proportion to diminution in wealth.

But chillies were not the country's original hot spice. Traditionally, the 'heating spices', the garam masala, were cinnamon, clove, cardamom, nutmeg, mace and black pepper. Everywhere I went in Delhi I inquired about a recipe for this mixture, the one which even uninformed Westerners associate with Indian food. Like the Italians, all Indians, whatever their level in society, have opinions about food and music, perhaps because both arts have their roots in the country's folk traditions, and the ability to enjoy them is distributed completely at random, irrespective of birth. Each person had a different masala recipe. Finally, I got a definitive answer.

'Is there one classic recipe for garam masala?' I asked a Delhi chef.

'Of course,' he said. 'But there are many versions of it.'

'You might as well ask what humans can do with language,' I was told by Robbi Chatterjee, a Bengali historian and musician now resident in Delhi. 'Or how many permutations are possible in a raga, the India melodic form: each artist extends the possibility.' In a country of 36,000 gods, there is no one way.

Ragas, like recipes, are melodic improvisations around a central structure, in which the performer's mood, his feelings for the place, season, even the time of day, change his interpretation of the music. Similarly one can take the garam masala and play infinite variations on it, depending on the weight one gives to each spice, whether they are fried whole in ghee at the beginning of cooking or toasted and sprinkled over at the end. 'I know of many dishes which I take off the heat and then put back on before serving,' Robbi said, 'and others I will never do this with.' Like the empty section in Indian classical rhythmn, in which the audience's clap is replaced by a wave of the hand.

The melodic structure of Indian food can be a simple one. 'We have a saying,' Vinod Nagpal told me, 'that all you need is a simple korma (meat curry) and *roti*. Everything else is self-indulgence of the rich.'

The old Delhi was a gentle, cosmopolitan place with manners that were a bench-mark for the rest of India. It was a court city and a city of learning, and its citizens were proud to belong to it. Today people hold court here but Delhi is no longer a court city, a loss of imperial power reflected in its cooking. Modern Delhi's culinary influences come from ambitious chefs in five-star hotels rather than from old family recipes.

'So is this the end of the spice road?' I asked Dr Panth.

'Ah no,' he said, with a guru's enigmatic smile, 'India's destiny is entwined with spices. In the West, and among some of the young here, there is a rising tide of interest in the old Ayurvedic holistic masalas. I am reminded of T.S. Eliot: In my end is my beginning.' A circular movement does not have to be closed, Robbi Chatterjee had said. It can also be a spiral.

Shoppers in Old Delhi's spice market are an indication of its cosmopolitan past: desert women from Rajasthan as vivid as bright butterflies.

Flavours of Delhi & the North
•
BREAD, ROOTS
AND LAYERS OF MASALA

*D*elhi is a multilayered paratha of culinary influences, to which each new invasion or wave of immigrants added another layer. There are the people who came down centuries ago from the Northwest Frontier Province, bringing with them Afghan tastes – black cardamom, roasted meats, bread scattered with nigella seeds. There is the original trading caste, who made up for their eschewal of onion or garlic by use of asafoetida. There were Muslims, doing everything from sweeping the streets to ruling them, whose cuisine at the highest level had such refinements as mild spicing and exotic flavourings like rose petals, nutmeg and mace, as well as a Turkish and Persian love of dried fruit and nuts. There was the local Hindu administrative class, with their own highly refined cuisine. And finally there are new arrivals, people from India's granary, the Punjab, who arrived after Partition. Having been at the forefront of the centuries of battles fought in this country, they had little time to develop refinements, but they brought with them their expertise with the tandoor clay oven – and their roots: carrots, radish, beetroot, potato, turnip.

CARDAMOM, Black: kali (black) elaichi, badi (big) elaichi.
BOT: *Elettaria cardamomum*
•

The big black wizened cardamom looks like a cross between a small prune and a goat's dropping. Its smoky, subtle aroma, popular in Rajasthan, Kashmir and the North, has none of the perfumed quality of the green cardamom. It is the poor man's flavouring, medicine and breath-freshener: the whole black cardamom is used in most meat dishes, and its musky fragrance greatly enhances the sweetness of onion- and tomato-based sauces; it is essential in garam masala, the spice mixture which is supposed to trigger off a sensation of heat in your body and prepare you for winter. According to Push Pesh Panth it is also a digestive with more medicinal properties than the expensive green variety. 'At least, so the poor here believe,' he said, 'although Western science does not perhaps distinguish between the volatile oils of these two. But our poor have always consoled themselves by thinking that the ingredients they could not afford were less beneficial then those they could.'

CORIANDER SEEDS: dhania
BOT: *Coriandrum sativum*
•

One of the most ancient and versatile spices in India, ground coriander seeds are the base note in many north Indian 'curries'. Toasted first to give them a nutty, spicy taste, and ground with fried onions and garlic, they are what thickens northern gravies instead of the flour used in Western countries. Unroasted or simmered whole in a sauce (as in Spring Lamb Stew with Baby Root Vegetables, page 171), they add a subtly sweet orange peel flavour. In northwest India and Pakistan there are many dishes, particularly tomato-based ones, where coriander seeds are simmered whole like this. It is the area where Alexander the Great marched in the third century BC. It is the area where carved stone Buddhas look like classical Greek gods. In classical European cooking, a dish simmered with whole coriander seeds is called à la Grecque.

Always buy coriander seeds whole – they lose their aroma rapidly when ground, and are much more interesting as a spice if ground coarsely rather than finely, after toasting.

CUMIN SEEDS, Black: *shahi jeera, kala jeera*
BOT: *Cuminum nigrum*

•

Resembling black onion seeds, and often confused with them, black cumin seeds bear no flavour resemblance to them or to the pale beige-coloured cumin seed. Mellow, sweet and herbal, even mushroomy, rather than spicy, black cumin's source – growing wild in Iran and Kashmir – is a key to its use: in Mogul/Persian pulaos and as an essential ingredient in garam masalas. Because of its delicacy, it does not require toasting first.

ABOVE: Layers of masala and bread in Old Delhi – whole garam masala spices reflect Persian and Afghan influences.

GARAM MASALA ('hot spice mixture')

•

A garam masala was the spice mixture prescribed for those in need of an elixir, a restorative. It speeded up your metabolism and triggered off a sensation of heat in your body, preparing you for winter or for hard physical exertion (thus for warriors as well as lovers). This was known as the *garam tahseer* (from the Arabic *assar*, meaning 'effect') and its original concept has now been lost. What happened, I was told by Push Pesh Panth, is that in the boudoirs of princely and Mogul India, over-indulgence in sex and food was common. 'Garam masalas' were prescribed by doctors to rejuvenate the appetites of weary nobles. This jaded the palate, more and more was needed, and eventually rich men's food became associated with enormous amounts of hot spices, resulting in the muddying of flavours (now commonly reflected in pretentious restaurants), and the loss of Indian cuisine's link with the seasons.

Spices considered to have a heating effect – to be used in moderation – cinnamon, cassia, black pepper, nutmeg, mace and cardamom are the ones which can overpower a dish. Add them with too heavy a hand and you might as well buy commercial curry powder, what Dr Panth called the last weapon of a colonial civilization.

There is no such thing as one definitive garam masala, but a rough rule of thumb is to divide the multitude of variations into two groups: the first, those associated with Punjabi and Uttar Pradesh onion- and tomato-sauced roots, chickpeas, kidney beans and black-eye peas, is heavier on the 'curry' spices like black cardamom, ordinary cumin and coriander seed; the second, those sweet, highly-scented spices such as nutmeg, mace, black cumin and dried ginger (sometimes including saffron and 'cooling' rose petals or fennel seeds), is used in conjunction with Mogul and Persian meat dishes rich in creamy yoghurt, dried fruits and ground nuts. The first set is toasted before use, the second 'sweet' set is not; both are ground to a dry powder and may be stored for months, unlike southern masalas which must be made fresh every day because they are ground with oil, water or coconut milk – a process known as 'touching the stone'.

Note If you grind your own spices in a small electric coffee grinder, as I do, you will give your coffee the aromatic taste of the East: spices grind to a finer powder than coffee – and cling. Don't be too obsessive about cleaning the grinder!

GARAM MASALA (1)

A nutty, 'curry' spiced masala, ideal for onion- and tomato-based dishes, with the smokiness of black cardamom in the background. Mix 1 teaspoon of this into fritter or pancake batters to liven them up, stir ½–¾ of a teaspoon into cooked chickpeas or lentils, sprinkle the same amount over stewed aubergines, courgettes and peppers or into garlicky tomato sauce.

2 teaspoons cumin seeds
3 teaspoons coriander seeds
1 teaspoon black peppercorns
7.5 cm (3 inch) piece cinnamon stick
8 black cardamom
1 teaspoon cloves
2 Indian bay leaves, broken up

Dry-roast spices over medium-high heat until they darken and smell aromatic. Cool and grind to fine powder. Store in the cool in an air-tight jar.

GARAM MASALA (2)

The following mixture gives a sweet and aromatic masala, ideal for creamy nut sauces and yoghurt marinades. I usually have two little jars of this – one quite coarsely ground, the bits of twig and bud still almost identifiable, for use as an Indian bouquet garni to simmer sauces from the beginning of cooking; the other finely ground, for mixing into dishes towards the end.

2 teaspoons black cumin seeds
1 teaspoon cloves, lightly toasted
1 teaspoon black peppercorns
5 cm (2 inch) piece cinnamon stick

4–6 black cardamom
seeds from 20 green cardamom
2 Indian bay leaves, broken up
½ teaspoon grated nutmeg
¼ teaspoon ground mace
¾ teaspoon ground ginger

Grind everything to a fine powder and store in an air-tight jar in a cool, dark place.

—— Uses ——

• A good tempering for cooked (or even canned) black-eyed peas or chickpeas is 1 tablespoon cumin seeds, 1 finely chopped onion, a thumb of ginger and a few cloves of garlic fried in 50 g (2 oz) ghee or 4 tablespoons sesame, olive or mustard oil. When brown, stir in 2 chopped fresh green chillies and 2 chopped tomatoes, let them thicken and mix with fresh mint or coriander and ½–¾ of a teaspoon Garam Masala (1). Stir into the black-eyed peas or chickpeas.

• For plain rice biryani, parboil basmati rice in boiling water for 2 minutes, then layer with fried onions, fresh coriander and mint, squeeze over the juice of 2 lemons or limes and a pinch of saffron dissolved in 6 tablespoons of hot milk. Sprinkle on 2 teaspoons of fine Garam Masala (2), cover tightly and steam for 30 minutes in an oven pre-heated to 170°C/325°F/Gas 3.

• Stir ¼ teaspoon of fine Garam Masala (2) into spinach purée or use instead of nutmeg in the classic Italian mixture of spinach, pine nuts and raisins.

• A good quick marinade for chicken to be bar-becued is fried onions and garlic, ground with a thumb of fresh ginger, 6 tablespoons of Greek-style yoghurt, cayenne pepper, salt and 1½ tea-spoons of fine Garam Masala (2). Marinate for an hour and grill, basting with marinade.

• Before serving steamed cauliflower or broccoli, toss in butter, lemon juice and ½ teaspoon of fine Garam Masala (2).

MOONLIT CHICKEN AND ALMOND KORMA

Serves 4–6 as a light main course

'White' food, cooked in creamy nut sauces, in which even the spices are white – white cardamom, white pepper, white poppy seeds, melon seeds, pumpkin seeds, almonds, the seeds from chillies – were popular in Mogul days, and are still among Rajput nobility. You can see these moonlit feasts, where everyone is dressed in white and there are white flowers as well to complete the lunar impression, in Mogul miniatures. This scented korma reveals its noble origins in its list of rich ingredients (cream, almonds, rosewater, coconut milk – rare in the North but not unheard of) and its lack of earthy roots like garlic and onions. In India it would be garnished with silver foil and fresh rose petals. Yellow chillies finely sliced crosswise, tossed with sea salt and fried until crisp, are a good, if less recherché, alternative.

65 g (2½ oz) blanched skinned almonds (or a mixture of melon seeds, almonds and white poppy seeds)
5 cm (2 inch) piece root ginger, chopped
¾ teaspoon salt, or to taste
2 tablespoons chilli seeds or 1 teaspoon ground white pepper
200 ml (7 fl oz) Greek-style yoghurt
450 ml (15 fl oz) canned coconut milk
200 ml (7 fl oz) chicken stock or water
1 teaspoon coarsely ground Garam Masala (version 2, page 158)
seeds from 10 green cardamom pods
900 g–1.25 kg (2–2½ lb) chicken breasts and thighs, skinned
juice of 1 lime
4 tablespoons double cream
1–2 teaspoons rosewater
fresh rose petals or yellow chillies, finely sliced crosswise, to garnish

Grind together very finely almonds, ginger, salt and chilli seeds or pepper. Whisk together with yoghurt, coconut milk and stock. Tie garam masala and cardamom into a small muslin spice bag or thin cloth. In a saucepan large enough to hold chicken as well, bring yoghurt and spices to a boil with spice bag. Slip chicken into sauce, cover tightly and lower heat. Simmer until tender (about 35–45 minutes).

If sauce is still quite thin, lift out chicken and keep covered. Discard spice bag. Raise heat and bubble sauce until reduced and thick enough to thinly coat the back of a spoon. Reduce heat, stir in lime juice, cream and rosewater, return chicken to pan and warm through. Serve napped with a few spoonfuls of sauce and garnished with rose petals or chillies.

GINGER, *Ground Dried: sont, sonth*
•

One of the spices associated with creamy Mogul sauces, dried ginger, like its fresh counterpart, is used to give a hot sour flavour and, in the case of the dried spice, a scented woodiness almost like sandalwood. It often forms part of the more elaborate garam masalas and is considered by Ayurvedic doctors to be efficacious in the treatment of flus and colds (because it promotes beneficial sweating, an effect noted by European herbalists of the Middle Ages). Although in terms of heat and sourness, 1 teaspoon of dry ginger powder is roughly equivalent to 1 tablespoon of ground fresh root, it is not a substitute, and is used for a different effect.

MACE: *javitri*
BOT: *Myristica fragrans*
•

Because of its price (higher than nutmeg), mace, the brilliant scarlet membrane covering the nutmeg, was rarely used in any but the most refined of the court dishes in Mogul India. Its sweet, nutmeggy aroma which has a slight edge of bitterness appears in conjunction with other precious ingredients such as almonds, dried fruits, cream.

NUTMEG: *jaiphul*
BOT: *Myristica fragrans*
•

Italians were not the first to notice the affinity nutmeg has for spinach and cream: Gujaratis used it in their milk and yoghurt puddings, and it was an essential in the Moguls' yoghurt sauces and in the masala sprinkled on their gingery spinach purées. Perhaps both Italy and India learned how to use it from the Levant, where it is often combined with cinnamon to flavour mutton. Although garam masalas containing nutmeg are generally prepared ahead of time to store, I find nutmeg loses its perfumed flavour very rapidly after grinding. Better to grate it into a dish just before serving. Myristicin, a component of its oil, is a hallucinogen and nutmeg-rich masalas are known to have a soporific effect.

ONION SEEDS, *Black, nigella seeds: kalaunji*
BOT: *Nigella sativa*
•

Bite into one of these little truffle-black seeds and the immediate sensation is of dried pepper and oregano rather than onion, despite their name. Not surprising, then, that they are popular in the hot, dry countries where oregano grows as well. They are used as a spice all over the Middle East and for sprinkling on tandoor foods and breads in Kashmir and the Punjab, or in stir-fried vegetables and dals. It is best to be sparing with them and to cook them gently as they can burn easily and become bitter.

ONION SEED POTATOES OR CAULIFLOWER

Serves 4 as a side dish

A recipe from a musician who stressed that food in India does not have to be complicated. In fact, the poorest people can take five simple ingredients and subtly alter them to fit season, mood or time of day, as one does with a *raga*, an Indian melody. In summer, he said, potatoes would be cooked in this way with tomatoes and onions (fried with the spices, before adding potatoes), or onion seeds, green chillies and salt would be brought to a boil with a cupful of water, the cauliflower cooked in this aromatic liquid until tender, then served simply with a squeeze of lemon. In Old Delhi roadside cafés, the dish would be started with a pellet of asafoetida, and finished with a few spoonfuls of yoghurt, stirred in and simmered until thickened.

450 g (1 lb) potatoes or cauliflower
2–3 tablespoons vegetable oil
½ teaspoon black onion seeds
¼ teaspoon ground turmeric
2 green chillies, finely sliced crosswise
½ teaspoon cayenne pepper
½ teaspoon salt, or to taste

Slice potatoes in 8 wedges lengthwise (if using cauliflower, break it into florets). Heat oil and sizzle onion seeds, turmeric and chillies over medium heat until they smell aromatic. Add potatoes, cayenne and salt and stir to coat well with spiced oil. Cover and lower heat. Cook until tender (10–12 minutes, less for cauliflower), then uncover pan, raise heat and stir-fry potatoes until brown and crisp. If using cauliflower, stir-fry just until most liquid evaporates.

PAPRIKA: *deghi mirch*
BOT: *Capsicum terragonom*

•

A brick-red powder made in the West from a pointed sweet Hungarian capsicum without the fieriness of red chillies. Look for good Hungarian brands which come in varying degrees of pungency from very mild and sweet to slightly hot, more like the Kashmiri paprika of northern India. Most often used in combination with turmeric to give tandoor dishes and earthy stews their colour.

SAFFRON: *kesar, zafran*
BOT: *Crocus sativus*

•

'Wretched is the stomach that has no saffron rice;' goes a quatrain by the fifteenth-century Persian gourmet poet, Bushaq, 'Its heart will be black like the Abyssinian with grief.' India's supply of the world's most expensive spice comes from crocus fields in Kashmir, although cooks there say that a superior quality, with more of the distinctive musky, honey and iodine perfume for which the spice is valued grows in Spain. An essential part of South Indian religious festivals and North Indian feasts – in Persian style pulaos and Mogul meat dishes, or soaked in warm milk and sprinkled over enriched breads towards the end of baking. Indians like it in sweet as well as savoury dishes, although it can give a cloying, medieval, almost medicinal flavour to puddings.

Buy it in small quantities in thread rather than powder form (to avoid the risk of adulteration). Despite its price (higher than gold), even poor people use it in India: as little as a quarter of a teaspoon gives a touch of luxury to a rice pudding or a pulao for eight.

Before using, soak it first for about 15 minutes in hot water or milk until the stigmas expand, then add towards the end of cooking – its aroma is dissipated in long exposure to heat.

Creamy Almond-Stuffed Saffron Pastry

Makes 4 dessert breads

This version of *sheermal*, a butter-rich bread from Lucknow, was originally served with savoury dishes in the old court, but for modern tastes its crisp cake-like texture and sweet marzipan filling makes a delicious alternative to French almond tart, especially if served with sharp fruit – apples cooked in butter with cardamom and brown sugar, say, or peaches warmed through in shreds of orange zest, then macerated in brandy.

225 g (8 oz) plain flour
pinch of salt
150 ml (5 fl oz) double cream
seeds from 8 green cardamom pods, crushed
2 tablespoons icing sugar
3 tablespoons milk
big pinch of saffron threads
4 teaspoons sweet almond paste
(brown sugar version, if available)
handful of flaked or chopped almonds,
toasted

Sift together flour and salt. Heat cream with cardamom and 2 teaspoons of sugar until sugar dissolves, then stir into flour to form a soft dough. Knead on a lightly floured surface for 7–10 minutes, until smooth and pliable. Wrap in cling-film and let rest 30 minutes.

Pre-heat grill to medium-hot, with a metal baking tray about 5 cm (2 inches) from grill. Heat 2 tablespoons of milk with saffron and leave to infuse. Divide dough into 8 balls and keep covered. Roll out 2 balls to 10 cm (4 inch) circles on floured surface. Flatten a quarter of almond paste as thinly as possible and place on top of one dough circle. Brush edges of dough with a little milk (not saffron milk), lay second piece on top and pinch edges together. Roll out again to 5 mm

(¼ inch) thick and prick dough with a fork to within 5 mm (¼ inch) of edge. Cover. Repeat process with remaining dough to make a total of 4 breads.

Lay breads on baking sheet (this crisps base) and grill until starting to brown (1–2 minutes). Brush with saffron milk and return to grill again until golden brown and beginning to darken in spots. Remove from oven, sprinkle over almond flakes and dust lightly with icing sugar. Serve with creamy yoghurt, fromage frais or fruit.

Baked Spiced Lamb and Almond Frittata

Serves 6 as a starter or light lunch

A link with Turkey and with Persia, an old dish popular in Old Delhi whose name – *sasranga* – and origins puzzled me. The name is still a puzzle but I discovered the origins when I was given a recipe and recognized it as a Turkish *eggah*, the Persian *kuku*, an exotic twist on what Tuscans would call a *frittata*, where eggs are used as a binder for a scented filling. It is eaten hot as a substantial dish, cut in wedges like a cake (which it resembles more than an omelette), or cold as a snack, cut in small pieces. I like to imagine some medieval Turkish spice merchant packing it on his first visit to the crossroads of Asia. This maharaja's version is the richest, but it can be made vegetarian and lighter in one of the variations listed on page 163.

350 g (12 oz) finely minced lean lamb
25 g (1 oz) ghee or butter or 2 tablespoons
vegetable oil
2 small onions, halved lengthwise and
finely sliced crosswise
1 teaspoon cumin seeds
25 g (1 oz) almonds, cut in slivers
25 g (1 oz) raisins

3–4 green chillies, finely sliced crosswise

2.5 cm (1 inch) piece root ginger, shredded

20 g (¾ oz) fresh coriander leaves, chopped

4 eggs, beaten

½ teaspoon Garam Masala (version 2, page 158)

juice of 2 limes, grated zest of 1

¾ teaspoon salt, or to taste

125 ml (4 fl oz) double cream or coconut cream

Pre-heat oven to 180°C/350°F/Gas 4. Lightly grease 20 cm (8 inch) tin and cut a piece of grease-proof paper to fit base. In a non-stick pan, stir-fry lamb until it is no longer pink and has begun to turn dark brown in spots. Lift out with a slotted spoon and spread half the meat evenly over base of tin. Reserve remaining meat.

Add ghee to pan and fry onions until caramel brown and crisp, stirring often to prevent burning. Lift out with a slotted spoon and drain on kitchen paper. Add cumin to pan and let it brown, then stir in almonds, raisins, chillies and ginger and stir-fry until lightly browned. Mix with coriander and onions.

Whisk together eggs, garam masala, lime and salt. Spread half the cream or yoghurt over meat, then half onion mixture, and pour over half the eggs, pressing down very well. Repeat with remaining ingredients and bake 30 minutes until set and golden. Eat warm or cold – it is a good picnic dish.

––––––––– *Variations* –––––––––

• For a vegetarian version, substitute 2 aubergines for the lamb: slice them thickly crosswise, drop in boiling water for 3 minutes, drain and layer as meat.

• A good variation is to use Greek-style yoghurt instead of cream and lime juice, and walnuts instead of almonds. You could also replace the lamb with lean beef.

GINGERY CHICKPEAS

Serves 8 as a side dish

A fresh-tasting dish. In summer, I keep a bowl of it in the fridge to have for quick lunches with a bitter green salad or some grilled red peppers. Canned chickpeas will do when you forget to soak the dried ones.

450 g (1 lb) dried chickpeas or 4×425 g (15 oz) cans chickpeas

½ teaspoon bicarbonate of soda (unnecessary for canned peas)

5–7.5 cm (2–3 inch) piece root ginger, ½ ground, ½ shredded

6 garlic cloves, ½ ground, ½ shredded

2–4 green chillies, ½ whole, slit lengthwise, ½ seeded and finely sliced

2 large onions, 1 whole, 1 finely sliced

50–65 g (2–2½ oz) ghee or butter or 4–5 tablespoons good oil (olive, sesame)

1½ teaspoons cumin seeds

3 good fresh tomatoes, seeded, cut in strips lengthwise (or handful of sun-dried tomatoes in oil, drained, cut in strips)

salt to taste

handful of fresh mint or coriander, roughly chopped

juice of 1 lemon or lime

Soak chickpeas with bicarbonate of soda for 24 hours in enough cold water to cover by at least 5 cm (2 inches).

After soaking, drain and rinse peas, cover in twice their volume cold water and boil hard for 7 minutes, removing any scum that forms. Reduce heat to a simmer, add ground ginger, ground garlic, whole chillies and whole onion and simmer until tender (from 1–3 hours depending on brand of chickpeas). If using canned chickpeas, drain off liquid, rinse, add 275 ml (9 fl oz) water and simmer for about 20 minutes with flavourings.

Depending on how long chickpeas have cooked, you may have to remove some water (save it for soup) – leave about one-third original quantity and purée it with enough of the chickpeas to make a sauce. Over medium heat, fry sliced onion in ghee (or oil if you are serving peas cold) until light caramel-coloured. Add remaining ginger, garlic, chillies and cumin seeds and cook until you can smell the garlic. Pour into chickpeas, add tomatoes, salt, herbs and lemon juice. Eat with gusto.

—————————— *Uses* ——————————

• Slightly mashed and re-fried in a few tablespoons of oil, this makes an excellent sauce for pasta – a Delhi version of the Italians' rustic *pasta e ceci*.

• Slightly crushed and mixed with more fresh herbs, you can use this to fill either the Spinach, Ginger and Garlic Balloon Bread (page 169) or the Spicy Beetroot Balloon Bread (page 170): simply crack the tops of bread open as you would an egg and spoon in some chickpeas.

• Slightly crush and pile into hollowed-out tomatoes or red peppers, lay in a baking dish, drizzle with oil and bake in a medium oven until crusty and browned on top. Serve with a salad of green beans.

GRILLED MONKFISH IN SPICE CRUST

Serves 4 as a main course with other dishes

'And if at any time you meet accidentally with any fish, the eunuchs, who love them excessively (I known not why) carry them presently away.' I know not why the eunuchs liked fish either, although it is just as rare in Delhi now as when the Great Mogul's doctor François Bernier wrote that in 1655. In Amritsar, however, cooks prepare a deep-fried meaty river fish with a carom seed batter (I have substituted fresh thyme which tastes less overpoweringly of thymol), and tandoor fish is a speciality at Delhi's splendid, atmospheric 1930s Imperial Hotel, one of the few left in Delhi with any character. The vinegar marinade in this recipe gives the fish a tangy flavour, and the crust keeps it juicy. If you want to deep-fry it, for Amritsar fish and chips, cut the monkfish into 5 cm (2 inch) chunks before marinating, then dip it in batter and fry. Even better over a barbecue.

2 tails, about 450 g (1 lb) boned monkfish
3 tablespoons white wine vinegar
1 onion, chopped
3 tablespoons mustard oil (or olive oil) or 40 g (1½ oz) ghee
5 cm (2 inch) piece root ginger, chopped
4 garlic cloves, chopped
¼ teaspoon ground turmeric
1 teaspoon cayenne pepper
½ teaspoon salt, or to taste
1 teaspoon coriander seeds, toasted and ground
½ teaspoon cumin seeds, toasted and ground
½ teaspoon paprika
25 g (1 oz) chickpea (besan/gram) flour
½ teaspoon fresh thyme, plus extra few sprigs to garnish

Remove and discard fine membrane covering the fish. Sprinkle fish with vinegar and marinate at least 30 minutes, preferably 1 hour.

Fry onion in oil until golden, add ginger and garlic and cook until softened, then stir in turmeric for a few seconds. Purée onion mixture with remaining ingredients, adding enough water (about 3 tablespoons) to make a batter thick enough to coat.

Pre-heat grill to medium-hot. Drain fish and pat dry. Tie up each tail separately with string (as you would a piece of meat). Boning splits the tail in half so put thin end against thick end to make pieces of fairly uniform thickness. Push a skewer through centre of each tail (this distributes heat better and helps in turning fish). Lay the 2 tails in a shallow oiled baking dish, and spread batter all over fish. Sprinkle over thyme sprigs and grill, turning twice, until fish is opaque right through and batter is browned – about 8 minutes. Slice in 4 and serve garnished with a few sprigs of thyme.

GRILLED LAMB CHOPS STUFFED WITH MINT OR CORIANDER CHUTNEY

Serves 4

Based on a far more elaborate recipe for minced lamb kebabs, this is faster and fresher tasting. I often substitute tangy sun-dried tomatoes for the original raisins.

> 8×4 cm (1½ inch) thick lamb chops each
> 75–100 g (3–4 oz)
> coarsely ground black pepper

> CHUTNEY STUFFING
> ½ small onion, finely chopped
> 2 green chillies, very finely chopped
> 2 tablespoons raisins, chopped, or 6 pre-soaked apricots or 6 sun-dried tomatoes in oil, drained, finely chopped
> 2 tablespoons finely chopped fresh mint or coriander or a mixture
> ½ teaspoon salt

Pre-heat grill or barbecue to hot. With a small, sharp knife, slice a deep pocket in each lamb chop. Mix together chutney ingredients, divide in 8 and stuff into pockets. Press pocket firmly shut and grind pepper over exterior of chops. Grill 3–4 minutes each side (rare to medium-rare). A good summer dish.

——— Use ———

• This same mint chutney is used to stuff a lamb kebab called '*goolar*' because it resembles the Indian wild fig of that name: mince 450 g (1 lb) cooked lamb very finely with 1 drained 425 g (15 oz) can of chickpeas, a thumb of fresh ginger, 3 dried red chillies, 2 teaspoons of fine Garam Masala (version 1, page 158), and salt to taste. Moisten with 4 tablespoons thick Greek-style yoghurt and form into 5 cm (2 inch) balls. Push some chutney into centre, form into 'fig' shape and then roll in poppy seeds. Deep-fry in hot oil until lightly browned (about 1½ minutes).

HERB-STUFFED POUSSIN KEBAB

Serves 2–4

This is unusual in that the herbs remain a bright emerald green inside the cooked birds. It is traditional to use coriander and mint, but when my pocket hanky-sized herb garden is going full blast in summer, I like to use a mixture of basil, lovage, sorrel, sweet marjoram, peppery dandelion and young rocket leaves mixed with a fist of ricotta – what is called in Genoa *preboggion*. Eat with the vivid green Spinach, Ginger and Garlic Balloon Bread (page 169) to match, and a glass of beer.

> 50 g (2 oz) fresh coriander, mint or other fresh-tasting green herbs
> 6 cloves, toasted and ground
> 5 cm (2 inch) piece cinnamon stick, toasted and ground
> 40 black peppercorns, toasted and ground
> seeds from 12 green cardamom pods, ground
> ¾ teaspoon salt
> 4–6 spring onions, green tops included, chopped
> 2 poussins (about 400–450 g (14 oz–1 lb) each)
> 100 g (4 oz) Greek-style yoghurt
> juice of 1 lime

Coarsely grind together herbs and half the ground spices, salt and onions. Stuff poussin with this mixture and either skewer or sew cavity shut. Purée remaining onions and spices with yoghurt and lime juice. Make several deep diagonal slashes down each side of birds' breasts and legs and marinate them in the yoghurt mixture for at least 1 hour.

Grill or barbecue (even better) until tender and well browned – about 15 minutes breast side down, 10–12 minutes breast side up. To serve for 2, cut through breast bone of bird with sharp shears and press open to reveal emerald green stuffing. For 4, cut birds in half through breast-bone and back and serve stuffing-side up.

INDIAN BREAD

Bread-making is an exact science, and like all sciences involving volatile ingredients, it requires experimentation to make the theory work in practice. We know, for example, that temperature control is less crucial for flat pan breads like *paratha* and *roti* than for yeast breads and risen breads such as Spiced Pizza Naan (page 184), a fact I learned the hard way in my cool northern kitchen. Not until I stood next to a tandoor oven in Old Delhi where the room temperature must have been at least 45°C did I understand why their bread rises in an hour and mine takes much longer.

To rise properly, yeasted dough should have a temperature of 23°–28°C – so if your kitchen temperature is 20°C, you will have to find somewhere warmer. Even non-yeasted breads have more texture and chew if rested in a warm place for 30 minutes before baking.

Flour, and the rate at which it absorbs water, is another variable. It can be affected by more than a damp climate. High-protein strong white flour used in bread-making (wholemeal flour reacts differently) absorbs far more liquid than the low protein flour used in cakes. Most Indian breads are made with a wholemeal flour, *aata* (also called chapatti flour, available in Asian markets) which is much more finely stoneground than any flour in the West. The entire wheat kernel is pulverised, then sifted to remove coarse bran flakes. Some European flour is so much more coarsely ground than American that it doesn't perform like flour – much of the gluten that gives dough its chewing-gum effect and makes it rise remains trapped inside the wheat kernels. If you want to see this chewing-gum effect in action, try the Rajasthani wheat gluten described on page 133.

Strong bread flour with 11½–14 per cent protein (you will see 11½–14 g per 100 g (4 oz) on package) is highest in the gluten-forming proteins that help bread rise, and more suitable for medium- to slow-risen Western breads. A mixture of plain white unbleached flour with 10–11½ per cent protein content per 100 g (4 oz) and stoneground wholemeal flour is best for the recipes in this book – pan breads like pooris, parathas and rotis, and medium-raised naans. And warm hands, anathema for pastry-makers, are a help.

SPICED CORNMEAL ROTIS

Makes 12×20 cm (7 inch) breads

Punjabi farmers make a cornmeal *roti* (chapatti) to eat with their gingery Spinach and Mustard Greens Cornmeal Purée (page 170) and glasses of frothy buttermilk. I have never found a corn flour in the West that performs as the Indian variety does but this bread, made with a mixture of fine yellow cornmeal (polenta), stoneground wholemeal flour and crunchy spices, gives some of the earthy sweet and nutty flavours of the original. Because Indian wholemeal flour is much more finely ground than the West's, I usually sift out the coarser bits of grain in Western flour, in which gluten remains trapped, preventing the dough

The percussive sounds of Old Delhi: multi-layered parathas and cornmeal rotis (breakfast of recent Punjabi immigrants) being slapped from hand to hand by a vendor in the Street of Parathas. Each layer of society in Delhi has its own bread and its own masala – the quantity of chillies rises as income falls.

from becoming as flexible as possible. If you can't bear to do this, your bread will still be good, but the dough will be stickier and the final bread less soft.

This is a very quick and easy bread to make. Try eating it wrapped around kebabs, or filled with yoghurt, fresh mint and onions caramelized in butter.

2 teaspoons coriander seeds
½ teaspoon cumin seeds
1 teaspoon black peppercorns
75 g (3 oz) plain unbleached flour, plus extra for dusting
75 g (3 oz) stoneground wholemeal flour, sifted
100 g (4 oz) fine yellow cornmeal (polenta)
¾ teaspoon salt
a little good vegetable oil (I always use olive oil but in the Punjab they would use melted ghee)

Toast spices until they crackle, then crush slightly to break peppercorns, and mix with flours, cornmeal and salt. Stir in about 200 ml (7 fl oz) warm water, or just enough to get flour to stick together. Knead on a floured board for 10 minutes, until smooth and pliable. Wholemeal dough is always sticky because the flour absorbs less water – keep dusting your hands with flour. Roll into a ball, brush with oil and leave in a plastic bag for 30 minutes.

Put a heavy frying pan over medium-high heat. Divide dough into 12 balls. Keeping remaining balls covered, squash 1 ball into a pillow, dip in flour and roll out to roughly 3 mm (⅛ inch). Cook on pan until edges of bread start to curl up (about 30 seconds). Turn over and repeat. When both sides are lightly freckled with brown, hold bread over the gas flame on your hob, first on one side of bread and then the other. It will puff up and freckle with black. If you have an electric hob, omit this step (which gives a final drying to the bread) and simply cook longer in pan – or put the breads under a hot grill. Brush with oil and keep warm. Repeat with remaining dough.

STUFFED CARROT PAN BREAD WITH ONION SEEDS

Makes 12 breads, enough for 4–6

One phenomenon that has levelled class layers in Indian society in recent years (as well as expanding the repertoire of Indian cooking) is the rise of women's magazines and women's pages in the former strict male preserve of newspapers. Lower middle-class women can now read about the recipes used by maharanis, women of the weaving class, if they are literate, can find out what middle-class women serve to their in-laws, and high-caste brahmin society women can learn the pleasures of Punjabi peasant breads. The following three recipes, loosely based on recipes from a Delhi newspaper, give some ides of that city's mastery of breads and roots. In this recipe, the carrot juice sweetens a dough studded with black onion seeds and its flesh becomes a moist savoury filling. A good lunch on its own with chutney or you can serve it as they do in Delhi's roadside cafés: fried, the top split open, an egg broken into it and the whole bread re-fried so you wind up with a fried egg in a bun.

This method is a fairly unconventional way of cooking parathas but I find it much easier than the Indian style. The following three vegetable doughs will keep fresh for up to a week in the fridge.

150 g (5 oz) plain flour
150 g (5 oz) wholemeal flour
¾ teaspoon salt
1½ teaspoons cayenne pepper
2 teaspoons black onion or black cumin seeds
4 tablespoons sunflower or olive oil
225 g (8 oz) carrots, scrubbed but not peeled
¼ teaspoon asafoetida powder
2 tablespoons chickpea (besan/gram) flour
vegetable oil, for frying

Sift together plain and wholemeal flour with half the salt and cayenne pepper. Mix with onion seeds and 2 tablespoons of oil. Purée carrots in a food processor and squeeze juice into flour, adding enough water (4–6 tablespoons) to make a stiff dough. Knead 10 minutes until smooth and pliable, brush with oil and wrap in a plastic bag. Rest 30 minutes.

Over medium heat, briefly sizzle asafoetida in oil, stir in grated carrot, remaining salt, cayenne and chickpea flour. Cook until dryish and soft. Cool. Divide bread dough into 12 balls. Keep remaining dough covered and roll 1 ball out to about 3 mm (⅛ inch). Put 1 teaspoon of carrot mixture in centre, lightly brush half of dough with oil and fold in half. Brush half again with oil, fold and roll out thinly again, starting from below bulge in 'nose' (so filling doesn't explode) and rolling to end of triangle. Breads can be prepared up to a day ahead to this point, separated by greaseproof paper, then kept wrapped.

Heat a heavy shallow pan with 5 mm (¼ inch) oil to just below smoking. Slip dough triangles into oil a few at a time – they must sizzle immediately or the oil is not hot enough. Fry them until edges start to brown. Turn over and fry a little longer, until crisp and golden. Remove and drain on kitchen paper. If oil gets too hot and parathas too brown, remove pan for a few seconds and allow it to cool.

Variations

• For a faster, easier version of this, simply mix all ingredients together (using 2 tablespoons less oil), add enough water to make a firm dough, knead and rest as above, then roll out into 5 mm- (¼ inch) thick round disks without folding and stuffing. Fry as above.

• A good, though not at all Indian, addition to these breads is the grated zest of an orange with a good oily skin (full of the orange oil) – put half in dough, half in stuffing.

SPINACH, GINGER AND GARLIC BALLOON BREAD

Makes 12 large breads, or 3 dozen bite-size

Small versions of these *puris* look like little turtles and are about the same colour after frying (see photograph, page 167). They break open to reveal a vivid green interior; delicious filled with home-made chutney or yoghurt cheese or cauliflower pickle. Plain wholemeal *puri* with fenugreek and tamarind chutney and potato curry made with whole toasted coriander seeds are the breakfast of Delhi. The test of a good *puri*, I was told, is that there should be no oil on your hands after eating them. This depends on oil temperature – keep it hot, but not so hot that they brown in less than 15–20 seconds. Much easier than it sounds. In India *puri* are rolled out one at a time, fine for a large version but tedious after a dozen. Stamping them out like biscuits works for me and is very quick.

150 g (5 oz) spinach
3 green chillies, chopped
4 cm (1½ inch) piece root ginger, chopped
6 garlic cloves, chopped
150 g (5 oz) strong white flour
150 g (5 oz) wholemeal flour
½ teaspoon bicarbonate of soda
1 teaspoon salt
3 tablespoons vegetable oil, plus more for frying

Wash spinach and cook in a covered pan just until it wilts. Squeeze out liquid (reserve for soups, breads, etc.) and purée spinach with chillies, ginger and garlic. Sift together dry ingredients and work in the oil, then spinach, adding enough spinach water to make a stiff dough (possibly as little as 1 tablespoon). Let rest 30 minutes.

Heat 2.5 cm (1 inch) oil in a small deep pan until a piece of dough sizzles immediately when

• Another variation, sharper and more pungent, is to substitute mooli (white radish) for carrot, in which case I prefer to use 2 green chillies, very finely sliced crosswise, instead of cayenne, and mix half of them into dough to give it a fleck of green.

dropped in (about 190°C/375°F). While it heats, roll out half the dough very thinly (about 3 mm (⅛ inch) and stamp out 5–7.5 cm-(2–3 inch) circles with a biscuit cutter. Cover with clingfilm while you fry bread in batches. Slip a couple of dough circles into oil. When they rise to surface, gently press them under oil with a slotted spoon to allow steam to puff them up. When edges brown, turn them over and cook 10–15 seconds more. Drain on kitchen paper. Keep warm while you make remaining breads.

SPICY BEETROOT BALLOON BREAD

Makes 16 ×18 cm (6 inch) breads, serves 4–6

Vegetable breads, when made with oil and plain flour (instead of strong flour) as in these recipes, have a 'shorter' texture than most Indian breads, more like pastry. A very little beetroot turns plain *puri* into this spectacular rosy-coloured version (see photograph on page 151), excellent with Kidney Beans, Beetroot and Walnut Oil (page 172). For a larger quantity, simply double the ingredients – and when you don't have the time or inclination to bake your own beetroots, you can even use drained pickled ones (about the only worthy use for them).

150 g (5 oz) plain flour
½ teaspoon salt
1 teaspoon cayenne pepper
4 teaspoons vegetable oil, plus extra for frying
4 tablespoons puréed cooked beetroot

Sift together flour, salt and cayenne and rub in oil. Work beetroot into flour with just enough water (1–2 tablespoons) to make dough cling together. Knead 10 minutes (this can be done with a dough hook in a food processor) until smooth. Dust with flour and wrap in plastic for 30 minutes.

Heat 2.5 cm (1 inch) oil in small deep pan until piece of dough dropped in sizzles immediately (about 190°C/375°F). While oil heats, divide dough into 16 balls and keep them covered. Squash 1 ball slightly, pat with flour and roll out very thinly (or roll them all out and keep separate with greaseproof paper). Drop the piece of rolled-out dough into the oil. When it rises to the surface, gently press down with slotted spoon to let it balloon with steam. When edges brown, turn it over and cook another few seconds. Drain on kitchen paper and keep warm. Repeat with the remaining dough.

SPINACH AND MUSTARD GREENS CORNMEAL PURÉE WITH GARLIC AND GINGER BUTTER

Serves 4–6 as a side dish

A mixture of Indian mustard leaves and wild greens is the classic accompaniment to Punjabi Spiced Cornmeal Rotis (page 166), but it makes an equally delicious stuffing or topping for those breads, and it is very good with Spring Lamb Stew with Baby Root Vegetables (page 171). Highly flavoured wild greens are readily available to Indians and Italians but the spices used here will give an Indian earthiness even to supermarket spinach. If you can find mustard greens, use them (they may need longer cooking), or mix them with spinach – or add a handful of fresh fenugreek leaves or 2 tablespoons of bottled fenugreek (methi) leaf purée, available in some Asian stores. If you can't find mustard greens, try mustard oil instead of ghee for pungency.

*900 g (2 lb) spinach or mixed spinach
and mustard greens*

4 tablespoons finely ground cornmeal

2–4 green chillies, chopped

¾ teaspoon salt, or to taste

*6 cm (2½ inch) piece root ginger,
½ chopped, ½ finely sliced*

¾–1 teaspoon cayenne pepper

*50–75 g (2–3 oz) ghee or 4–6 tablespoons
good oil (mustard, olive, sesame)*

6–8 garlic cloves, finely sliced lengthwise

Wash greens well. Put into a deep saucepan with cornmeal, chillies, salt, chopped ginger, cayenne and 450 ml (15 fl oz) water. Cover, bring to boil and cook for 10 minutes. Remove lid and simmer until spinach is thick and dryish. Purée and keep warm. Heat ghee until sizzling and stir-fry garlic and remaining ginger to a golden brown. Pour immediately into spinach, stir and serve.

SPRING LAMB STEW WITH BABY ROOT VEGETABLES

Serves 4–6 as a one-pot meal

Lamb and turnips cooked in spicy tomato juices is a popular dish in Hyderabad and Delhi. Made with tiny new-season's turnips, carrots and onions, as it is here, it becomes something very like an Indian version of the classic French stew, *navarin printanier*. The original slow-cooking and puréeing of the onion gives the sauce its rich, deep flavour, as well as thickening it, and this is balanced by the pungency of the mustard oil. Cooking the young vegetables separately (not at all an Indian thing to do) means they keep their sweetness. Good with Spiced Cornmeal Rotis (page 166).

*225 g (8 oz) small new turnips, scrubbed
but not peeled*

*225 g (8 oz) small new carrots, scrubbed
not peeled*

225 g (8 oz) small new onions

550 ml (18 fl oz) stock or water

*6 tablespoons mustard oil (or other good
oil e.g. olive, sesame)*

*900 g (2 lb) lean boned lamb, cut in 5 cm
(2 inch) chunks*

1 large onion, sliced

*5 cm (2 inch) piece fresh root ginger,
chopped*

8 garlic cloves

½ teaspoon ground turmeric

*½ teaspoon cumin seeds, toasted and
ground*

1 teaspoon black peppercorns, cracked

*4 black cardamom or 3 green cardomom
pods*

2.5 cm (1 inch) cinnamon stick

2 teaspoons coriander seeds

1 teaspoon cayenne pepper

¾ teaspoon salt, or to taste

1×425 g (15 oz) can plum tomatoes

handful of fresh mint, chopped

Cook vegetables until tender in boiling stock or water. Lift out and reserve cooking liquid.

Pre-heat oven to 180°C/350°F/Gas 4. Over medium-high heat brown meat in oil. Lift out with a slotted spoon. Cook large onion in same oil, stirring often. When caramely brown, grind to a purée with ginger and garlic. Return to the pan, add spices (except cayenne) and stir-fry over medium heat until they start crackling. Stir in cayenne, then tomatoes and reserved cooking liquid. Bring to a boil, add meat, cover and cook in oven for 1–1½ hours, until meat is tender.

You can simply add vegetables and heat stew through, but for a less soupy conclusion, remove meat and simmer sauce until it is thick enough to coat back of a spoon. Return meat and vegetables to pan, heat through and stir in fresh mint.

KIDNEY BEANS, BEETROOT AND WALNUT OIL

*Serves 4 as a vegetarian main course,
with other dishes*

A sixteenth-century Persian cookery book describes *bughra* as a stew made with beetroot, pomegranate juice and fresh mint – a celebration of colour – just as this dish is, with its rich, earthy flavours and vivid magenta of beetroot and matching kidney beans. Once a favourite at *dhabas* (truckstops) on the Punjabi and Delhi stretches of the old Grand Trunk Road that runs from Kabul, kidney beans are now too expensive for any but the rich, who have never taken to them. Kashmiris love them – and beetroot as well, and are famous for their high-quality walnuts and walnut oil, which enrich the sauce here. A lazy version of a slow-cooked dish – you can use previously cooked beetroots as long as they are not chopped first or pickled.

3 beetroots or 6 baby beetroots
3 tablespoons peanut, sunflower or olive oil
2 onions, halved lengthwise, finely sliced crosswise
4 garlic cloves, crushed
5 cm (2 inch) piece root ginger, half grated, half cut in fine shreds
½ teaspoon ground turmeric
1–1½ teaspoons cayenne pepper
1×425 g (15 oz) can plum tomatoes
2×425 g (15 oz) cans red kidney beans, drained and rinsed
¾ teaspoon salt, or to taste
1–2 tablespoons walnut oil
handful of walnut pieces
1 teaspoon cumin seeds
1 teaspoon paprika

To cook beetroots, leave whole with roots and stalks. Rinse well under water, wrap all together in foil and bake in a pre-heated oven at 180°C/350°F/Gas 4 until tender. This takes from 1–3 hours depending on age and size of beetroot. Peel when cooked, trim off roots and stalks and cut in 6–8 wedges lengthwise.

Fry onions in vegetable oil oven medium heat until caramel brown, stirring often. Add garlic and grated ginger and cook until softened. Stir in turmeric and cayenne and let sizzle for a few seconds. When they smell less raw, add tomatoes, kidney beans, beetroot and salt. Simmer for about 20 minutes, half-covered, for flavours to blend, adding ginger julienne for last 10 minutes. Before serving, lightly brown walnuts in walnut oil over medium heat. Stir in cumin seeds and paprika and when brown and aromatic pour into beans.

Variation

● If you can get beetroot with their green tops still on, these are delicious. Trim the tops, wash well and cook in a dry, covered pan until they wilt. Just before serving the beans, mound the beetroot greens on top and pour over walnuts and oil. You can do the same with 225 g (8 oz) spinach instead of the beetroot tops.

The roots of Delhi cooking: the city's cooks have a thousand recipes for carrots, beets, radishes and turnips – many of them add the roots' leaves at the end of cooking for flavour and colour.

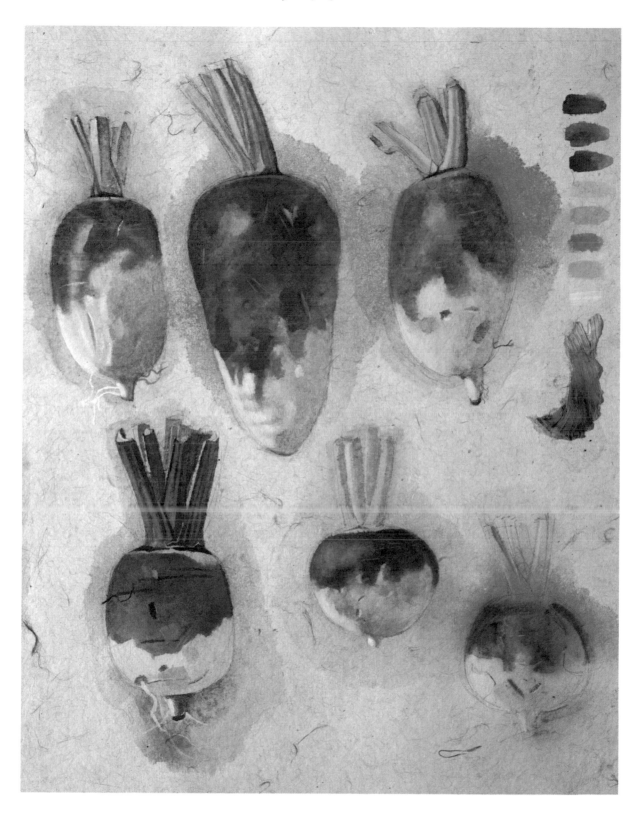

coriander
fennel · dill

cauliflower · maize
broccoli · pumpkin

capsicums
pineapples

chillies
papaya

Sun

potatoes
tomatoes

North Frigid
Zone
Arctic Circle
North Temperate
Zone
North Tropic
(Tropic of Cancer)
Torrid or tropical
Equator | | Equator
Zone
(Tropic of Capricorn)
South Tropic
South Temperate
Zone
Antarctic Circle
South
Frigid Zone

MONDE CONNU
des Anciens.

VASCO da GAMA

CHAPTER EIGHT

A
SPICE SEA
CHANGE

•

Masalih/masallah: interests, benefits; substances of any sort
used alone or combined to improve both intrinsically and outwardly.
DEFINITION FROM THE ARABIC, PERSIAN AND URDU LEXICON.

Sometimes, on a wintry day, when my garden lies dormant and all the colours are dulled under a grey blanket sky, I get down a jar from the cupboard, unscrew the top – and smell the kitchens of India.

It's a simple trick: you take the darkest, most unrefined sugar you can find, the one closest to India's own bittersweet jaggery, and you put it in a jar with crushed seeds from several cardamom pods – the pods plump and green, their seeds burnt caramel-coloured and slick with essential oil – and you add some very finely ground roasted pistachios, having first rubbed off their maroon skin. Then tighten the lid and shake the jar until pale green flecks of pistachio are thoroughly distributed through the deep brown sugar. I like it on buttered toast, still hot enough that the sugar melts into the butter; or on cold and creamy Greek yoghurt – or just to smell. The longer you leave it, the more India's scents of cardamom and pistachio will permeate the sugar. I have a row of these jars now, labelled 'Hyderabad: rose petal masala', 'Gujarat: mint and sesame chew' and 'Mysore: five-nut blend' – each one a whiff of historical connections.

Just about the time cooks in India perfected their skills with American chillies, tomatoes and capsicums, Indian colour and fragrance virtually disappeared from Western kitchens. In the seventeenth century, François Bernier, physician to the Great Mogul, may have inspired his friend Molière with tales of Delhi's court intrigues, but at the same time La Varenne, father of French classical cooking, was banishing all spices except salt, pepper and a scraping of nutmeg from France's kitchens. Thus he wiped out the influence of his predecessor Guillaume Tirel, known as Taillevent, whose rule as France's master chef spanned virtually all of the fourteenth century and popularized the taste for a *poudre fin* closely resembling curry powder.

Most extraordinary of all is the paucity of spices used in eighteenth and nineteenth century England, and in Italy (with the exception of Arabic Sicily), which had traded with India since Roman times. Whereas ancient Rome's cooking, like India's, was defined by spices, Italy's in the late eighteenth century had become increasingly defined by herbs, as it still is.

Why this happened remains a mystery. Some say that Oliver Cromwell banned the importation of spices simply because they were foreign. Some say the loss of spices in England, France and Italy is the result of losing the spice race to Portugal and Holland. If so, there is little evidence of this victory in Dutch and Portuguese kitchens. It has been claimed that aristocrats, previously the main consumers of spices, no longer valued them when they became less costly (but this didn't stop the same aristocrats from using salt and pepper). Perhaps improved culinary and food preservation methods meant that we no longer liked such strong flavours, or needed them to cover the taste of spoilt meat. Or perhaps – as the archivist to London's ancient Grocers' Guild has suggested – new trade with the West Indies gave us a taste for sugar instead of spice.

Even after generations of Europeans had made the trip to India and back, the basic characteristics of their cuisine were not altered. Instead, a form of culinary apartheid applied: pies, gravies, *potages* and omelettes on one level; curries, masalas and chutneys on another, lower level. The English, with a love of categorization matched only by the subcontinent's, simply bottled India. In his delightful book, *Culinary Jottings*, written for the English housewife in Madras in 1878, 'Wyvern' remarked, 'All native cooks dearly love the spice box and they all reverence Worcester Sauce.' With good reason: Sir Marcus Sandys' distillation of India (one of the few pungent Anglo-Indian sauces to have survived their nineteenth century heyday) contains tamarind, shallots, garlic and spices, things a South Indian cook could understand.

Wyvern mourned the decline in the skill of making curries, which he attributed to the fact that curries had lost caste, had been demoted from the banquet table to dishes suitable only for breakfast, luncheons and cosy dinners at home. 'The old cooks, who studied the art, and were encouraged in its cultivation, have passed away to their happy hunting grounds; and the sons and grandsons who now reign in their stead have been taught to devote themselves to more fashionable dishes.' He worried that the 'Oriental Depot' on the south side of Leicester Square, with its sundry casks of curry-stuffs and chutneys, might have been swept away with Northumberland House, Temple Bar and other renowned structures. He suspected that it was patronized largely, at the best of times, by London grocers who adulterated the Oriental's fine masalas with arrowroot to produce their own miserable concoction 'that can hardly with justice be called "genuine Madras curry-powder", notwithstanding its being bottled in a very pretty bottle and priced at two and six' (a sentiment that could have been expressed yesterday).

In the West, and in spite of such talented missionaries as Madhur Jaffrey and Julie Sahni, we still know very little about the history and technique of India's cooking. Because its recipes come out of a verbal and visual tradition rather than a written one, they are like stories whose plots have changed in the re-telling. Few cooks have tried to marry Indian masalas to Western

paneer nigella
poori pappadum naan
paratha raita kheer pakora

aubergine eggplant
cucumber saffron
asafoetida cloves

black cumin
turmeric
fenugreek
black pepper
ginger root
Cardamom

snake gourd
yoghurt
mango
mace
onion and
garlic okra
ghee barley
millet

mustard seeds
garam masala
cinnamon
cassia leaves

basmati rice
karela gourd
cashew nuts coconut milk
sesame seed peanuts

als; toovar red lentil channa
ickpea peas black gram
ad dal) muna bean
lnuts pistachio rose
mond banana
dish (mooli

recipes. Of course, the subcontinent's flavour patterns are not always clear. Indians have a purely religious fondness for bright red and yellow, for example, and since a lot of their protein comes from pulses, they are quite naturally interested in spices that prevent wind. Moreover, the correct use of spices is less easily grasped than, say, the use of herbs. A tablespoon here and there of basil will not substantially alter a dish, whereas the same cannot be said for cardamom.

Many classically trained chefs have the same disdainful view of Indian recipes as they have of the long lists of spices used in Roman times, a false vision of past and present that can be blamed on bad translations. Classical cookery books such as those of Apicius have always been translated either by non-chefs or by chefs with an inadequate grasp of the language. Certainly they have never been translated by Indian chefs, who probably could shed more light on them than even a gastronomic classicist.

The final stop on the Indian spice trail may be California, where cooks uninhibited by a classical chefs' training have always felt more free to experiment than have their European counterparts. With the influx of Asian cooks and ingredients of the last forty years, they have already achieved not so much a new cuisine as a new perspective on traditional techniques. The result is what has been dubbed 'Pacific Rim' cooking, a fusion of Orient and Occident – the latest innovation being such Indian-inspired food as fried oysters in curried cucumber, and lamb ravioli with cardamom tomato chutney. In Europe, too, there has been a sort of spice sea change. Chefs are beginning to realize the affinity of 'curry' spices for hotpot and tortillas and the possibilities of introducing cardamom and turmeric into a 'ratatouille' of aubergine and okra and Indian bitter gourd.

The danger in adding a pinch of masala here and there is that it can result in the worst kind of homogeneity. I was reassured by the theatre producer Jatinder Verma. His family, originally from the Punjab, emigrated to Kenya in the early years of this century and was forced to flee the troubles there in 1968, when he was fourteen.

'When I blend Indian and European traditions, I don't worry much about losing my roots, because my starting point is always: where are my roots? Emotionally they lie somewhere in the flow of the Ganges, actually they are in Africa, and yet what forms me is Britain. So I speak in one language, my heart is in another and my birth is in some other language altogether. Today we are all subjected to a vast range of influences – more, perhaps, than in any other age, and so we acquire things: we always have done. Added to that, I am convinced that theatre as a form is an impure one, as is cooking, the edible manifestation of Indian theatre. But the whole world is impure. History is a catalogue of borrowing and adaptation – it's just that we do it more quickly now.'

Flavours of East & West
•
FUSION

I came to Indian cooking after a love affair with Italian and southern French peasant food, so it could be said that the following recipes were born somewhere on the spice roads between the sub-continent and the Mediterranean, and what forms them is my own love of vivid tastes and colours, inspired by the wide palette that is part of India's sensuality and visual stimulation.

MEDITERRANEAN TANDOOR PASTE

*Enough for 4 poussins or fish, 2 chickens or
6–8 naan*

To achieve a natural version of the garish commercial tandoor flavouring, purée sweet red peppers with Middle Eastern harissa and add sun-dried tomato paste. This is not traditional, but better than ground beetles (cochineal); which is what the better 'Tandoori' brands use for colouring.

For tandoor chicken or poussin, make several 1 cm-(½ inch) deep diagonal slashes in flesh, prick remaining flesh well with a sharp fork and rub lemon juice in (2 lemons per chicken), then marinate for 30 minutes. Drain, brush with olive oil or melted butter and spread thickly with tandoor paste. Marinate for at least 1 hour, preferably 8, before cooking. Heat oven to 240°C/445°F/Gas 9 and keep your nerve while cooking – the paste should blacken in places. It will not be the same as food cooked in a clay tandoor oven, but the black cardamom and grilled red peppers give it a similar smoky taste. In Old Delhi, baked kebabs are hung up to dry, brushed with melted ghee and given a final baking. Try it with barbecued poussin – the ghee dripping onto coals makes the birds even smokier.

2 red peppers
3 tablespoons sun-dried tomato paste (available at Italian delicatessens)
1–2 teaspoons red chilli paste or harissa
6 garlic cloves, chopped
7.5 cm (3 inch) piece root ginger, chopped
½ teaspoon ground turmeric
4 black cardamom pods, ground to a powder
3 tablespoons Greek-style yoghurt
2 tablespoons olive oil
salt to taste (if pastes do not contain it)
2 teaspoons black cumin seeds

Grill peppers over a gas flame or under a hot grill, turning often until blackened on all sides. Put in a plastic bag and leave to cool. Peel, discard stem, core and seeds, drink the juice and purée flesh coarsely with everything except cumin seeds. Stir these in after. Refrigerate, tightly covered, until use.

——————— *Variations* ———————

• Spread paste on spatchcocked quail or skewered pieces of boned chicken or lamb before grilling or barbecuing.

• *Better than liver paté* Marinate 225 g (8 oz) chicken livers and 225 g (8 oz) lambs' liver, sliced to the same thickness as chicken, in tandoor paste for 1 hour. Skewer and put under a very hot grill or on a barbecue for 3 minutes, turning once and brushing with marinade or melted butter, until livers are browned outside but still pink within. Mix with fresh mint or coriander and roll up in the Spiced Cornmeal Roti (page 166). Or serve with Bombay Ketchup (page 100) or Fruity and Pungent Smoky Chutney (page 100).

• *Tandoor-spiced fish* Mix the paste with a big handful of coriander leaves and spread thickly over pomfret (Indian flat fish) or other whole flat fish such as small sole. Put under very hot grill until browned. Check that flesh is opaque right through and squeeze on plenty of lime juice.

• *Tandoor pizza naan* Spread a layer of tandoor paste on unbaked Spiced Pizza Naan (page 184), top with rounds of mozzarella and bake.

GRILLED ROOT VEGETABLES WITH TANDOORI YOGHURT SAUCE

Serves 4–6 as a side dish

Make this with small, young vegetables.

900 g (2 lb) mixed root vegetables (new potatoes, carrots, baby turnips or small parsnips, small onions, plump garlic cloves), scrubbed

8 tablespoons Mediterranean tandoor paste (page 179)

1–2 tablespoons olive or sesame oil

Pre-heat grill. Cook vegetables in boiling water until just tender but not soft. No vegetable should be thicker than 2.5 cm (1 inch) so slice or cut them up attractively if they are. Whisk together paste and 1 tablespoon oil, mix with vegetables and spread them out in a layer on a metal baking tray. Drizzle a little more oil over and grill for about 15 minutes until brown and beginning to blacken in spots, stirring and rolling vegetables around several times during cooking to brown evenly. Drizzle with more oil before serving.

GINGERY SPINACH FRITTATA

Serves 6 as a light starter

An Indian version of an Italian idea – try making it as well with new-season's baby broccoli, with its leaves and tender stalks finely sliced, and serve with spoonfuls of Mediterranean Tandoor Paste (page 179), warmed through until fragrant.

2 tablespoons peanut or light vegetable oil

2 teaspoons melted ghee or butter

2 onions, finely chopped

4 cm (1½ inch) piece root ginger, cut in fine shreds

2 green chillies, sliced finely crosswise

¼ teaspoon ground turmeric

350 g (12 oz) spinach (including stalks), chopped

6 eggs

salt to taste

In a wok or heavy frying pan with lid, fry onions in oil and ghee over medium-high heat until they are golden and browning on edges. Stir in ginger, chillies and turmeric for a minute or two, until they start to smell fragrant. Add spinach, cover and cook for 5 minutes – just enough to wilt the leaves and soften the stalks.

Beat eggs lightly with salt. Uncover spinach, turn up heat and stir-fry the leafy mixture until all liquid evaporates. Pour in eggs, mixing them into the spinach very well, and continue cooking as for an omelette, loosening the eggy edges as they set, and tilting the pan to let raw egg run underneath. When the bottom is well browned, slip the pan under a hot grill to brown the top.

SPICY MOREL STOCK

Makes about 1.2 litres (2 pints)

From Italy's *brodo* to Delhi's *akhni*, a good stock is the root of all great cuisines. This mahogany-coloured broth, with its earthy base of morels (typical of Kashmir), is delicious with beans, lentils and roots. For a summer taste, ideal for poaching fish, leave out the funghi and add a handful of fresh coriander and the juice of a lemon 15 minutes before end of cooking.

1 large unpeeled onion, quartered

2 carrots, sliced

1 fennel bulb, sliced

1 green chilli

2 unpeeled garlic cloves, crushed

5 cm (2 inch) piece root ginger, sliced

2 teaspoons cumin seeds

2 teaspoons coriander seeds

1 teaspoon black peppercorns

1 teaspoon sea salt

6 green cardamom pods

1 cinnamon stick, roughly crushed

15 g (½ oz) dried morels

Over medium-high heat, cook vegetables, chilli and garlic in a large saucepan until onion begins to brown. Stir in spices and continue cooking until they release their fragrance. Add morels and 2 litres (3½ pints) cold water and bring to the boil. Partially cover pan, lower heat and simmer for 1 hour. Leave overnight to infuse. Strain, pressing down well to extract juice. Keeps for up to a week, refrigerated, or freeze in ice-cube trays.

PUMPKIN KEDGEREE RISOTTO

Serves 4–6

A beautiful dish – the combination of golden yolks and rice with earth-red spice and orange pumpkin is splendid both to look at and to eat. This recipe is playing games with an Italian technique and a purely Indian flavour pattern of rice and caramelized onions, although the onions would usually be browned in butter in India.

RISOTTO

2 large onions, finely sliced, tossed with

1 teaspoon salt

4 tablespoons olive oil

1 small pumpkin or firm squash, cut in 1 cm (½ inch) chunks

about 1.2 litres (2 pints) Spicy Morel Stock (this page) or other home made stock

40 g (1½ oz) butter

1 cm (½ inch) piece root ginger, ground to a paste with 2 green chillies and 1 garlic clove

350 g (12 oz) arborio rice

pinch of saffron threads, dissolved in 125 ml (4 fl oz) hot water

50 g (2 oz) grated Parmesan (optional)

GARNISH

6 hard-boiled eggs, quartered

3 tablespoons toasted sesame seeds, ground coarsely with ½ teaspoon each toasted coriander seeds, sea salt and cayenne pepper

Over medium-low heat in a heavy pan, cook onion in oil, stirring often to prevent burning, until caramel brown. With a slotted spoon, lift out and drain on kitchen paper. Simmer pumpkin in broth for 5 minutes until just tender. Lift out and reserve.

Bring broth to a low simmer in a pan. Put half the reserved onions in a saucepan over medium-high heat with 15 g (½ oz) butter. Stir in ginger paste, then rice, until it is well coated (1–2 minutes). Pour in a good splash of broth (about 135 ml (4½ fl oz)) and stir constantly until liquid is completely absorbed. Continue stirring in splashes of broth, adding saffron water after 15 minutes, then the pumpkin, 5 minutes later. Start testing rice after 20 minutes, using less stock from this point on. Your aim is a classic risotto texture – firm to the tooth but creamy on the tongue. If you run out of broth, continue with water. The risotto should take 25–30 minutes.

When rice is cooked, remove from heat and stir in remaining butter (and Parmesan, for a less Indian flavour). Season with more salt if necessary and pour onto warm plates. Dip eggs in spiced seeds and arrange on top of rice. Scatter over remaining onions.

LAMB IN SPICY LENTIL AND RED PEPPER CRUST

Serves 4–6

Western cooks put lentils in soups and salads, and under roasts, but never think of turning the process upside-down, as Indian cooks do, and grinding the lentils with spices to form a peppery nutty-flavoured crust – used for vegetables in India, for roast lamb in this recipe. The ideal accompaniment is a mound of spinach cooked in butter until it wilts and tossed with a spoonful of toasted black mustard seeds.

LENTIL CRUST
100 g (4 oz) split red lentils
juice and grated zest of ½ lemon
4 cm (1½ inch) piece root ginger, grated
1 garlic clove, chopped
2 dried red chillies, crumbled (or chilli flakes)
65 g (2½ oz) cold butter
1 red pepper, finely chopped

25 g (1 oz) pistachios, roasted and coarsely ground
2 racks best end of neck (7 bones each), chined
salt and pepper

Cover lentils with water by 2.5 cm (1 inch) and soak for 4 hours. Drain lentils and purée in a food processor with all crust ingredients except red pepper and nuts. Add these at end – they should still have texture. Season with salt and divide in half. Roll out each half 5 mm (¼ inch) thick, into rough shape of lamb racks ('dough' will be crumbly). Wrap in foil and chill until firm.

Pre-heat oven to 230°C/450°F/Gas 8. Trim all but a little visible fat from lamb and scrape ends of bones. Season all over with salt and pepper and then cook in a roasting tin for 6–8 minutes, flesh-side down. Turn over and roast for another 8 minutes. Remove from oven and cover loosely with foil – it can remain like this for up to an hour.

Ten minutes before serving, press lentil crust onto fleshy side of lamb. It will be crumbly, but any bits that break off can be stuck back again without affecting the dish. Cook 7.5 cm (3 inches) from medium-hot pre-heated grill until crust is a deep golden brown (about 7–10 minutes) – better to have a few black spots than to undercook it. Serve each person with a few cutlets and a couple of spoonfuls of crust.

——————— *Variations* ———————

• *Green herb crust* Substitute green chillies and green pepper for the red chillies and pepper and add a big handful of finely chopped fresh coriander. Good with chicken breasts.

• *Baked trout in herb crust* Spread either red pepper crust or green herb crust on 4–6 large trout fillets. Place in an oiled baking dish, pour in a glass of wine and bake for 10 minutes at 200°C/400°F/Gas 6, finishing under hot grill if necessary to brown. Whisk pan juices with 4 tablespoons of olive oil and pour around fish.

• *Stuffed yellow peppers* Halve 4–6 yellow peppers, remove anything that isn't yellow and cook in a roasting tin with ½ glass of white wine and 2 tablespoons of olive oil, skin-side up under hot grill until skin begins to blacken. Turn over, spread with thin layer of lentil dough and grill until browned. Serve with pan juices.

• *Lentil tart bases with anchovy and yogurt topping* Roll out lentil dough, chill until firm and cut into 10 cm (4 inch) rounds. Put under a hot grill until browned, turn over and brown on other side, then top with marinated fresh anchovies. To make them yourself use 100 g (4 oz) anchovies in oil, drained and marinated in ½ teaspoon of popped black mustard seeds, 1 finely chopped red pepper, 1 tablespoon of lime juice and ¼ teaspoon of toasted cumin seeds. Spread tart bases with Greek-style yoghurt and arrange anchovies in a wheel on top.

ROAST COD WITH SPICED CORIANDER SAUCE

Serves 4

A good sauce for any white fish.

4 cod fillets, 2 cm (¾ inch) thick (about 150–175 g (5–6 oz) each)
sesame oil
black pepper
salt
6 tablespoons Spicy Morel Stock (page 181)
25 g (1 oz) cold butter, cut in small pieces
2 tablespoons Greek-style yoghurt
3 tablespoons finely chopped fresh coriander
1 ripe tomato, peeled, seeded and finely chopped

Pre-heat oven to 180°C/350°F/Gas 4. Brush cod with oil and grind on pepper and salt. Roast 7 minutes or until flesh is opaque. Keep warm under buttered greaseproof paper. Bring stock to low boil and whisk in butter. Reduce heat and stir in yoghurt. Off heat, stir in coriander and tomato, pour over cod and serve.

SCALLOPS MULLIGATAWNY

Serves 4 as a main course

Inspired by the recipe of a friend, Shaun Hill, this plays with the old Madras Club favourite (whose members in the nineteenth century were known as 'mulls' because of their fondness for mulligatawny soup) producing instead of turmeric-yellow stodge, a pale apricot-coloured lentil sauce with griddled scallop 'croûtons'. Where I have used slivers of fresh ginger and scallop coral in sesame oil to finish the dish, Indians would melt butter with masala spices – and Italians would do the same with fresh herbs and olive oil.

SAUCE
50 g (2 oz) tamarind paste
2 tablespoons olive oil
1 onion, finely chopped
2 garlic cloves, chopped
5 cm (2 inch) piece fresh root ginger, grated
½ teaspoon ground coriander
½ teaspoon ground cumin
½ teaspoon cayenne pepper
75 g (3 oz) split red lentils
2 carrots, chopped
1 teaspoon sea salt, or to taste
8–12 large scallops, with coral
sesame oil
1 lime or lemon
1 cm (½ inch) piece root ginger, cut in slivers
fresh coriander, to garnish

To make lentil sauce, pour 250 ml (8 fl oz) boiling water over tamarind and leave to soak 30 minutes. Over medium heat, soften onion, garlic and ginger in oil. Add spices, lentils, carrots and 650 ml (1⅛ pints) cold water and bring to boil. Reduce heat and simmer 30 minutes. After 15 minutes, pour tamarind through sieve into lentils, rubbing well to extract pulp. When lentils are cooked, purée and add salt to taste.

Separate coral from scallops and cook coral for 2 minutes in a cupful of simmering water. Drain (add water to lentils), refresh in cold water and slice in strips.

Brush both sides of scallops with sesame oil. Heat heavy non-stick pan over medium-high heat and cook scallops 30 seconds each side. Put in bowl, squeeze lime juice over, cover with buttered paper and keep warm. Add 2 tablespoons of sesame oil to pan and stir-fry coral and ginger. To serve, ladle re-heated soup into warm plates with scallops, spoon on gingery coral and oil and top with fresh coriander.

The lentil sauce keeps several days, refrigerated, and freezes well.

--- *Variations* ---

● Double the quantity of lentils and tamarind and you have a good sourish South Indian soup to preceed tandoori Spiced Pizza Naan (this page).
● Substitute chunks of monkfish or cod – or even grilled tofu – for the scallops, and stir-fry 1 cm (½ inch) piece root ginger, cut in slivers, to garnish.
● On frantic days, leave out the fish altogether and serve soup with chunks of soft goats' cheese melted in it and a spoonful of Green Coconut and Coriander Chutney (page 92).

SPICED PIZZA NAAN
Makes 2 large or 4 small pizzas

A rich bread that has a crisp surface and almost cakey texture if made with plain white flour and a chewier, breadier feel if made with strong white bread flour (in which case it may need a bit more milk). It exudes clouds of spice while you knead. You can get a bit of the tandoori naan's smokiness by heating your oven to its highest setting and baking on an earthenware pizza brick – even more if you finish the dough on the barbecue.

To serve more than one kind of pizza, divide dough in half and roll out separately, pulling dough into rounded tear shapes. Spread each with any of the toppings and bake side by side.

100 g (4 oz) butter
1½ teaspoons garam masala (page 158, or a good commercial brand)
450 g (1 lb) plain flour, sifted
½ teaspoon salt
1 tablespoon white sugar
1½ teaspoons 'Easybake' or other quick-rising dry yeast
135 ml (4½ fl oz) plain low-fat yoghurt, at room temperature
135 ml (4½ fl oz) whole milk, lukewarm

TOPPING (or use one of the variations)
3 tablespoons olive or mustard oil
1 teaspoon coarse sea salt
2 teaspoons black mustard, cumin or black onion seeds

Melt butter with masala and allow to cool until still liquid but no longer hot. By hand or in a food processor, blend flour, salt, sugar, yeast and butter until mixture forms crumbs. Gradually add yoghurt and enough milk for mixture to form ball. Turn out onto lightly floured surface and place remaining milk in a bowl nearby. Dip the

knuckles of one hand into milk and punch into dough, gathering dough up with your other hand. Continue like this for 10 minutes, dipping your knuckles into milk, punching it into dough and giving it a turn and a knead. Stop adding milk if dough becomes sticky (flour absorption of liquid is unpredictable) and sift over a very little flour. Total kneading time is about 12 minutes.

Put dough in a lightly oiled bowl, cover with clingfilm and leave for 1 hour in a warm place.

A Muslim Pathan woman from Lahore uses traditional flavours that can be applied to a modern Pizza Naan with onions and garlic or (bottom) another naan with eggs and parmesan.

Half an hour before cooking, pre-heat oven to highest setting (about 240°C/475°F/Gas 9) and put in either a flour-dusted pizza brick or a heavy metal baking sheet brushed with oil. Knead dough for 2–3 minutes to get some spring back into it, and divide in half. Keep half covered in clingfilm while you make first bread. On a lightly floured surface roll out to a large 5 mm (¼ inch) thick circle. Prick all over with a fork to within 1 cm (½ inch) of edge.

Lift dough onto baking brick, brush well with oil and sprinkle over salt and seeds. Cook 5–6 minutes, until starting to brown, then lower heat to 200°C/425°F/Gas 7 and cook a further 5–10 minutes until browned. Repeat with second piece of dough. Cut in wedges to serve.

———— Alternative Toppings ————

• *Caramelized onions* The traditional Indian way to make these is to finely slice 2 large onions, toss with 1 teaspoon of coarse salt and fry for 15–20 minutes in 4 tablespoons of butter, ghee or oil (I use olive or sesame oil) stirring often, until mahogany brown. This will give a sweet and caramely flavour. For a sharper, more oniony taste, simply slice the onions finely and deep-fry in 1 cm (½ inch) of hot oil until brown and crisp. Drain, spread on pizza bread and sprinkle with mustard seeds. Or spread bread first with soft goats' cheese and then top with onions.

• *New season's purple sprouting broccoli and deep-fried onions* One of the simplest and best toppings is to pile dough with the first baby broccoli that appear at the end of winter: trim off toughest ends of stalks and separate stalks into individual branches of about 6–7 inches. Drop them into boiling water and cook until just tender (about 5 minutes). Drain well. Finely slice an onion and drop into 1 cm (½ inch) of hot sunflower oil. Fry the pieces until they are brown and crisp. Stir-fry 2 garlic cloves, 2.5 cm (1 inch) shredded root ginger, 2 crumbled red chillies and 1 teaspoon of black onion or cumin seeds in a little olive oil. When soft, toss with broccoli and pile on top of bread, sprinkle over onions, a little oil and coarse sea salt. You could add a handful of pine nuts but this is gilding the lily.

• *Aubergine and onion* 1 large aubergine, sliced thinly, sprinkled with salt and left to drain off bitter juices for 30 minutes (you can leave this step out if you are in a hurry). Rinse and lay on dough after its first 5 minutes baking, top with 1 large onion and 1 dried red chilli, both very finely sliced. Drizzle with oil, sprinkle with coarse sea salt and black mustard seeds. After 5–10 minutes cooking, finish off under grill to caramelize. Put a dollop of yoghurt in the centre and sprinkle with fresh coriander before serving.

• *Tandoori egg on toast* A good late-night snack even with bought naan and some of the Mediterranean Tandoor Paste (page 179): spread naan thickly with tandoor paste, leaving a slight hollow in the centre. Break an egg into this hollow and put whole naan under a hot grill. Grill for a few minutes, just until egg sets, then shave over some Parmesan and sprinkle with fresh basil. A beautiful colour contrast to the Purple Sprouting Baby Broccoli and Onion Pizza Naan (left).

TANDOORI-SPICED LAMB

Enough to cover 1 pizza naan thickly or 2 thinly

This mixture of fresh and dried spices ground with lemon and yoghurt is a classic one for giving meat or chicken a tandoori flavour. Indians add red colouring for purely aesthetic reasons. I prefer the red of sun-dried tomatoes. If you have some already prepared, you can use 4–5 tablespoons of the Mediterranean Tandoor Paste (page 179) instead of this yoghurt mixture.

½ teaspoon ground cumin
½ teaspoon garam masala (page 158) or a commercial brand
¾ teaspoon salt, or to taste
4 cm (1½ inch) piece root ginger, grated
1 teaspoon paprika
½ teaspoon cayenne pepper
2 garlic cloves, grated
juice of ½ lemon
3 tablespoons Greek-style yoghurt
2 large lamb chops, weighing about 275–350 g (10–12 oz), boned and trimmed of fat
½ onion, finely sliced
1 quantity Spiced Pizza Naan dough (page 184)
6 sun-dried tomatoes in oil
fresh coriander, to serve

Mix together spices and garlic and slowly add lemon juice, working it into spices with a pestle or the back of a wooden spoon. Stir in yoghurt. Slice lamb thinly across the grain and stir into yoghurt with onion. Leave to marinate for 2 hours at room temperature or 4–6 hours refrigerated.

To cook, pre-heat oven for at least 30 minutes to its highest setting with a floured pizza brick or well-oiled heavy metal baking tin.

Prepare 2 pizza naan as directed and bake 5 minutes, or until they begin to brown, then lower heat to 200°C/425°F/Gas 7 and cook for another 7 minutes. Drain lamb, spread over bread, leaving 1 cm (½ inch) free around outer edge. Scatter over tomatoes and grill until lamb starts to blacken at edges. Scatter with fresh coriander and serve.

STUFFED PIZZA NAAN

Makes 8

This is close to *consum*, the stuffed breads found in Romagna, which are the folded version of *piadini*, the Italian answer to pan-fried chapatti.

STUFFING
100–175 g (4–6 oz) feta or soft goats' cheese, mashed
6 sun-dried tomatoes in oil, chopped
4–6 tablespoons finely chopped fresh coriander
1 garlic clove, crushed
2 green chillies, chopped
2.5 cm (1 inch) piece fresh root ginger, finely chopped
½ teaspoon cumin seeds, toasted
½ teaspoon salt, or to taste
Spiced Pizza Naan dough (page 184), made with bread flour
olive oil or melted butter
black cumin, onion or sesame seeds

Pre-heat oven to 200°C/400°F/Gas 6 with floured pizza brick or oiled metal baking tray.

Mash together stuffing and set aside. Divide dough into 8 pieces, roll each piece into a ball and keep covered while you proceed. On a lightly floured board, roll out each ball of dough into 5 mm (¼ inch) thick oval, then stretch it as thin as it will go without tearing. Spread one-eighth of stuffing in centre, fold dough in half and seal edges tightly. Brush with oil and sprinkle with seeds. Repeat with remaining dough. Bake 20–25 minutes until well browned.

Orange Cardamom Indian Custard

Makes 600 ml (1 pint)

Rabadi, the milk sauce used for so many Indian sweets, does not need sugar to sweeten it or eggs to thicken it. The milk's own sweetness is enough and its custardy consistency is achieved by the simplest of all techniques – reduction. Traditionally it is flavoured with ground cardamom, but I like to put a strip of orange or lemon peel in while it cooks, and to use it in ways more French than Italian. A good dish to make while cooking something else because it does not require Michelin-standard skills, just the occasional stir.

1.75 litres (3 pints) whole milk
pared zest of 1 orange
seeds from 8–12 green cardamom pods, ground
orange liqueur (such as Cointreau or Grand Marnier), to taste

Bring milk to boil with orange zest in wide shallow pan – a Chinese wok is ideal. Boil gently for 45 minutes (remove zest after 20 minutes), breaking skin as it forms and stirring in.

At the end of cooking, you will have a curious substance full of milk shreds – do not worry. Allow the milk to cool slightly, then purée with cardamom to taste (this will depend on size of pods, but the end result should be fragrant without being too perfumed), until smooth and frothy. If you prefer thicker custard, reduce for further 15 minutes over medium heat, but remember that it will thicken on cooling. Flavour with orange liqueur and chill well. Wonderful with bitter chocolate cake or lemony rice pudding. The thicker version is served on its own in India in silver bowls, scattered with crushed pistachios, rose petals and toasted almonds.

Bitter Chocolate Kulfi with Praline

Makes 900 ml (1½ pints) – serves 6–8

Kulfi is Indian ice-cream that is frozen without beating (therefore much easier to prepare than ordinary ice-creams). Adding bitter chocolate to it changes its character without spoiling the fragrance, and gives it a texture very similar to an American fudgsicle, a dense, almost crisp chocolate ice lolly.

1 quantity Orange Cardamom Indian Custard (left)
100 g (4 oz) bitter chocolate, broken in pieces
about 3 tablespoons muscovado or dark brown sugar
Indian Praline, to serve (page 189)

Before processing custard recipe, melt chocolate into milk and sweeten with sugar. It should taste slightly sweeter than an ordinary custard (because freezing dulls sweetness), but not sickly. Process to a smooth cream and pour into metal bowl, or into a decorative metal mould if you have one. Freeze without stirring until firm.

To serve, dip bowl briefly in hot water and tip the ice-cream onto plate. Scatter with either Indian Praline or with almonds sprinkled with brown sugar and toasted in a pan until the sugar caramelizes.

PISTACHIO AND CARDAMOM SPICE SUGAR

I keep a jar of this in the cupboard permanently, to caramelize under a grill on custard for crème brûlée, to sprinkle over zabaglione or chocolate ice-cream – and just to smell from time to time.

15 g (½ oz) shelled pistachios, roasted
6 tablespoons muscovado or dark brown sugar
seeds from 6 green cardamom pods, ground

Rub off as much as possible of pistachios' red skin and grind nuts very finely. Mix with sugar and cardamom and store in an air-tight jar. This is enough to make brûlée for 6 small ramekins – if you increase the quantity, add cardamom to taste rather than doubling/tripling etc., otherwise it can be overwhelming.

——————— *Variation* ———————

• *Indian praline* Heat 1 quantity Pistachio and Cardamom Spice Sugar in a small heavy saucepan with 1 tablespoon of water until sugar melts. Pour onto cold surface and let set, then roughly crush with rolling pin. Delicious sprinkled on cakes and ice-creams – or mix it into half-frozen Bitter Chocolate Kulfi (page 188) for crunchy bites.

SAFFRON BREAD AND BUTTER PUDDING WITH CARAMEL ALMONDS

Serves 6

A wedding of English bread and butter pudding, Italian or French brioche, Lucknow's classic *shahi tukra*, and Gujarat's *shrikand* of drained and beaten yoghurt. *Shahi tukra* was originally made in Lucknow with a brioche-like saffron bread, so this is not that removed from the original idea. Serve it with dried apricots that have stewed with cardamom, sugar and brandy.

250 g (8 oz) brioche or panettone
25–50 g (1–2 oz) butter
200–225 g (7–8 oz) caster sugar
90 g (3½ oz) dried apricots, soaked overnight in rum, sliced in strips
3 eggs
750 g (1½ lb) Greek-style yoghurt
big pinch of saffron threads
handful of blanched almonds, sliced in 3 lengthwise
seeds from 4–6 cardamom pods, crushed

Slice brioche into 6 rounds. Butter both sides, sprinkle lightly with sugar and fry on each side until lightly browned. Overlap slices in an oven-proof dish with apricots in between.

Pre-heat oven to 175°C/350°F/Gas 4. Beat eggs and 175 g (6 oz) of sugar until frothy and light. Lightly beat in yoghurt. Put over low heat with saffron, stirring constantly, until mixture thickens – it must not boil. Pour this over bread and bake 30 minutes or until barely set – it should wobble in dish. Chill. Put almonds, cardamom and 2 tablespoons of sugar in a non-stick pan and stir until almonds start cracking and browning. Pour onto a piece of foil and leave to cool. Before serving, spoon a thin layer of sugar over pudding and put under hot grill to caramelize. Sprinkle with cardamom and almonds.